Two Hundred Years of Pushkin

Volume II

Alexander Pushkin:
Myth and Monument

STUDIES IN SLAVIC LITERATURE AND POETICS

VOLUME XXXIX

Edited by

J.J. van Baak
R. Grübel
A.G.F. van Holk
W.G. Weststeijn

TWO HUNDRED YEARS OF PUSHKIN

VOLUME II
ALEXANDER PUSHKIN:
MYTH AND MONUMENT

Edited by

Robert Reid
Reader in Russian
Keele University

and

Joe Andrew
Professor of Russian Literature
Keele University

Rodopi

Amsterdam - New York, NY 2003

The paper on which this book is printed meets the requirements of "ISO 9706:1994, Information and documentation - Paper for documents - Requirements for permanence".

ISBN: 90-420-0874-1 vols. I-III
ISBN: 90-420-1135-1 vol. II
©Editions Rodopi B.V., Amsterdam – New York, NY 2003
Printed in The Netherlands

Contents

VI

Preface

The chapters in the present volume, like those in the companion volumes, *Two Hundred Years of Pushkin, Volume I: 'Pushkin's Secret': Russian Writers Reread and Rewrite Pushkin* and *Pushkin's Legacy*, arise primarily from a conference 'Two Hundred Years of Pushkin: A Bicentennial Conference', held under the auspices of the Neo-Formalist Circle at Mansfield College, Oxford from 13-15 September 1999. The editors of the three volumes warmly thank all the participants in that conference for their contributions. We are also grateful to those who assisted us at the conference and in the preparation of these three volumes, especially Pearl Aldridge of Mansfield College, and Angela Merryweather and David Sherwood of Keele University.

The chapters are grouped thematically, rather than chronologically, to reflect the principal manifestations of myth in Pushkin's work. Chapters 1-5 reveal the extent to which Pushkin's classics were inspired by some of the great mythic archetypes of European culture - Psyche and Cupid and Dante's *Inferno* in *Evgenii Onegin*, Cleopatra in the poem of that name and Don Juan in *The Stone Guest* and *The Queen of Spades*. Chapters 6-9 centre on what has been termed Pushkin's 'sculptural myth', as manifested in *The Bronze Horseman* and the image of St Petersburg more generally. The last two chapters examine the interaction of history and myth in Pushkin via the *History of Pugachev* (chapter 10) and a more general philosophical overview of the presentation of time in such works as *The Tales of Belkin*, *The Gypsies* and *The Bronze Horseman* (chapter 11).

Titles of well-known Russian literary works have been given in established English translation only; for lesser known works the cyrillic original has been supplied on first mention. Quotations from Pushkin and other writers are given in English translation, except (as in poetry, for instance) where reference to the original was considered essential. Citation of Russian titles in the notes is via transliteration, the system used being that of the Library of Congress without diacritics.

Robert Reid and Joe Andrew
Keele University

2003

Notes on Contributors

Robin Aizlewood is Senior Lecturer in Russian at the School of Slavonic and East European Studies, University College, London. He is author of *Verse Form and Meaning in the Poetry of Vladimir Maiakovskii* (1989) and *Two Essays on Maiakovskii's Verse* (2000), as well as articles on Russian thought and literature and language course design.

Michael Basker is Reader in Russian at the University of Bristol. He has published widely in both English and Russian on Nikolai Gumilev, Anna Akhmatova and other Russian poets. His recent work on Pushkin includes an edition of *The Bronze Horseman* (Bristol Classical Press, 2000).

David M. Bethea is the Vilas Research Professor of Slavic Languages at the University of Wisconsin-Madison. He has written broadly on issues of Russian literature and thought. Among his major publications are: *Khodasevich: His Life and Art* (1983), *The Shape of Apocalypse in Modern Russian Fiction* (1989), *Puškin Today* (ed.) (1993), *Joseph Brodsky and the Creation of Exile* (1994), *Realizing Metaphors:Alexander Pushkin and the Life of the Poet* (1998), and *The Pushkin Handbook* (ed.) (forthcoming). Presently he is at work on a four-volume critical biography of Pushkin.

Leon Burnett is Reader in Russian Literature at the University of Essex. His research and publications are mainly in Comparative Literature. He has recently edited *Word in Time: Poetry, Narrative, Translation* (1997) and is currently working on a book-length study *Faces of the Sphinx: Literary Encounters between Russia and the West*. From 1992 to 2000 he was the main editor of *New Comparison: A Journal of Comparative and General Literary Studies.*

Priscilla Meyer, Professor of Russian at Wesleyan University, Middletown, Connecticut, is the author of *Find What the Sailor Has Hidden: Vladimir Nabokov's 'Pale Fire'*, and editor of books on Bitov, Gogol and Dostoevskii. Recent articles are on Dostoevskii and Janin; Gogol and Hoffmann; Stoppard and Nabokov. She is currently writing a book on 'How The Russians Read The French: Origins of the Russian Novel'.

Marguerite Palmer is a postgraduate student of Russian literature at Keele University. She is currently writing her doctoral dissertation on Pushkin and Dante.

Robert Reid is Reader in Russian at Keele University. His main research interests are in Russian Romanticism and, as well as a number of articles and essays, his principal publications in this area are *Problems of Russian Romanticism* (ed.) (Gower, 1986), *Pushkin's 'Mozart and Salieri': Themes, Character, Sociology* (Rodopi, 1995) and *Lermontov's 'A Hero of Our Time'* (Bristol Classical Press, 1997).

Alexandra Smith is Senior Lecturer in Russian at the University of Canterbury, New Zealand. She is author of *The Song of the Mocking Bird: Pushkin in the Work of Marina Tsvetaeva* (Peter Lang, 1994) and numerous articles on Pushkin, Russian Modernism and Postmodernism (including Tsvetaeva, Akhmatova, Pasternak, Nabokov and contemporary women's writing).

Tatiana Smoliarova is a researcher at the Institute for Higher Studies in the Humanities in Moscow and has also researched at Harvard. Among her academic interests are the history of the solemn ode in France and Russia, literary disputes in France and Russia and the reception of antiquity in neo-European culture.

William Mills Todd III is Curt Hugo Reisinger Professor of Slavic Languages and Literatures and Professor of Comparative Literature at Harvard University. His publications include *The Familiar Letter as a Literary Genre in the Age of Pushkin* (1976), *Fiction and Society in the Age of Pushkin* (1986) and several edited books including *Sovremennaia amerikanskoe pushkinovedenie* (1999).

André van Holk is Professor Emeritus of Slavic Languages at the University of Groningen, The Netherlands. His academic interests include Russian syntax and the semiotics of literature. His approach to literary analysis is set out in his book *Theme and Space: Text-Linguistic Studies in Russian and Polish Drama. With an Outline of Text Linguistics* (Rodopi, 1996).

Introduction: Pushkin: Myth and Monument

by

ROBERT REID

This is the second of three volumes to come out of 'Two Hundred Years of Pushkin', a conference held at Mansfield College, Oxford, in September 1999 to commemorate the poet's bicentenary. The first volume concentrates on Pushkin's impact on his literary successors illustrating, with reference to writers as diverse in style and genre as Turgenev, Tsvetaeva, Nabokov and Brodsky, the all-pervasiveness of Pushkin's influence on subsequent Russian writing, a phenomenon which confirms (and constitutes) his stature as a national and world writer.

The present volume focuses more specifically on the nature of Pushkin's own inspiration and creative preoccupations. In this context it is probably true to say that Pushkin criticism has often oscillated between the imperative to maximize the creative originality of the poet and a tendency on the part of literary historians to locate him along the predictable ley-lines of literary influence: Byronism for the romantic poetry; French classicism for the prose etc. This latter tendency has also had the effect of 'biographizing' criticism of the writer, who is seen as having passed through the successive stages of classicism, romanticism and realism (generically signposted by lyric poetry, narrative poetry/closet drama and prose).[1] The essays gathered here, however, reflect a growing and welcome tendency to view Pushkin within a much broader range of fundamental influences: as an autonomous and unmediated reader of the accumulated inspirational fund which is European culture. Such an approach defines him as an equal to his great European predecessors, rather than their brilliant student.[2] At the same time it does not question Pushkin's position at the centre of Russian culture, but rather enhances and justifies it.

The chapters which comprise this book are all broadly concerned with the mythic dimension of Pushkin's work. The striking recurrence in his œuvre of myths and archetypes may be interpreted in part as a manifestation of Pushkin's overall stylistic economy, wherein myth fulfils on the thematic level the same inferential function as metonymy on the stylistic. Jakobson, in particular, famously demonstrated not merely the specific functioning of one such myth but, by tracing its recurrence and reformulation, established its presence as a structural principle throughout Pushkin's œuvre.[3] The degree of mythic coherence in Pushkin's work, suggestive as this might be of inherent 'system', is a matter of dispute. Advocates of mythic coherence might agree with Savely Senderovich that '... two myths within the bounds of one mythology may reveal a common superstructure. The network of such superstructures, permeating the whole œuvre of a given author, allows the consideration of his œuvre as one integral mythological system'.[4] There is, of course, a long tradition of resisting the extraction of over-arching *meaning* from Pushkin's œuvre, but this position (Tomashevskii provides an extreme instance) thrives only when the opposing arguments are unsophisticated.[5] A protean poet is open to protean critical approaches and this is precisely what we see in the work of contemporary commentators such as Greenleaf and Bethea. Greenleaf's substitution of 'autoportraiture' for autobiography reflects a preference for 'isolated, immanent cross-sections' and the suppression of discourse over 'an explanatory theory of the self's coherent existence in time'. The critic's attention focuses on recurring 'clusters' of 'imagos' or 'psycho-dramas' which travel over 'generic and content boundaries'.[6] Bethea, while an admirer of Jakobson, finds that the structural articulation of his sculptural myth neglects important dimensions of Pushkin's creativity ('the poet's awe and enchantment before the idea of *living form*') and therefore concludes that he was not 'successful at *realizing* the sculptural metaphor in the larger context of the poet's personal mythology'.[7] Bethea, in fact, may be regarded as supplementing and expanding Jakobson's basic myth by the addition of others, as his chapter in the present work illustrates.

The studies which comprise this volume point in general towards two distinct Pushkinian orientations towards myth: 1. appropriation and reinterpretation of existing European myths either at an explicit or subtextual level: Cupid and Psyche, Cleopatra, Dante and Beatrice, Don Juan; 2. the creation of original mythological figures out of the raw material of Russian history and culture: the protagonists of *Evgenii Onegin, The Bronze Horseman* and *The Captain's Daughter* (and, in an alternative formulation, *The History of Pugachev*). Importantly, these two categories are constantly melting into one another, with the first often implied by the second and the second valorized by the first; their interpenetration is part of the wider dialogue between European culture in general and Russian culture in particular. We should, however, posit a third mythological pole: Pushkin inserted himself into some of these myths which are not fully interpretable without reference to him. This must be true of *Evgenii Onegin,* for instance, where it is arguable that he is 'the primary historical personage of his own novel'[8] or, as Sandler puts it '[his] life was lived between the chapters'.[9] Thus Pushkin is raised (or raises himself) to something like mythic status, acquiring his own heroic plot, 'a drama played out by other people', one might say *for* other people.[10] This heroic myth is inalienable from Pushkin and a cultural fact quite distinct from either his biography or biographically structured critiques of his work. Transcendent national significance is part of heroic myth, as is a space in which the myth can be imagined and realized. It is St Petersburg which becomes the urban equivalent of 'Pushkin country' to borrow (if paradoxically) an increasingly common British designation for poetical space. Acmeism was partly founded on the implications of this creative symbiosis. Later scholars have explored the relationship more analytically. Over half the contributors to the present volume address this phenomenon either directly (Alexandra Smith) or via *The Bronze Horseman*. Like the Promised Land possession had to be wrested from a predecessor's grasp: St Petersburg, as Pushkin realized, was first of all 'Peter's creation'; Pushkin had first to recognize this before transcending it. Alexandra Smith quite rightly sees here a special form of the anxiety of influence (of which more later) - in this instance, however, transferring the private agon of literary emulation to the grand cultural arena. Pushkin acknowledged this problematic 'Petri-faction' by absorbing it into the wider symbolic system of petrifaction wherein the living may survive monumentally and the monumental becomes and remains at a certain level - alive.

Myth in general exhibits such quasi-vital properties, particularly in its capacity for evolution as it is successively re-appropriated and re-animated into contemporary significance. *The Queen of Spades*, for instance, becomes the archetext for a number of subsequent Russian works[11] (Robin Aizlewood speaks of the work's 'protean influence' in subsequent Russian literature). The plot and character structure of *Evgenii Onegin* becomes a fundamental axiom of the Russian realist novel and the spectral St Petersburg inhabited by the alienated Evgenii in *The Bronze Horseman* provides the core around which Gogol and Dostoevskii further develop the myth of the city. These, the results of successors poring over his works, are an essential part of our understanding of Pushkin, not an annexe to it: if Pushkin is indeed a rich mine of myth this is verifiable as much by what is extracted from him by later Russian writers as by the insights of criticism. One may conclude that the various explanations for this sublime influence - pure genius, experimentation in a wide number of genres, cultural acuity, linguistic innovation - come together in the single quality of *inferentiality*: maximal receptional scope: multi-predication between signified, signifier and interpretation; irresolvable aporia; the capacity for inexhaustible re-reading.

Reading is a process and what is readable is the object of that process. But it is not merely the object which is present to be read in Pushkin, but the process itself. Pushkin furnishes, as well as myth, the secret of transforming the myth. For while there is a nexus of intertextual transformation which runs seamlessly from Pushkin's own appropriation of myth to his successors' appropriation of that appropriation, there is, between the termini of this semiosis, a process of self-appropriation on Pushkin's part, a revisitation of the same mythic archetypes and multiple re-scripting of the same mythic core. This is what A.L. Bem, in another context, called 'self-imitation'.[12] It is certainly possible to approach the manifestations of the sculptural myth in Pushkin's œuvre from this point of view which clearly differentiates itself from the notion that such manifestations represent multiple recurrence to a central conceptual hub (rather than sequential re-scriptings which can be traced back to a primal mythic source).

The appropriation (or elaboration) of pre-existing myth, as the basis of either plot or character, as opposed to conscious innovation in those areas, or a studied realism, might be thought to be essentially classical in orientation. It suggests deference to pre-existing form. On the other hand Pushkin's way of dealing with such archetypes is recognizably romantic. The forms are taken, but the writer passionately engages with them so that they become simultaneously self-standing myths and intimate aspects of the transforming artist: they are subjectivized. It is not, as in classicism, that the artist must do homage to the priority of myth; the myth itself is made to do homage to the artist. This is the Copernican revolution wrought by romanticism. However only an animated myth can perform such homage and thus we have in Pushkin the several instances in which the mythic or temporally prior is conjured to life: the Stone Guest, the Bronze Horseman, the animated card and the Countess in *The Queen of Spades*.[13] Each of these animations corresponds to the deepest wishes or fears of the perceiving subject. Bethea sees affinities between this process and the Pygmalion myth which foregrounds the animation of artefact by artist (rather than, as in Jakobson's scheme of things, the nature of the animation itself).[14] Yet such animations transcend artifacts and are better seen as the result of a certain kind of *artefaction* of the objective world. If we cast the net thus widely we can include here the animation of his hoard by the Covetous Knight and that of the Neva by the narrative voice of *The Bronze Horseman*.[15] This desire to animate, indeed *animism*, is typically romantic - as are the often unpredictable and deadly consequences of such animation or the desire for it. Its relative circumscription and rationalization in Pushkin's work may be attributable to the restraining influence of classicism, rather than the aesthetic demands of emergent realism.[16] Certainly the reverse of this process - *petrifaction* rather than *artefaction* (where art animates) - evokes the rigidity of classicism. The archaic has a dead quality, but it is a hard deadness that makes it endure: the living corpse of the Countess in *The Queen of Spades* and Salieri with his austere aesthetic (which itself involves dissecting music like a corpse) are spooky symptoms of outmoded canons which will not give way. Bethea is right to call the sculptural myth 'double-sided'.[17] However it is arguably true that Pushkin's myth in general contains this potential for reversibility. It is systemic: the systole requires a diastole and there is therefore no didactic closure in this mythologizing. Between mortification and animation, rigidity and freedom, past and present, authority and autonomy, Pushkin seeks less to choose than to conditionally emphasize. The myths themselves remain animate through this very refusal of closure.

Of the chapters which comprise the present volume Bethea's probably most closely engages with what has been said above. Bethea here analyses a myth complementary to that of Pygmalion which formed a central part of his *Realizing Metaphors*. The two are complementary and might be said to represent an ongoing project by the author to 'map' the mythological deep structure of Pushkin. The attractiveness of Pygmalion is that it is an artist's myth (and one moreover which runs radically counter to the prevalent aesthetics of ancient Greece).[18] The Cupid and Psyche myth (from Apuleius' *Golden Ass*, a work well-known to Pushkin) is interesting when read against Pygmalion: it can be seen as the creature's reciprocal desire to know the creator. Love is the animating power in both myths, but whereas love concludes the Pygmalion story, it is merely the starting point for Cupid and Psyche.

The power of the Psyche myth is that it encapsulates both anthropological and psychological features of human sexuality. The first of these is not of principal concern, although the myth curiously conflates two forms of anonymity in the courtship process: that enforced in some cultures on the betrothed of both sexes *before* marriage and that enforced on the male in some Caucasian tribes: that he should, for the first months of his marriage visit his wife only at night and as secretly as possible. However, the psychological implications of the myth are developed by Bethea to explore, in particular, the character of Tatiana, for, if Pygmalion is peculiarly fitted to the predicament of the artist, the Psyche myth is especially bound up with the self-realization of its heroine. The myth sets up a binary between having one's lover but not knowing his identity and knowing his identity but not having him. As Bethea rightly perceives, Psyche's self-knowledge is dependent on her knowing who her lover really is (since she has been falsely led to believe that he is a demonic being).[19] Psyche chooses to find out the identity of her lover and so drives him away; Bethea sees this myth as underlying Tatiana's thrust towards self-knowledge in *Evgenii Onegin*. In particular strong and convincing analogies are drawn between Psyche's enlightenment and that which is acquired by Tatiana when she pores over the books and ornaments in Onegin's study after the death of Lenskii.

Remarkable though the myth is in terms of Pushkin's transformation of content, the formal conditions of the appropriation are also striking. Where Psyche's plot follows the following order: 1 told her lover is a demon; 2 in love (after pricking herself with Cupid's arrow); 3 discovers his identity; 4 is rejected; 5 seeks him out, Tatiana's plot represents a re-arrangement: 1, 2, 5, 4, 3. This remarkable discrepancy shows the importance of plot sujetization in the revision and re-animation of myth; in this case the inversion of the three terminal components suffices to provide the modern heroine with an intellectual dialectic denied to her mythic archetype. The curiosity which animates both heroines recalls Hobbes' contention that it is a uniquely human quality (in that it directs animal desire to a purely intellectual end: knowledge for its own sake).[20] This goes to the heart of Pushkin's use of myth; it is not merely for æsthetic effect: these 'unexpected changes and metamorphoses ... go to the centre of a hero or heroine's identity'.[21]

A different myth, applied to the same novel by Marguerite Palmer activates a quite different metaphorical system, intimately involving the creative status of the hero himself. Palmer sees *Evgenii Onegin* as deeply structured by Dante's great work on two distinct levels: the relationship between the poet and his heroine; the relationship of the poet to other poets. The second of these - a poet's preoccupation with his own canonical status - was clearly a matter of æsthetic as well as personal concern to Pushkin. Bethea, for instance, has dealt elsewhere convincingly with Pushkin's consciousness of his own literary position vis-à-vis Derzhavin in terms of Bloomian anxiety of influence.[22] However, there is evidence too that Pushkin viewed the artist's relationship to his predecessors and successors as fundamental to creative consciousness. *Mozart and Salieri* is clearly a meditation on this theme but with strikingly original elaborations.[23] Two Bloomian anxieties manifest themselves in Salieri, an 'orthodox' urge to emulate his predecessors, and a far more profound reaction to the threat posed by Mozart. Mozart, of course, threatens to deprive Salieri of his influence on later generations and he himself is younger in years and possessed of youthful vitality. *Mozart and Salieri* therefore realizes in a particular artistic context that more generalized anxiety between old and young which is typically Pushkinian and pervades works as diverse as *The Stone Guest*, *Evgenii Onegin*, *The Queen of Spades* and *The Bronze Horseman*.

Palmer starts from the position that Dante's negotiation of the Inferno under Virgil's guidance represents for Pushkin the archetypal relationship between poet and predecessor and models the creative relationships in *Evgenii Onegin*. The most obvious such relationship in the novel is that between Pushkin and Lenskii and it is Lenskii who is sent Lethe-wards by his creator, while the latter is left to elegiacally lament his passing. However, Palmer contends that there is a creative triangulation in the novel between Pushkin, Lenskii and Onegin and argues in favour of the poetic credentials of the latter. Lenskii is briefly the satellite of Onegin and 'could be viewed as a parody of Virgil, allowing Onegin to adopt the role of Dante'. Here we encounter the other major Dantean motif - Tatiana as Beatrice and therefore muse. In the emulation between these three male figures, victory goes to him who wins the favour of this muse incarnate - a privilege reserved, inevitably, for Pushkin himself.

If Tatiana embodies a chaste and virtuous form of female empowerment, Cleopatra is its demonic counterpart. The incomplete narrative poem of this name (1824) is founded on the apocryphal tradition that the Egyptian Queen sold herself to those who were willing to sleep with her for a single night and to pay with their lives the next morning. This is enhanced as a myth of female empowerment when read against the more widely known *One Thousand and One Nights* in which it is a woman who is to pay this forfeit. Although this work is fragmentary and unfinished, Burnett sees it as importantly anticipating *The Queen of Spades* in its linking of risk, sexual attraction and financial gain. Here is a good example of mythic evolution in Pushkin. The characterization of Cleopatra, who is introduced as vocal and animated, but then, seemingly responding to the crowd's 'idolization' of her, becomes impassive and statue-like, aligns the work with later ones based on the statuary myth: *The Stone Guest* and *The Bronze Horseman* as well as with those lyrics (*Exegi monumentum, The*

Poet and the Crowd) which grow out of the theme of mass appraisal or adulation. In this respect the three-stage semiotics of the poem are interesting: while living she is treated as an idol; when, however, she responds like an idol the crowd grows apprehensively silent; in response to this silence she re-animates, but as something demonically superhuman. The three distinct personas which participate in this dialectic - the living person, the idol and the living idol, are functionally similar to those that are found in *The Bronze Horseman*. This dynamic structure may indicate something fundamental about Pushkin's view of the historical process and its relation to myth, but only because the contexts are here historical, even imperial. However, we see variations of this same process in contexts shorn of explicit historical significance (*The Queen of Spades*, *The Stone Guest*). Burnett is inclined to view the work from the much wider perspective of eros and thanatos, but he also argues that it highlights tensions in Pushkin's æsthetic between the pathos of rapture and passion and the detachment or serenity which Pushkin felt necessary for the appreciation of beauty.

There is both a specious and genuine goal to Cleopatra's actions: while her victims fancy they will enjoy her charms for their own sake, Cleopatra sees herself as an acolyte of Aphrodite (Kiprida): they are to take part in a sacred, rather than a profane act, and the death which seems Cleopatra's whim is a sacrifice to the god and therefore the end and justification of the process.[24] *The Stone Guest* shares with *Cleopatra* a theme which focuses on obsessive eros, but whereas in *Cleopatra* there is rationalization to be found in the enactment of sacrificial mysteries, no such logical explanation presents itself for the amorous activities of Don Juan. However, one may argue that none is required: Don Juan is himself the archetype of promiscuous male behaviour and, as such, serves nobody but himself. He is exemplar rather than example. He is moreover a romantic, rather than classical myth, thus representative of self-definition rather than derivation from higher authority. André van Holk sees this in processive terms as 'the agent's orientation towards a goal or object ... [and] the orientation from object or goal back to the agent...' The romantic system envisaged here only works if it is fully circular, so that the subject's emotional output is matched by reciprocal input from the goal sought. This is a useful model and we can test it against a number of love plots in Pushkin, where (as in *Evgenii Onegin*) the reciprocity fails or (as in *The Blizzard*) it is deferred. Van Holk argues that 'the compactness and intensity' of *The Stone Guest* marks it out 'as one of the jewels of Pushkin's œuvre' and he makes a convincing case in favour of its structural elegance, particularly as regards characterization.[25] *The Stone Guest* exhibits typical features of recurrent Pushkinian motifs: the triangle of Don Juan, Anna and the Comendador has a similar structure and psychological dynamics to that of Onegin, Tatiana and Tatiana's husband. However, here it is the third of these figures who is foregrounded and the play thus also resonates against other of Pushkin's works which centre on the problem of precedence, priority and the dominant persistence of the past. As in *Cleopatra* and *The Bronze Horseman* it is the onlooker who animates. However in contrast to these works it is the blasphemous insouciance of the immoral Don Juan which brings the idol to life, coupled with the catalogue of dishonour which he has suffered (and continues to suffer) at Don Juan's hands. To that extent he is an objective agent of retribution who comes to re-assert the laws which the hero has violated. The continuing mastery of the present by the past, symbolized by an animated petrifact, is not unique to *The Stone Guest*; however the work's almost provocative romanticism æstheticizes the temporal confrontation: in Don Juan we see the quintessentially romantic hero, the breaker of every rigid convention, disciplined and destroyed by the rigid effigy of priority and precedence. It is substantially the same confrontation as in *The Stone Guest*'s stable-mate *Mozart and Salieri* and lays bare Pushkin's problematic relationship to the two dominant æsthetics which shaped him.

The most complex reconfiguration of the mythic elements of *The Stone Guest* is to be found in *The Queen of Spades*. Hermann, like Don Juan, wrestles with the past, but it is a complex past which contains the ambiguous romantic image of Napoleon as well as the relics of pre-romanticism; his implied imitation of the former and violation of the latter produce a belated reprise of the confrontation in *The Stone Guest* but on a more broadly cultural level. Robin Aizlewood investigates the relationship between these two works in depth and analyses the multi-layered parallels between them. In particular, he stresses the 'desacralization' of *The Queen of Spades* relative to its predecessor: although questions of life and death, good and evil, are present in the story, they are clouded in ambiguity and, whereas Don Juan is 'an archetypal transgressor' Hermann represents something more morally ambiguous and less easily definable. Aizlewood's study of doubles in *The Queen of Spades* lays bare the polyvalent nature of Pushkin's mythology. Hermann, for instance, functions as a Don Juan to both Lizaveta and the Countess as well as a death-bearing stone guest; on the other hand the Countess herself also has idol-like qualities both before and after her death. Interestingly Aizlewood concludes that the 'very obviousness' of the onomastic doubling of Hermann and St Germain in the story suggests that it is functioning less as a double in its own right than as an 'emblematic sign of doubling' - a laying bare of the device. Significantly the full gamut of doublings in *The Queen of Spades* only emerges intertextually, when read against *The Stone Guest* which functions in this comparison less as archetext than parallel manifestation of common mythic substructures determining plot and characterization, among them petrifaction (and its reverse) in both literal and figurative form.

Four of the contributors to this volume chose to write about the most celebrated manifestation of this substructure - *The Bronze Horseman*. Jakobson, as is well known, referred to Pushkin's treatment of statuary as 'the sign of a sign'.[26] Tatiana Smoliarova places *The Bronze Horseman* in a broad and ancient tradition of *ekphrasis* - poetry about artefacts - which has classical origins. The æsthetics of ekphrasis imply not merely the description of statues, pictures or buildings, but eulogy, since what has been chosen for description must have been deemed worthy of description. At the same time, as Smoliarova points out, 'the crucial notion, the key-word for such a description would be the Greek word *pneuma* ... the animation of the statue in question. One should say that it is energetic as if it were alive ... as if it has just jumped or will be jumping in the next few minutes'. Thus traditional ekphrastic æsthetics foregrounds not so much realistic representation as transformational potential: the statue is not merely life-like; it seems about to come to life - in Bethea's terms the æsthetics of Pygmalion. Smoliarova demonstrates that Falconet himself aimed for just such an effect in sculpting Peter's monument, wishing to extract from his spectators the ultimate ekphrasis: 'It's alive!' However, Pushkin elaborates this semiotics in such a way that it is impossible to conclude that Evgenii in the *Bronze Horseman* is somehow an æsthetically correct viewer of the statue. Pushkin adds a preliminary metaphoric semiotic in which Evgenii (and Don Juan) address their statues *as though* they were alive; it is this provocative communication which animates their statues; or by corollary one may conclude that Pushkin verbalizes the æsthetic criterion of ekphrasis - to be life-like is to understand words. Moreover, as Alexandra Smith notes, some contemporary commentators (breaking the canons of Lessing) referred to Peter's statue as 'Falconet's epic poem', a sculpted ekphrasis of a virtual text, so that Pushkin's poem becomes (to paraphrase Jakobson) an 'ekphrasis of an ekphrasis' or the re-animation of a text fixed in stone.

The theme of the statue's animation is a focused aspect of the broader theme of Peter the Great's continual survival in the fabric of his city - petri-faction in both senses of the word.[27] Alexandra Smith, however, argues that there is also a Pushkinian Petersburg and that, in the broadest terms, the city can be seen as the joint creation of these two figures. In a sense it is Pushkin who imparts cultural and historical perspective to the city: in different but complementary ways *The Queen of Spades* and *The Bronze Horseman* chronicle its growth and evolution, while (via, for instance, *Evgenii Onegin* and again *The Bronze Horseman*) Pushkin's own paradigmatic biography is inscribed in it in phases which also mirror the country's political evolution.

Yet, as Basker and Meyer demonstrate, Pushkin himself had shadowy co-adjutors in the creation of the civic myth, and the poem as a whole is more indebted to literary influence than is often suggested. Basker's scrutiny of Pushkin's notes to *The Bronze Horseman* reveals an implied acknowledgment of Mickiewicz whose poems about the city touch the same mythic chords (flood and monument) to produce anti-imperialist undertones which are thus mutedly present in Pushkin's work too. Meyer detects in Pushkin's description of the flood the influence of Aimée Harelle's 'The Flood at Nantes'. Here again, however, subversive ideas adhere to the intertext: the Nantes description is bound up with French revolutionary ideas and the description of Nantes suggests a city in which there is a wide gulf between rich and poor. For Meyer these resonate with the later Pushkin's broad political interests: Peter the Great (as destroyer of the old); the Decembrists (as revolutionaries); the Pugachev revolt (as mass democratic movements).[28] This intertextual dimension if anything complicates a definitive reading of the poem. Meyer sees it as synthesizing these major concerns of Pushkin; Basker's reading leads him to conclude that Pushkin, in affirming creativity, aligns himself with the creative Peter 'rather than Evgenii's descent into meaningless incoherence'. Smith inclines to the view that there is no clear ideological position in the poem.[29]

Mythologizing is at some level invariably connected to historical perspective: individual attainment of mythic status implies historical process. The situation therefore frequently arises when, as Nebolsin puts it, the artist is a historian despite himself.[30] Contrariwise, to quote Mills Todd, the reader may approach *Evgenii Onegin* as a historical novel in which social tyranny replaces the brutality of more dramatic historical events.[31] In his contribution to the present volume, Mills Todd focuses on *The History of Pugachev*, a work which is inevitably read against its fictionalized counterpart *The Captain's Daughter*. Curiously, however, as Todd points out, there is a well-established critical view that Pushkin's novel somehow better catches the spirit of the Pugachev period than the *History*; in particular *The History* fails to convey the personality of Pugachev himself which cries out for dramatic, even romantic treatment. Todd argues that Pushkin deliberately wrote his *History* using 'self-effacing conventions of normal history' although this was at odds with the prevailing taste for the ornamentations of romantic history. This 'narratorial reticence', as Todd terms it, was, of course, a feature, too, of his fictional prose. By studiedly refusing to maintain an omniscient point of view, Pushkin creates a complex interplay of multiple perspectives on a historical episode which many of his contemporaries felt should have evoked an unequivocal and passionate authorial judgement. The 'polyperspectivalism', and 'ironic and troubling lack of confusion' which the work creates is a receptive outcome familiar enough in Pushkin's fictional works, but is unconventional in historical discourse where the reader is not used to applying 'cognitive effort'.

However formulated, even the most abstract co-ordinates which make a historical perspective possible may be found on closer scrutiny to be furtively anthropomorphized. The persistence of myth in culture, and the continued emergence of myths, is only an extreme instance of this tendency. As Reid seeks to demonstrate, Dilthey's views of time are of particular relevance here because they associate the three temporalities - past, present and future - with major human cognitive processes (understanding, value, and purpose respectively). The most crucial of these modes is value: by valuing past events and experiences we maintain them in presentness. This is equally true of negative valuation (hatred or revenge for instance). Reid shows that many of Pushkin's narratives hinge upon the hero's elevation of a past event or experience to a level of unparalleled personal significance, thus permitting it to abide in the presentness of consciousness. Such intensely valorized episodes are not allowed to escape into the inertia of the past; they remain animate. This is as true on the personal level (Hermann's obsession with the Countess' winning secret) as on the civic (Russia's continuing obsession with Peter the Great).

Many of the mythic images in Pushkin do indeed come from the obsessive retention in the present of realia, persons or concepts which objectively reside in the past.[32] It is the values of the protagonist - the intensity of his ethos - which invest these elements with such power: it is a measure of Don Juan's passionate nihilism, causing him to violate the most basic social taboos and restrictions, that it can bring the outraged dead to life; it is a measure of Evgenii's despair and hatred that it can animate a monument to a historical figure, thus emphasizing the continuing presentness of that figure for the whole nation; it is a measure of Hermann's mental obsession with a past secret that a ghost visits him to resolve it for him. But there is also reciprocity in these animations: for the dead too must somehow transcend the past in order to be able thus to requite or avenge posthumous insults.

While it is not possible to derive the sort of coherent moral and philosophical conclusions from Pushkin which we can, for instance, from Tolstoi or Dostoevskii, a sense of value, mediated through characters animated by strong desires and passions, is a pervasive feature of his narratives. This exploration of passionate action, shorn of judgment or conclusion, is something Pushkin's works share with myth; but this is as it should be - Pushkin, as we have seen, is drawn to myth for this very reason, builds upon its existing foundation and himself adds to the mythic fund.

NOTES

1. This is not necessarily to validate the insights produced by either of these approaches. Briggs, for instance, combines them in an original manner. His study addresses head-on the over-assertion of Pushkin's originality or 'Pushkinolatry' by daring to point to the overestimation of the poet's romantic works in particular. This leads him to stress the positive nature of the development away from Byronism towards the realism of *Count Nulin* and *The Bronze Horseman*. See A.D.P. Briggs, *Alexander Pushkin: A Critical Study*, Croom Helm, London, 1983, p. 103.

2. Bethea and Davydov's article is an important landmark here. Among the many useful points it makes about the *Tales of Belkin* in particular there is the more general one about Pushkin's orientation towards the influence of literary movements and styles: the fates of the protagonists being wry warnings about the dominance of a range of romantic and pre-romantic mind sets. The Pushkin that emerges from such a reading is self-emancipated from the influences often attributed to him. See David Bethea and Sergei Davydov, 'Pushkin's Saturnine Cupid: The Poetics of Parody in *The Tales of Belkin*', *PMLA*, XCVI, 1, 1981, pp. 8-21.

3. Roman Jakobson, *Puškin and His Sculptural Myth*, edited and translated by John Burbank, Mouton, The Hague, 1975.

4. Savely Senderovich, 'On Pushkin's Mythology: The Shade-Myth' in Andrej Kodjak et al., eds, *Alexander Puškin, Symposium II*, Slavica Publishers Inc., Columbus, Ohio, 1980, pp. 103-15 (104).

5. See B.V.Tomashevsky, 'Interpreting Pushkin' in D.J. Richards and C.R.S. Cockrell, eds and translators, *Russian Views on Pushkin*, Willem A. Meeuws, Oxford, 1976, pp. 153-61.

6. See Monika Greenleaf, *Pushkin and Romantic Fashion: Fragment, Elegy, Orient, Irony*, Stanford University Press, Stanford, California, 1994, pp. 341-4.

7. David Bethea, *Realizing Metaphors: Alexander Pushkin and the Life of the Poet*, University of Wisconsin Press, Madison, Wisconsin, 1998, p. 97.

8. William Mills Todd III, *Fiction and Society in the Age of Pushkin: Ideology, Institutions, and Narrative*, Harvard University Press, Cambridge Mass. and London, 1986, p. 123.

9. Stephanie Sandler, *Distant Pleasures: Alexander Pushkin and the Writing of Exile*, Stanford University Press, Stanford, Cal., 1989, p. 207.

10. Id., 'Pushkin as Sign in Contemporary Russian Culture: the Example of Film' in Robert Reid, Joe Andrew and Valentina Polukhina, eds, *Structure and Tradition in Russian Society: Papers from an International Conference on the Occasion of the Seventieth Birthday of Yury Mikhailovich Lotman*, Slavica Helsingiensia, 14, Helsinki University Press, Helsinki, pp. 138-52 (141).

11. On this see Neil Cornwell, *Pushkin's 'The Queen of Spades'*, Critical Studies in Russian Literature, Bristol Classical Press, 1993, p. 59 and pp. 70 ff.

12. Bem applied this to Lermontov: see '"Samopovtoreniia" v tvorchestve Lermontova' in *Istoriko-literaturnyi sbornik. Posviashchennyi V.I. Sreznevskomu 1891-16*, Rossiiskaia Akademiia nauk, Otdelenie russkogo iazyka i slovesnosti, 1924, pp. 268-90. Imitation and self-imitation are the twin sources of poetic inspiration: one exogenous and the other endogenous (or in strict intertextual terms direct and self-mediated influence).

13. Kodjak argues that the animation of the card in the eponymous *Queen of Spades* puts it on a par with the sculptural animations discussed by Jakobson: Andrej Kodjak, '*The Queen of Spades* in the Context of the Faust Legend' in Andrej Kodjak and Kiril Taranovsky, eds, *New York University Slavic Papers*, I: *Alexander Puškin, A Symposium on the 175th Anniversary of His Birth*, New York University Press, New York, 1976, pp. 87-118 (113).

14. Bethea, *Realizing Metaphors*, p. 109.

15. Lezhnev sees the psychologized tropes used in the nature description in *The Bronze Horseman* as being typically poetic. This is in contrast to the view, typified by Bayley, that *The Bronze Horseman* is in scope and aspiration typical of a 'modern' work of prose despite its poetic form. See Abram Lezhnev, *Pushkin's Prose*, translated by Roberta Reeder, Ardis, Ann Arbor, 1983, pp. 36 ff.

16. On this see N. Vickery, *Alexander Pushkin*, Twayne Publishers, New York, 1970, p. 189.

17. Bethea, loc.cit.

18. For instance *Phaedrus*, 275 c-d: '... for the characters of painting stand like living beings, but if one asks them a question, they preserve a solemn silence'.

19. In this respect the parallels between this myth and Lermontov's *The Demon* are very striking, and, as far as I know, unexplored.

20. Thomas Hobbes, *Leviathan*, ed. John Plamenatz, Fount Paperbacks, Collins, Glasgow, 1983, p. 92. Serbo-Croatian is the only language known to me which actively captures this meaning - *znatiželnost*: 'desire to know'.

21. We also see here the beginnings of that psychological realism which will come to full development in Tolstoi and Dostoevskii. As Debreczeny points out Tatiana's reading is a complex process embracing author, character and reader: 'In Tatiana we watch a fictional character reading fiction. Not only is she adapting her reading matter to her needs as she creates the narrative of her life, but the whole description is coloured by Pushkin's ironic view of the kind of literature she reads'. See Paul Debreczeny, *Social Functions of Literature: Alexander Pushkin and Russian Culture*, Stanford University Press, Stanford, California, 1997, p. 28. The reader is made to see Tatiana as a fellow reader and thus she is animated by a kind of lectorial *cogito* (of powerful rhetorical, if of dubious logical force): I read and (therefore now) exist; she too reads and therefore exists. The suppressed axiom is that reading implies intellection.

22. Bethea, op.cit., pp.137 ff.

23. On the æsthetics of *Mozart and Salieri* see the present author's *Pushkin's 'Mozart and Salieri': Themes, Character, Sociology*, Rodopi, Amsterdam and Atlanta, 1995.

24. We see this bifurcation in *The Queen of Spades* too: the erotic plot in which Lizaveta will spend a night with her Napoleon which is but a means to the real plot which has the Countess and her 'mysteries' as its goal and Lizaveta, predictably, as merely the acolyte.

25. This is in marked contrast to Briggs' appraisal of it as Pushkin's weakest masterpiece: Briggs, op. cit., p. 178.

26. Jakobson, op. cit., p. 31.

27. Simmons regards the plot of *The Bronze Horseman* as a 'fantastic device' and 'pure poetry' in contrast to the 'realistic' imagery and language. Paradoxically, however, the animative theme of the poem appears fantastic only if subjected to an uncompromisingly realist or reductionist reading. See Ernest J. Simmons, *Pushkin*, Vintage Books, 1964, p. 357.

28. Lotman summarizes all of these categories in terms of Pushkin's general interest in historical cataclysm: Iu. M. Lotman, 'Biografiia pisatelia' in id., *Pushkin*, Iskusstvo, St Petersburg, 1997, pp. 19-184 (169).

29. If Andrew Kahn (*Pushkin's 'The Bronze Horseman'*, Critical Studies in Russian Literature, Bristol Classical Press, 1998, p. 4) is right in maintaining that Pushkin wrote *The Bronze Horseman* because he felt 'stymied in his historical work', we should indeed expect this text to be less historical than para-historical.

30. S.A. Nebolsin, *Pushkin i evropeiskaia traditsiia: Istoriko-teoreticheskie raboty*, Nasledie, Moscow, 1999, p. 41.

31. Mills Todd, op. cit, p. 12.

32. One may link this perhaps to the aristocratic Pushkin's sense of a dying aristocracy. On this see Sam Driver, *Puškin: Literature and Social Ideas*, Columbia University Press, New York, 1989, chapter 2.

Pushkin's Mythopoetic Consciousness: Apuleius, Psyche and Cupid, and the Theme of Metamorphosis in *Evgenii Onegin*

by

DAVID M. BETHEA

Pushkin was possessed of a richly mythopoetic consciousness. He was also, as numerous friends attest, intensely superstitious. Indeed, for a poet of Pushkin's range and energy, it is not surprising that some of his finest works are motivated thematically on the dual and interpenetrating notions that myths can, literally, come to life and that forces beyond one's control can prearrange one's destiny. Yet Pushkin never made the connection between certain crucial myths (or beliefs, superstitions) and his own unfolding biography *explicit*. He was protected from this not only by his own *amour propre* but by the carapace of what Lidiia Ginzburg terms 'genre consciousness'.[1] Stories about the fortune-teller Kirchhof or the hare and the monk seen by the poet as he was preparing to depart for St Petersburg on the eve of the Decembrist uprising are tantalizing facts of Pushkin's biography (*if* they are facts),[2] but their potential status in Pushkin's works, where everything having to do with the historical person is artistically masked, is highly problematic. In other words, Pushkin could be as serious as he wanted within the bounds of a lyric poem, and given the date of composition of a work such as *The Prophet* (1826) it is hard to believe we as readers cannot make a connection between the violent change in the speaker and the shock of recognition in the real-life post-Decembrist Pushkin, but according to the rules of 'genre consciousness' we cannot in good faith elide the historical man with the constructed voice. Thus we can speak of *The Prophet* as a poem of conversion, but any discussion of a converted 'Pushkin' has to be placed in quotes.

There is a way, however, to get closer to Pushkin's mythopoeticizing consciousness and to see it in action, as it were. Pushkin used different angles of vision or 'voice zones' - title, epigraph, dedication, text proper, and footnotes - to suggest ways of vectoring in on competing truths (romantic, historical, etc.) within one work, say, *Poltava*.[3] No one truth holds sway in *Poltava*; its 'story' is the different truths' spirited coexistence within the bounds of a single text, which in turn is a model of the world. Likewise, we as readers can compare Pushkin's references to a single myth (or related myths) within a relatively short time period and from different generic voice zones. It would also help of course if the time period were one fraught with certain life choices and heightened by fear and anxiety. My purpose here is not to break down entirely the walls of 'genre consciousness' (not that different from the precepts of New Criticism, after all) and engage in another instance of undisciplined postmodern intrusiveness, but rather to demonstrate, through a careful parsing of the evidence, that Pushkin *returned* to a certain mythopoetic core, let us call it the idea of *metamorphosis*, that he needed to guide some of his greatest works, including *Evgenii Onegin*, and the creative life that fed them.

Two myths dominate Pushkin's thinking at the time of his marriage and his 'descent to prose'. These myths are complementary and they have one important structural element in common: metamorphosis, or a radical 'change in form' that is simultaneously a change in substance. The first has to do with the female statue that comes to life (the Pygmalion story); the second has to do with the female soul in search of love and knowledge (the Psyche and Cupid story). It is important to note, with regard to different angles of vision, that the Pygmalion story, first appearing in Ovid's *Metamorphoses*, is told from the point of view of the legendary king/sculptor receiving the gift of the living statue, while the Psyche and Cupid story, first appearing in Apuleius' *Metamorphoses, or The Golden Ass*, is told from the point of view of the young princess who marries, unbeknownst to her, the god of love. My focus in this study will be primarily on the Psyche and Cupid story, as I have discussed the Pygmalion myth at some length elsewhere.[4] Briefly stated, the change that is the needy Pygmalion's gift is the one given the male narrator (or stylized 'Pushkin') in *Evgenii Onegin*, where the muse comes alive when a modest village maiden is 'miraculously' transformed into a beautiful and wise princess; the change that is the equally needy Psyche's gift, on the other hand, is the one given the heroine Tatiana - *knowledge* of eros. How these changes relate to Pushkin the person (and bridegroom) will be noted in the course of my analysis.

During his first and most prolific Boldino autumn Pushkin was, as we know, simultaneously contemplating his upcoming marriage and anxiously corresponding across fourteen quarantines of a cholera epidemic with his fiancée in Moscow. He feared for himself, feared more for Natalie caught in the plague-infested city, and all the while wondered whether he, with his past (both its wander and its lust), was fit for domestic life with this exquisite beauty. Literal and figurative matchmakers and gravediggers/coffinmakers populate many of the works of this feverish period, from *The Tales of Belkin* to the *Little Tragedies* to the famous poem *The Devils* (*Бесы*).[5] This was also the time Pushkin completed (except for Onegin's letter to Tatiana) the last chapter of *Evgenii Onegin*. With this in mind, let us turn to another document Pushkin wrote that autumn. Referred to in the scholarly literature as 'Refutation of Criticisms' ('Опровержение на критики'), this piece was Pushkin's way of setting down his own responses to the faults others had found in his works over the years. His tone was often tetchy and much of what he wrote was never meant to be published. But one section he did publish the following year, in *The Morning Star* (*Денница*), was both finished and important enough to see into print. The excerpt begins with reference as to why his *Poltava*, which he felt to be completely 'original' and better than much of his earlier work, was a failure in the eyes of his critics. It was, first and foremost, because 'no one has ever seen a woman fall in love with an old man and, therefore, Mariia's love for the old hetman [Mazepa] ... could not have existed'.[6] The paragraph that follows is key to my argument, so I will quote it in full:

> I couldn't remain content with this explanation: love is the most capricious of passions. I'm not even speaking about the ugliness and stupidity that are preferred daily to youth, intelligence, and beauty. Recall the mythological legends, the metamorphoses of Ovid - Leda, Philyra, Pasiphae, Pygmalion - and admit that all of these fantasies [вымыслы] are not devoid of poetry. And Othello, the old Moor [негр], who captivated Desdemona with stories of his wanderings and battles ... And Myrrha, who inspired the Italian poet [Alfieri] with one of his best tragedies?[7]

How this argument implicates the speaker personally, who was obviously fretting over the May-December aspects of his union with the eighteen-year-old Natalie, is clear. As always with Pushkin, he speaks more about himself when he speaks about others.But this passage is also illuminating in the way that it presents Pushkin's deeply mythopoetic consciousness orienting itself toward the twin notions of metamorphosis and the writing of eros into life or 'plot'.

If we look a little closer, two things strike us about Pushkin's list proving love's 'capriciousness'. First, all the examples from Ovid involve females except one - Pygmalion.[8] And second, the story of Othello and Desdemona does not belong to Ovid at all, but to Shakespeare (via Cintio's *Ecatommiti*). The common denominator in all of these is the *unnaturalness* of the union. Leda is ravished by Zeus in the form of a swan; because Minos refuses to sacrifice the beautiful bull given him by Poseidon, the god causes Minos' wife Pasiphae to become enamoured of the bull, with which she couples and gives birth to the Minotaur; likewise, Philyra lies down with Saturn, who has transformed himself into a horse, and produces the centaur Chiron. The unnaturalness in the case of Myrrha is that of incest: in the original Ovidian version, she conceives a fatal passion for her father Cinyras, tricks him into making love with her in the dark, is impregnated by him, and for her crime is transformed into the myrrh tree. The metamorphosis that Pushkin senses at the centre of *Othello* is for us especially pertinent: not only does the story involve the 'inexplicable' love of the beautiful Desdemona for the 'monstrous' Moor, with both family (Brabantio) and society (led by Iago) condemning the couple for 'making the beast with two backs', but deeply implicated in the plot of the tragedy is Apuleius' tale of Psyche and Cupid, only in reverse. At the climax of Shakespeare's play it is the male spouse who, coming in the dark to murder the

female one, is concerned with lamps ('Put out the light, and then put out the
light'), lets fall on the comely sleeper (thus waking her) not a drop of boiling oil
but his own hot tear, and, *contra* Apuleius (hence the tragedy), does succeed in
killing what is most dear to him.[9] When Pushkin says that 'these fantasies are not
devoid of poetry', what he means is that desire is by definition unexpectedly,
even shockingly, specific (a beautiful woman who, aroused, makes love to a bull
or her father or an exotic blackamoor), just as it is both potentially 'beautiful'
and potentially 'beastly'.

How these stories link up to the actual Pushkin of the first Boldino
autumn is, as we noted, fraught with conceptual problems, but perhaps not
impossibly so. First, let it be said that, given his 'protean' genius and the
remarkable capaciousness of his imaginative empathy, Pushkin could insert
himself, or his 'textual desire', into multiple roles. One of the hallmarks of a
Pushkin work is that the poet is everywhere and he is nowhere: he is Aleko and
the Old Gypsy, Peter and Evgenii, Petrusha Grinev and Masha Mironova and
even Pugachev himself. Indeed, at risk of contradicting myself, I would suggest
that there are certain characters in Pushkin who are especially imbued with their
author's desire: Grigorii Otrepev, Tatiana, and Don Juan, for example. But this
statement can be proved only by a methodical sifting of textual (artistically
shaped) and non-textual (artistically unshaped and in many cases deriving from
the observations of others) evidence that in any event is beyond the bounds of
my analysis here. For now, suffice it to say that Pushkin was clearly smitten with
the Othello story and read it into his own biography more than once in the
second half of the 1820s, in the years leading up to his marriage: perhaps most
persuasively for our purposes, he worked its major themes and plot peripeteias
into his most autobiographically suffused narrative - *The Blackamoor of Peter
the Great* (1827-28). In that unfinished (because it was *too* autobiographical?)
historical novel we find a nexus of associations that is both familar
(Shakespearean) and new and specific (Pushkinian): passionate Abyssinian
blood; family patriarch celebrated for his feats in battle;[10] love for a beautiful
woman of the best society who is not only not put off but is actually aroused by
the black man's 'terrifying' exterior; a noble, trusting nature ('one that lov'd not
wisely but too well' and 'one not easily jealous, but being wrought / Perplex'd
in the extreme') that, fearing betrayal, is nearly devoured by the 'green-eyed
monster'. Add to this the evidence, presented convincingly by Tatiana
Tsviavlovskaia, that Pushkin experienced the end of his affair with Elizaveta
Vorontsova and his exile from Odessa to Mikhailovskoe as a kind of re-
enactment of his great-grandfather's story ('black-white' coupling,
'Proserpinian' undercurrents of jealousy and betrayal, a natural child who is
racially 'unnatural', return to 'Russia' and 'Russianness' from 'abroad'), and we
begin to see how crucial this notion of a 'beauty and the beast' metamorphosis
was to Pushkin's interpretation of the facts given to him by the twin fates of
biography and history.[11] That the Desdemona of Shakespeare was young,

inexperienced, deeply in love with the Moor, and despite Iago's machinations, ultimately faithful was not lost on Pushkin. Where *Blackamoor* breaks off, that is, after Ibrahim has finally begun to get over his affair with the lovely yet anything-but-monogamous 'Parisian'[12] Countess D. and to set his sights on the 'unspoiled' and echt-Russian maiden of old boyar stock Natalia Gavrilovna Rzhevskaia, is also not far from the place that Pushkin the unlucky suitor had arrived with his own feelings by the late 1820s. The wishful thinking (artistic licence) that has Russia's greatest tsar assuring his godson of his inherent worth and dignity and informing the Rzhevskii family that it is the tsar's will that they make peace with the bridegroom they call a 'black devil' strikes the reader as nothing short of divine intervention. It is as though this Othello has help from a fairy godfather as he prepares to win his homegrown Desdemona with tales of his adventures.

We know from a variety of sources, including his own private statements, that Pushkin was, from a very young age, sensitive about his appearance. But this knowledge gives the modern reader no special privilege, no psychoanalytic wedge, that pries open like a hinge the poet's 'inner life'. Pushkin's ugly-duckling appearance was no secret,[13] while that inner life was. His 'blackamoorish ugliness' ('арапское мое безобразие'),[14] which some women found so repellent as to be attractive,[15] is simply a fact, though a not insignificant one, of his biography. What does concern us, however, is how Pushkin turned this perceived lack into gain by placing it at the centre of his personal mythology through the theme of metamorphosis: undesirable transformed into desirable, nature rewritten as culture. Perhaps an example taken from his early verse can give a more vivid sense of what I have in mind:

> While I, an eternally frivolous scapegrace,
> An ugly descendant of Negroes,
> Raised in wild simplicity,
> Not knowing the sufferings of love,
> I am pleasing to youthful beauty
> With the shameless fury of desire;
> With an involuntary flame in her cheeks,
> Not understanding herself [why],
> [So too] does a young nymph furtively
> Look at times on a faun.[16]

Here we see the principle of metamorphosis at work. The speaker, the stylized young 'Pushkin' of 1820, is addressing his friend F.F. Iurev, a co-member of the Green Lamp society, who is dashing and handsome in all the traditional ways. With his black moustache and pleasing smile, this budding 'Adonis' (Myrrha's son) and 'favourite of Venus' (баловень Киприды) does not have to try in the games of love. Women's longing glances seem to 'flock' (летят) to him of their own accord. But in the second half of the poem, the portion cited above, the speaker creates an antithesis to Adonis as his own signature myth. This anti-Adonis is not beautiful on the outside, but rather an 'ugly descendant of Negroes'. There is something about him that is clearly 'monstrous'. And the monstrousness is in turn *transformed* into the attractive bestiality of the Pan-like faun, who, half-man and half-goat, is the epitome of lubricity and who is known to arouse irrepressible lust in women and to haunt them in their dreams. The nymph in the poem blushes because she wants the faun but does not know why and suspects that that desire is shameful or 'unnatural'.

APULEIUS IN *EVGENII ONEGIN*

So far we have been discussing mainly the male attributes of desire.[17] The changes in the Tatiana of chapter 8, as she is transformed from village maiden to high society princess, are changes that arouse *him*. At some basic level she is his, the author-narrator's, creation: *he* explains her origins as the latest incarnation of his muse at the beginning of chapter 8, *he* 'unveils' her at the 'светский раут' ('grand rout/reception'), *he* makes this ice goddess both universally desirable and secretly passionate and needful, and at the end *he* withholds her ('my Tatiana') from the hero and gives her forever to the reader (which is to say, to himself). But in Pushkin's novel-in-verse the heroine is both the poet's creation and a psychologically realized character in her own right - she is both 'poeticized' and 'novelized'. In this respect, and always keenly aware that turnabout is fair play, Pushkin was equally interested in the female attributes of desire: he wanted to be able to imagine for himself and his readers (many of whom were women) a heroine who was not merely a male's Promethean self-projection but who really did appear to think and feel and need in a manner consonant with her 'kind'. For this Pushkin had to turn to another powerful story of metamorphosis, this one focusing on the female.

        In the very first lines of chapter 8 Pushkin takes us back to his poetic awakening at the Lyceum:

> In those days when in the Lyceum parks
> I insouciantly blossomed out,
> Read willingly Apuleius,
> But didn't read Cicero,
> In those days in the secret vales,
> In the springtime, to the calls of swans,
> Near the water glimmering in the quiet,
> The Muse began to appear to me.[18]

This reference to Apuleius is, arguably, one of many in a work that is throughout intertextual. In the drafts, for example, Pushkin also toyed with using as rhyme partner for 'лицея' ('of the Lyceum') 'Елисея' ('of Elisei'), another work replete with humour, bawdiness, and ancient gods and goddesses: Vasilii Maikov's *Елисей, или раздраженный Вакх (Elisei, or Bacchus Enraged*, 1771).[19] However, I submit that this return to the past is foregrounded in more than the usual way. In the end Pushkin opted for Apuleius as the one author he, or at least his stylized youthful self, read *with pleasure* during the sacred period of his Lyceum tutelage and brotherhood. And in yet another draft, this one dated December 24, 1829, he portrayed himself reading Apuleius not simply 'willingly' ('охотно'), as in the published version, but 'on the sly' ('украдкой'), the idea being that there was something delightfully prohibitive about *The Golden Ass - украдкой* was the same word used to describe the nymph's blushing response to the faun - from the beginning.[20] The naturally evocative surroundings, the appearance of the Muse out of them, and the reading of Apuleius all go hand in hand. We are further entitled to consider the influence of *The Golden Ass* on the storyline of *Evgenii Onegin*, especially its climax, because Pushkin was using the Psyche and Cupid story, mediated by Bogdanovich, to investigate another metamorphosing heroine's psychology in *Peasant-Lady*, a story composed during the same Boldino autumn that the poet was completing his novel-in-verse. If the young noblewoman Liza Muromskaia is intrigued to see what it would be like to 'become' a peasant in order to attract a handsome young squire (Aleksei Berestov), then Tatiana can be seen to follow a similar course of self-reinvention, only in the opposite direction: from 'уездная барышня' ('country maiden/miss') to mistress of the highest reaches of society.

So why was Apuleius potentially such an intriguing text to Pushkin?[21] First of all, *The Golden Ass*, written probably in the first half of the second century A.D., was a novel. Rather than the mellifluous hexameters of Ovid's *Metamorphoses*, it was composed in a rather sophisticated prose framework that allowed for rapid shifts in tone, narrative irony, and the interplay between inserted texts and the outer storyline. But what must have attracted Pushkin most of all was its central theme of metamorphosis. Lucius, its hero, is turned into an ass when the too curious young man is drawn into sorcery experiments and given the wrong magic ointment. Thereafter he falls into the hands of robbers and undergoes a series of adventures, often being abused and variously humiliated. He feels intense mortification for his ugliness and brutishness and for the fact that he can no longer speak. In one later episode, which was sure to delight the same schoolboy Pushkin who read Barkov, Lucius the ass is called upon by his then keeper to have sex with a noble lady inflamed by his immense organ and willing to pay a large fee for his services. As opposed to Ovid, where similar 'beauty and the beast' scenes are never explained or 'fleshed out' with realistic motivations, here the accommodation of the beastly to the human is described in salacious detail.[22] At the end of the novel, in the now strangely rhapsodic (and much disputed) Book Eleven, Lucius is finally returned to his human form when he prays to the universal feminine deity Queen Isis and, blessed with a vision of her, agrees to serve her chastely for the rest of his life.

If *The Golden Ass* were just about the metamorphosis of Lucius, it would be entertaining but fairly one-dimensional. Its real liveliness comes from the inserted tales, which can span different books and create complex narrative structures, and Lucius' and other characters' reactions to them. It is also through these inserted tales that we find thematic allusions to other works by Pushkin, particularly *Ruslan and Liudmila* and its later sibling *Evgenii Onegin*. For example, at one point during his captivity Lucius is brought together with a young captive, Charite, who relates to the robbers' ancient cook how she was kidnapped from her husband Tlepolemus on their wedding night: 'a sudden invasion of armed men . . . burst straight into our room in a tightly packed mass . . . [and] snatched me, half dead with pitiful fright. . . . That is how my marriage, like those of Attis and Protesilaus, was broken up and brought to nothing'.[23] This sounds uncannily like the boisterous opening of *Ruslan and Liudmila*, especially if we take into account the fact that the wretched groom, like Ruslan, has lost his bride somehow shamefully, right at the moment of consummation, and is 'loudly lamenting the rape of his beautiful wife and calling on the people to help him'.[24] But the story of Charite and Tlepolemus frames the story of Psyche and Cupid, which is in turn told by the old woman: it ends on a tragic note of fidelity that interacts subtly both with the ultimately comic adventures of Psyche and with the low burlesque tales of concealed lovers and routine cuckoldry heard by Lucius on his asinine way.

In Book Eight, after Tlepolemus has heroically rescued Charite (and Lucius) from the robbers and begun, presumably, to live 'happily ever after', we learn that the young husband has been killed by his friend Thrasyllus while boar hunting. The traitor, who wants Charite for himself, makes it look like the victim was gored by a boar, when in fact it was he who stabbed him. Shortly thereafter Tlepolemus comes to the grief-striken Charite in a dream:

> 'Wife', he said. 'I call you by the name which only I have the right to use, if any memory of me still remains in your heart. But if my untimely death has caused you to forget the ties of our love, marry whom you will and be happier than I could make you; only do not accept Thrasyllus' impious hand. Have nothing to do with him, shun his bed and board. Fly from the bloodstained hand of my assassin. The wounds from which you washed the blood with your tears are not those of the boar's tusks; it was Thrasyllus' spear that took me from you' - he told her the rest, revealing the whole enactment of the crime.[25]

This is the theme of the dead or absent husband/bridegroom in danger of having his conjugal rights usurped by an interloper, which runs through Pushkin's *œuvre* like a red thread.[26] Pretending to reciprocate his advances, Charite then drugs Thrasyllus and plunges a hairpin deep into both his eyes, thus blinding him but leaving him alive. 'This is how you have found favour with a chaste woman,' rages the righteous wife, 'this is how the marriage-torches have lighted your bridal chamber. Your matrons of honour shall be the avenging Furies, and blindness your best man, and the prick of conscience will haunt you to eternity'.[27] While Charite ends by stabbing herself and joining her husband in the grave, the careful reader notes how salient topoi from the preceding Psyche story are here reversed and, rather than erotically poeticized, rendered ironic and, so to speak, 'novelized'. Instead of the male's favoured weapon, the sword, which Psyche takes up to kill the 'monster' in her bridal bed, the female hairpin, which is then actually used; instead of the 'male courage' Psyche pleads for, cunning female resourcefulness; instead of the marriage torches (cf. Psyche's oil lamp) lighting the way to the bridal chamber, the all-encompassing darkness of the blind; and instead of the prick of Cupid's arrow (eros), the prick of conscience that is synonymous with Thrasyllus' blindness and an everlasting reminder of his perfidy. So in a novel otherwise rife with tales of bawdy wives, simpleton husbands destined to wear horns, and bold lovers (the role the young Pushkin enjoyed imagining, and not only imagining, himself in), here was a story of fierce fidelity and vindication.

But without doubt the sections of *The Golden Ass* most apt to draw the young Pushkin's attention were those describing the adventures of Psyche and Cupid: Books Four-Six. Just as Lucius' story has a metamorphosis (human beast) as its central conceit, and just as Charite's and Tlepolemus' story has certain 'changeling' twists at its core ('Hæmus' appears to take command of the robbers' band only to turn into Tlepolemus and rescue Charite; Charite pretends to be in love with Thrasyllus in order to disguise her true intent as avenging fury), so does the Psyche and Cupid story have a shifting identity as its chief motivation, only in this instance the male hero does not become a beast but is revealed to be a god. More important, however, this story revolves around *the woman's* adventures, and misadventures, as she seeks self-knowledge, which is synonymous in the myth with not being kept in the dark about the true lineaments of her husband. Psyche is the traditional third, and loveliest, daughter of a king. But 'for all her striking beauty, [she] had no joy of it … Though all admired her divine loveliness, they did so as one admires a statue finished to perfection'; hence Psyche 'stayed at home an unmarried virgin'.[28] When the father, despairing over his daughter's unhappiness, prays to Apollo for help, the god answers:

> On mountain peak, O king, expose the maid
> For funeral wedlock ritually arrayed.

No human son-in-law (hope not) is thine,
But something cruel and fierce and serpentine;
That plagues the world as, born aloft on wings,
With fire and steel it persecutes all things;
That Jove himself, he whom the gods revere,
That Styx's darkling stream regards with fear.[29]

Thus Psyche, acting out the mythical fears of every nubile maiden commanded to enter into an arranged marriage and knowing nothing about her proposed spouse, is taken to the mountain top as 'a living corpse'. Believing her groom to be a monster, 'something cruel and fierce and serpentine,' she makes her approach to the place of sacrifice as one going 'not to her wedding procession, but her own funeral'.[30]

Rather than being ravished by the monster on the mountain top, however, Psyche is carried by the breath of Zephyr down into a deep valley, whereupon she falls 'sweetly asleep'. Now left alone, without her parents or sisters to advise her, Psyche's adventures begin in earnest. Once she awakes she proceeds to a magnificent palace, a 'pleasure-house of some god' that holds the 'vast treasure of the entire world' but is not secured by 'a single lock, bolt, or guard'.[31] 'Becoming a little bolder,' she crosses the threshold into the palace's empty splendour, where she is greeted by disembodied voices that tend her every whim. She examines the new surroundings in detail, is addressed as 'mistress', and is informed that 'all of it is yours'. But as she is being prepared for her bridal bed Psyche is naturally uneasy. She 'quails and trembles, dreading, more than any possible harm, the unknown'. At last 'there enters her unknown husband; he mounts the bed, makes her his wife, and departs in haste before sunrise. At once the voices that were in waiting in the room minister to the new bride's slain virginity'.[32] The point of this marriage night description and indeed of the entire Psyche and Cupid story is *who* is this husband/lover. She does not know he is Cupid, a god, who has fallen in love with a mortal and who must conceal his identity because his mother, Venus, is jealous of Psyche's beauty. And she is faced with a dilemma: no matter how sweet this lover's embraces seem, is he a 'monster', as Apollo's prediction suggested and as her jealous sisters subsequently insist, or is he the wonderful being that visits her in the dark? She has given herself, but there is something about him she is prohibited to know, and what this is is inextricably tied to her self-knowledge and 'enlightenment'. As the invisible Cupid warns her, 'their [the sisters'] one aim is to persuade you to try to know my face - but if you do see it, as I have constantly told you, you will not see it'.[33]

Psyche's condition becomes archetypal of every woman who must depend on the male, on *who he is*, to define herself. She must disobey his prohibition and see things in the light because that is where her curiosity, which is more powerful than the urge to live in erotic captivity, however splendid, drives her. She must go back on her word - 'As to your face, I ask nothing more; even the darkness of night does not blind me; I have you as my light'[34] - in order to *become herself*. So the sisters' arguments about the unknown husband being 'an immense serpent, writhing in knotted coils, its bloody jaws dripping deadly poison' win out:

> For I have never seen my husband's face and I have no idea where he comes from; only at night, obeying his voice, do I submit to this husband of unknown condition - one who altogether shuns the light; and when you say he must be some sort of wild beast, I can only agree with you. For he constantly terrifies me with warnings not to try to look at him, and threatens me with a fearful fate if I am curious about his appearance.[35]

Torn between rage and despair, 'in one and the same body ... loath[ing] the monster and lov[ing] the husband', Psyche at last agrees that she must expose the unknown one's identity and kill him while he sleeps. But when she comes to do the deed and shines the light, 'the secret of their bed becomes plain, [and] what she sees is of wild beasts the most soft and sweet of monsters, none other than Cupid himself, the fair god fairly lying asleep'.[36] It is at this moment of *cognitio* in both the literal and figurative senses that Psyche inadvertently pricks herself with one of her husband's arrows and 'without realizing it ... through her own act falls in love with Love'.[37] Immediately thereafter, that is, as she feels 'ever more on fire with desire for Desire' and as she proceeds to 'devour' her sleeping beauty with 'quick sensuous kisses', she drops the boiling oil from the lamp on Cupid's right shoulder, causing him to wake and, as promised, fly away. Thus Psyche's desire for her husband is now inevitably linked with a forbidden knowledge that translates into separation. 'But if you do see it [my face], as I have constantly told you, you will not see it.'

Banished from her paradise, Psyche goes out in search of the Cupid she has, through her own act, forced to flee. The remainder of her story has to do with the trials, imposed by Venus, that she endures in order to remove the prohibition. Pan, seeing that she is 'desperately in love', advises her to win back her husband's favour 'through tender service.'[38] (Again, the parallel in the parent text involves the rehabilitation of Lucius, who can reassume his human form only after suffering various travails and then agreeing to worship unswervingly Queen Isis.) Whether sorting through a huge hill of seeds from different grains, or obtaining some golden wool from fierce sheep, or retrieving an urn of black water from a deadly spring on a mountain top, or finally journeying to the underworld to Proserpine and returning with a small casket filled with 'beauty', Psyche rises to the occasion, showing courage and ingenuity. She is also of course aided by various magic helpers. But on her last assignment her 'reckless curiosity',[39] which is also a salient theme in Lucius' adventures, again gets the best of her: having made it safely in and out of the dark halls of Proserpine and succeeded in filling the box with its mysterious contents, she cannot restrain herself and opens the lid on her return trip, whereupon she immediately turns into a sleeping corpse.[40] She is revived, however, by another prick from Cupid's arrow, and the two lovers are at last reunited when Jupiter listens to the young god's plea and, cautioning him to curb his earlier hot-blooded pursuits, presides over the now official epithalamium. Psyche in turn is greeted into the ranks of the immortals and the daughter issuing from their union is called Pleasure.

Let us now return to *Evgenii Onegin* and to the psycho-erotic arc of Tatiana's own adventures as a heroine. There are numerous moments in the novel that are revealing of Tatiana's character: her initial appearance, her dream, her name-day party, her wanderings in the countryside, her 'sermon' to Onegin after receiving his letter, etc. But two in particular stand out as turning-points in the sense that they show Tatiana entering a *new* stage of self-knowledge. The first occurs chapter 3 when she realizes she has fallen in love with Onegin and writes him a letter, and the second takes place in chapter 7 when she visits Onegin's library and learns something there that allows her to move on with her life, including in this case agreeing to be taken to Moscow to the 'marriage market.' In both instances the crux of Tatiana's engagement with the eroticized other has to do with that other's identity - who he is, what his motives are, why he has come into her life. And if in the first case what we see is Tatiana *falling in love with Love*, being *on fire with desire for Desire*, then in the second case what becomes clear is that she hasn't fallen out of love - indeed, far from it - but rather has learned something that translates knowledge of the heart into eternal separation.

To begin with, as an embodiment of the female 'psyche', Tatiana shares certain traits with her mythological sibling: she takes no joy in her beauty or in those that admire it, she stays at home an unmarried virgin while her more gregarious and worldly sister succeeds in finding a mate,[41] and she is melancholy and lonely by nature. She is searching for something - something unavailable to her at home or in her known surroundings. When she meets Onegin she quickly falls in love, not with him specifically, because she hardly knows him, but rather with *the idea of love*.

> Tatiana listened with irritation
> At such rumours [of Onegin's interest in her]; but in secret
> With an inexplicable joy
> She thought involuntarily about it;
> And into her heart the idea sank;
> The time had come - she had fallen in love.
> Thus into the earth a fallen grain
> Is enlivened by the heat of the spring.
> For a long time her imagination,

Burning with languor and melancholy,
Had hungered for the fatal food;
For a long time the longings of the heart
Had constricted her young breast;
Her soul … awaited someone,

And found him … Her eyes were opened;
She said, 'It's him!'[42]

The point of this strophe, and of the enjambement of self-discovery that slips into the following one, is that Tatiana has for some time, and without really knowing why until now, been preparing to *fall in love with Love*. That her imagination is described as 'burning with languor and melancholy' captures perfectly that state of being 'on fire with desire for Desire' of Psyche's original self-inflicted wound (again, Cupid did not fire his arrow at her, but she found it, and pricked herself on it, on her own).

The parallels with Psyche become even stronger when Tatiana, increasingly inflamed, sits down in her nightshirt to write to Onegin. Suddenly she switches from the formal 'вы' ('you') to the intimate 'ты' ('thou', whose archaic flavour in English I have kept in the following literal translation):

Another! … No, to no one else on earth
Would I give my heart!
Such has been decreed in the highest council …
Such is the will of heaven: I am thine;
All my life has been but a pledge
Of a true meeting with thee;
I know thou hast been sent by God
And art my guardian to the grave …
Thou appeared to me in dreams,
Unseen, thou wert very sweet,
Thy wondrous glance caused me to pine,
In my soul thy voice was sounding
Long ago … no, it was not a dream!
As soon as thou entered, I recognized in an instant,
I was completely overcome, felt on fire
And in my thoughts said, 'It's him!'
Isn't it true? I heard thee:
Thou spoke to me in the silence
When I was helping the poor
Or when I softened the anguish
Of my agitated soul with prayer?
And in that same instant

> Didst thou not, sweet vision,
> Flash by in the transparent darkness,
> Press up quietly to my bedside?
> Didst thou not, with joy and love,
> Whisper words of hope to me?
> Who art thou, my guardian angel
> Or a perfidious tempter:
> Resolve my doubts.[43]

As many commentators have noted, Tatiana's expression of desire is here far in excess of that allowed by the epistolary norms of her class and status as unmarried young lady.[44] Indeed, not only is Tatiana taking a great risk in initiating this correspondence in the first place, but the very way she addresses her interlocutor is tantamount to undressing before him. But even more than that, what we see here in this exchange of words is a spontaneous act of love, a soulful 'coupling', that is highly eroticized in terms of the Psyche-Cupid encounter. This Cupid came to her in her dreams and, as the dramatic shift to ты signifies, 'slew her virginity' well before he appeared in the flesh. That is why he is referred to as both 'unseen' and a 'sweet vision' that moves around her in the darkness and presses up against her bedside to whisper in her ear. The sexual nature of this love letter is never in question - for Tatiana the search for a soul-mate is never about sex *per se* or the offering or withholding of herself as partner - but what is in question is the identity of the phantom lover, the one who, in the Psyche myth, 'enters [as the] unknown husband … mounts the bed, makes her his wife, and departs in haste before sunrise'. When Tatiana asks him, 'Who are you, my guardian angel / Or a perfidious tempter: / Resolve my doubts', she is trying to learn whether he is, on the one hand, a Cupid, 'of all wild beasts the most soft and sweet of monsters', or, on the other, 'something cruel and fierce and serpentine' ('коварный искуситель' has satanic connotations).

To sum up our findings thus far, the Psyche-Cupid story is motivated by two turning points that are especially 'magnetized' with female desire. These turning points happen at virtually the same instant in the text and are powerfully interrelated - indeed, each seems in a tantalizing way to be a mirror extension of the other. The first is when Psyche shines the lamp on her husband while he sleeps and, 'curious as ever', takes an arrow from his quiver and tries the point on her thumb, but because her hands are trembling she applies too much force and pricks herself. This is the moment when she 'falls in love with Love' and there is no turning back. It is important to realize that it is not the body of the god, however beautiful in its dormant state (for example, 'golden hair', 'rosy cheeks', 'milk-white neck', 'dewy-white wings'), that arouses Psyche until she is 'carried away by joy and sick with love'; it is rather the point of the arrow, whose wound somehow 'happens' of its own accord. The second turning point is likewise not the product of Psyche's volition:

But meanwhile that wretched lamp, either through base treachery, or
in jealous malice, or because it longed itself to touch such beauty and
as it were to kiss it, disgorged from its spout a drop of hot oil on the
right shoulder of the god. What! Rash and reckless lamp, lowly
instrument of love, to burn the lord of universal fire himself, when it
must have been a lover who first invented the lamp so that he could
enjoy his desires for even longer at night! The god, thus burned, leapt
up, and seeing his confidence betrayed and sullied, flew off from the
loving embrace of his unhappy wife without uttering a word.[45]

The lamp, whose motives here are treated with mock-epic indignation, has a
mind (and heart) of its own. It not only lights up the darkness, revealing the
identity of what was hidden, but it spreads its scalding contents on the god of
love, causing his flight. To want to know who, in the darkness of his soul, your
lover is is to chase him away. But then not to want, to *desire,* to know is
impossible - the lamp that is as essential to Psyche's identity as Cupid's arrow
is to his *wills* it.

   I would like to suggest in this last portion of my study that Tatiana's
visit(s) to Onegin's library in chapter 7 is a novelized version of Psyche's
adventures in Cupid's palace. During this visit Russia's favourite heroine
displays the same 'boldness' and 'curiosity' as her mythological counterpart. She
comes upon the 'пустынный замок' ('vacant castle') as if by chance; she
crosses over a threshold that is guarded by 'wild animals' (barking dogs[46]); she
enters the forbidden space of the male's living quarters while the master is
absent; she is tended to by a servant, a 'keeper of the keys' ('ключница'), only
this one is in the flesh; and she examines all the 'priceless' items of this interior
space, including a bed and a 'померкшая лампада' ('dimmed lamp'), as one
'enchanted'. Most convincingly, however, she has found her way to Onegin's
home in order to discover at last, after various false starts, *who her lover is.*
Where then is the wilful lamp, the scalding oil, and the fleeing god? This is a
novel-in-verse, which means that Pushkin cannot play literally on mythical
expectations, but must reflect and refract them through the alternating
poeticizing and prosaicizing prism of his hybrid form. The light from Psyche's
oil lamp has now become the reflected illumination of Onegin's *library,* his
books, the windows to his soul in a modern world where you are, more and
more, what you read.[47]

   After being left alone in the 'silent library', Tatiana first has a long cry
('И долго плакала она'), presumably over what might have been. But then she
turns to the books themselves:

> At first she was not drawn to them,
> But their selection seemed
> Strange to her. Tatiana gave herself up

> To reading with a greedy spirit;
> And a new world opened up to her.[48]

The reader immediately notices that Tatiana is pulled along by her curiosity, by her will to know. Difference - the 'strangeness' of the books' selection - plainly excites her. She doesn't rush in to apply her own categories of knowing to the new reading material, but rather allows the latter to draw her into its orbit. By the same token, the 'greediness' she exhibits seems very close to the wellsprings of desire itself. And Tatiana is rewarded for her pursuit by seeing a 'new world' open before her. On a literal level this is of course the contents of Onegin's favourite books - the stories by the 'singer of the Giaour and Juan' as well as 'two or three' contemporary novels that we learn about in the next stanza. But it is not the identity of Byron or some fellow novelist of the time that is in question here, which is probably the reason why Pushkin left the account of the actual items in Onegin's library, after experimenting with more explicit versions, intentionally vague and underdeveloped.[49] No, Tatiana is interested in *how* Onegin reads these books (and their authors), what he shows about himself in the reflected light of his interactions with their texts. On a figurative level, this is the moment in the Tatiana-Psyche story when she, holding the lamp, sees her lover exposed.

What does she find? In the original Psyche and Cupid myth the heroine dramatically illuminates the physical form of the god of love: his hair, neck, cheeks, shoulders, wings. Now, in this later novelized version of the same myth, Tatiana casts her light on the *inner* physiognomy of her lover:

> On many pages were preserved
> The sharp mark of his fingernails;
> And the eyes of the attentive maiden
> Were trained on them ever more keenly.
> Now trembling, Tatiana sees
> With which idea or remark
> Onegin happened to be struck,
> With what he silently agreed.
> On the pages' margins she encounters
> The traces of his pencil.
> Everywhere Onegin's soul
> Involuntarily expresses itself
> With a short word, with a cross,
> With a question mark.[50]

Tatiana is 'attentive' and her eyes are trained 'keenly'. The pages she is looking at 'хранить' ('preserve') the outline of his spiritual movements as though he were an invisible body leaving fugitive impressions on its surroundings. She is discovering for the first time which ideas Onegin responds to as significant, which he questions, which he ignores and passes over. The hero's 'soul' displays itself 'involuntarily', which is to say, it lets out the secret it would prefer to keep to itself. And this new information causes the inquirer to tremble because it is intimate, it is like seeing the other lying undressed and asleep. The psychic energy of this revelation is caught in the alliterative scudding and internal rhyme - the к+р+с+т sounds of 'То кратким словом, то хрестом, / То вопросительным крючком' - of the last two lines. For Pushkin, and for Tatiana, perhaps his most self-referential character, nothing is more private and more revealing of one's core identity than one's reading habits.

But it is not until the next, climactic, stanza that the new information becomes understanding, *knowledge*:

> And little by little my Tatiana
> Begins to understand
> At last more clearly - thank God! -
> The one for whom she is fated
> To sigh by a powerful fate:
> A sad and dangerous eccentric,
> A creation of heaven or hell,
> This angel, this haughty devil,
> Who is he then? Could he really be an imitation,
> A paltry phantom, or even
> A Muscovite in Harold's cloak,
> An interpretation of others' fancies,
> A lexicon full of fadish words? ...
> Is he not just a parody?[51]

In the mythological world, which is also the world of poetic expectation (nymphs fall in love with fauns and gods of love fall in love with mortals), the 'monster' is shown to be 'of all wild beasts the most soft and sweet' and thus flies away when his changeling status is revealed. There is no burn on Cupid's shoulder in Pushkin's stanzas, but there are the marks of Onegin's pencil, which wound in their own way. To repeat, the notion of shifting identity/metamorphosis (the reader does not know that the monster is Cupid until Cupid is himself exposed) is tied both to the female's will to knowledge and to the idea of punishment and separation (male prohibition). In the world where 'novel time' is emerging out of 'poetry', the changeling identity of the hero is no longer between 'monster' and 'Cupid', devil and angel, but involves a third, more prosaic possibility: Onegin is an 'imitation', a 'parody', that interacts with its created alter-egos in a profoundly uncreative way. At this, for Tatiana pivotal, juncture in the plot, Onegin 'copies' the texts that he reads into his life and merges all too neatly with the roles he encounters on the printed page. To say he is a 'Muscovite in

Harold's cloak' is to say that he tries to be *like* Childe Harold (*that* is his identity), which is a relation of lesser to greater, rather than *being himself* while still knowing Byron's text. The '*яснее*' (to understand 'more clearly') means that Tatiana at last sees what has lain hidden in her desire. This, I would suggest, is the precise moment in Pushkin's novel when Cupid *leaves* Psyche: 'if you do see it [my face], as I have constantly told you, you will not see it.' This is another way of saying that the 'he' ('It's him!') who was Tatiana's male muse and the object of her most ardent desire still exists in her 'psyche', but has from this point forth fled as something actively embodied in the person of Evgenii Onegin. The myth of Psyche and Cupid has entered novelistic space and 'my Tatiana', regardless of future trials, is not fated to be reunited with the sweet vision of her dreams.

The point about metamorphoses with which I began this discussion and to which I now return in conclusion involves the *unexpected*: the unnatural coupling of Pasiphae with a bull or Philyra with a horse (Saturn), the shocking passion of Myrrha for her father. It was Pushkin's very 'poetic' understanding - 'these fantasies [metamorphoses] are not devoid of poetry', as he said in 'Refutation of Criticisms' - that every genuine desire is characterized by the quality of seeing (and feeling) something that others don't. The same holds true with the story at the centre of Pushkin's most complicated and ambitious work. If in *The Golden Ass* Psyche goes to her marriage bed waiting to be ravished by a monster, she wakes up, so to speak, having made love, and now *wanting* to make love again, to a god. Yet in *Evgenii Onegin* these expectations have been further undermined and frustrated: the hero is neither god nor monster, but an all too predictable human being, while the heroine still wants to sleep with the deity she imagined to be there. In the first Boldino autumn of 1830 Pushkin gives us not one but three competing versions of quintessentially female 'Psyches' who learn secrets about the male embodiments of eros courting them: Doña Anna and Don Juan (*The Stone Guest*), the Tatiana and Onegin of chapter 8, and Liza Muromskaia and Aleksei Berestov (*Peasant-Lady*). Not for nothing is each male lead closely tied to the Don Juan story or to 'Byronism' (Onegin collects the works of the 'singer of Giaour and Juan' and Aleksei appears in the province suspiciously 'gloomy and disenchanted' and wearing a death's-head ring) or to both. And likewise, given the author's personal concerns that autumn, it is not by chance that the heroines' anxieties and conflicts are intimately bound up with their sexual identities and with being true to themselves in different stages or statuses of life: maiden, wife, widow. (Recall again Pushkin's words to his future mother-in-law: 'God is my witness that I am ready to die for her [Natalie], but that I should die to leave a dazzling widow, free to choose a new husband tomorrow - this idea is hell'.) All of these plots, varying in tone from the tragic to the tragicomic to the comic, centre on unexpected changes, metamorphoses that go to the centre of a hero's or heroine's identity: Juan, the cynical and seemingly insatiable sexual athlete, claims to have become someone else, someone who has fallen in love for the first time and been reborn ('я весь переродился'); Tatiana, freely admitting that she still loves Onegin yet not yielding to his entreaties, turns 'miraculously' from pining provincial maiden to majestic princess; and Liza, following her thematic sibling Dushenka ('little Psyche'), keeps changing disguises until she is found out by Aleksei and can at last just 'be herself' ('In all costumes are you, Dushenka, pretty').[52]

Finally, both the inner (Psyche and Cupid) and outer (Lucius) story-lines of *The Golden Ass* open with the theme of 'ill-starred curiosity' (self-knowledge) and close with the theme of faithful service to a more elevated notion of love. And so it is with the magic-box structure of *Evgenii Onegin*. Tatiana refuses to be simply the object of male desire, which of course makes her only more desirable. She loves to know and she knows to love and she will not accept a relationship where the erotic and the cognitive are decoupled. Her creative reading habits are precisely what her loved one's are not.[53] Onegin, for his part, cannot live in the glare of Tatiana's urge to know. And the narrator, the burnisher of the 'magic crystal'? He is the force whose restless curiosity and will to know constantly challenge our expectations and eroticize all that they touch, including the provincial maiden who was prepared to give herself when she was not wanted and the *grande dame* who is no longer willing to give herself when she is. This source of energy lies somewhere between the golden ass who is crudely indistinguishable from his oversized organ (the bared device, so to speak) and the chaste priest who comes to pray to Queen Isis. Neither Psyche nor Cupid, he is closer to the prick of the arrow or the drop of the boiling oil. Which is to say, he is closer to desire *in the act of becoming* - a wanting that is articulate and that literally knows no end.

NOTES

1. 'Myshlenie zhanrovymi kategoriiami': see discussion in L. Ginzburg, *O lirike*, second edition, Sovetskii pisatel', Leningrad, 1974, p. 183.

2. The *locus classicus* in this case is Pushkin's friend S.A. Sobolevskii's article 'Tainstvennye primety v zhizni Pushkina', first published in *Russkii arkhiv* in 1870 and subsequently excerpted (that is, the relevant section about Kirchhof's prophecy) in V.E. Vatsuro et al., eds, *Pushkin v vospominaniiakh sovremennikov*, 'Akademicheskii proekt', St Petersburg, 1998, II, pp. 9-11. See also I.S. Chistova, 'K stat'e S.A. Sobolevsksogo "Tainstvennye primety v zhizni Pushkina"' in M.N. Virolainen, ed., *Legendy i mify o Pushkine*, 'Akademicheskii proekt', St Petersburg, 1994, pp. 249-56.

3. See discussion in Iu.M. Lotman, 'Posviashchenie "Poltavy" (adresat, tekst, funktsiia)' and 'K strukture dialogicheskogo teksta v poemakh Pushkina (problema avtorskikh premechanii k tekstu)', in *Izbrannye stat'i*, 'Aleksandra', Tallinn, 1992-93, II, pp. 369-88.

4. See David M. Bethea, *Realizing Metaphors: Alexander Pushkin and the Life of the Poet*, University of Wisconsin Press, Madison, 1998, pp. 10-17, 89-117.

5. See David M. Bethea and Sergei Davydov, 'Pushkin's Saturnine Cupid: The Poetics of Parody in *The Tales of Belkin*', *PMLA*, 96,1, January 1981, pp. 8-21.

6. A.S. Pushkin, *Polnoe sobranie sochinenii*, B.V. Tomashevskii, ed., 10 vols., 'Nauka', Leningrad, 1977-9, VII, p. 132. This edition will be referred to subsequently as *Pss*.

7. Ibid.

8. Pushkin had at least three different editions of Ovid, two French and one Latin, in his library as catalogued by Modzalevskii: 1) *Amours mythologiques, traduits des Métamorphoses d'Ovide par De Pongerville*, second edition, Paris, 1827 (No. 1231 in catalogue); *Œuvres complètes d'Ovide*, ed.'imprimée sous les yeux et par les soins de J.Ch. Poncelin', Paris, 1799 (No. 1232 in catalogue); and *Publii Ovidii Nasonis opera*, ed. 'recognovit, et argumentis distinxit J.A. Amar', Paris, 1822 (No.1233 in catalogue). See B.L. Modzalevskii, 'Biblioteka A.S. Pushkina' in *Pushkin i ego sovremenniki. Materialy i issledovaniia*, 9-10, 1910, p. 304.

9. See commentary in P.G. Walsh, 'Introduction' in Apuleius, *The Golden Ass*, intro. and transl. P.G. Walsh, Oxford University Press, Oxford, 1994, pp. xlvi-vii.

10. To be accurate, Abram [Ibrahim] Petrovich Gannibal's prowess as a military engineer (he eventually rose to the rank of general of the army/*general-anshef*) would come much later, and is not part of the story-line of *The Blackamoor of Peter the Great*. But as is clear from Pushkin's famous note to stanza 50 of the first chapter of *Evgenii Onegin*, these exploits were well-known to the great-grandson and reinforced, as historical background or 'horizon of expectations', the connection with the Othello story in the uncompleted *Blackamoor*. *Pss*, V, pp. 430-1.

11. T.G. Tsiavlovskaia, 'Khrani menia, moi talisman', in R.V. Iezuitova and Ia.L. Levkovich, eds, *Utaennaia liubov' Pushkina*, 'Akademicheskii proekt', St Petersburg, 1997, pp. 295-380. Tsiavlovkaia's piece first appeared in *Prometei*, X, 1974, pp. 12-84.

12. Elizaveta Ksarver'evna Vorontsova ('Elise') was of Polish origin and Pushkin seems to have been playing off her 'western' charms as he developed the figure of Countess D. in the novel. The same use of the Poles as western 'others' plays an important role in *Boris Godunov*, for example.

13. 'Vrai singe par sa mine' ('a real monkey in the face'), he writes while describing himself in the early Lycée poem *Mon Portrait*, *Pss*, I, p. 80. *Mon Portrait*, written in French, was not published in Pushkin's lifetime.

14. Letter to his wife of 14-16 May 1836, in *Pss*, X, p. 452.

15. As Countess Dar'ia (Dolly) Fikel'mon (Fiquelmont) wrote in her diary, 'The writer Pushkin conducts a conversation in a charming fashion, without pretence, [but] with animation and fire. It is impossible to be more ugly: he is a mix of the exterior of a monkey and a tiger. He is descended from African ancestors and he has retained a certain blackness [chernota] in his complexion and something wild in his glance' (N.B. Izmailov, 'Pushkin v dnevnike gr. D.F. Fikel'mon', *Vremennik Pushkinskoi komissii*, 1962 [1963], p.33).

16. *K Iur'evu* (*To Iur'ev*, 1820), *Pss*, II, p. 42: 'А я, повеса вечно праздный, / Потомок негров безобразный, / Взращенный в дикой простоте, / Любви не ведая страданий, / Я нравлюсь юной красоте / Бесстыдным бешенством желаний; / С невольным пламенем ланит / Украдкой нимфа молодая, / Сама себя не понимая, / На фавна иногда глядит.'

17. For the purposes of this study I am speaking about *heterosexual* desire.

18. *Pss*, V, p. 142:'В те дни, когда в садах Лицея / Я безмятежно разцветал, / Читал охотно Апулея, / А Цицерона не читал, / В те дни в таинственных долинах, / Весной, при кликах лебединых, / Близ вод, сиявших в тишине, / Являться муза стала мне.'

19. *Pss*, V, p. 460.

20. *Pss*, V, p. 462.

21. Pushkin had two different editions of Apuleius' *The Golden Ass* in his library: *Œuvres complètes d'Apulée*, transl. M.V. Bétolaud, Bibliothèque Latine-Française publiée par C.L.F. Pannkoucke, Paris, 1835 (No. 613 in catalogue; Pushkin had the first two volumes, the ones containing *Métamorphoses* of the four volume set); and Apulei, *Lutsiia Apuleia platonicheskoi sekty filosofa prevrashchenie, ili zolotoi osel*, transl. Ermil Kostrov, Universitetskaia tipografiia u N. Novikova, Moscow, 1780-1. The Kostrov translation of Apuleius was one of the books that Modzalevskii determined to have been in Pushkin's library at one time but then subsequently lost. B.L. Modzalevskii, *Biblioteka A.S. Pushkina* (*Bibliograficheskoe opisanie*), Tipografiia Imperatorskoi Akademii Nauk, St Petersburg, 1910, p. 160; and B.L. Modzalevskii, *Biblioteka A.S. Pushkina: Prilozhenie k reprintnomu izdaniiu*, 'Kniga', Moscow, 1988, p. 12.

22. The episode takes place in Book Ten. See Apuleius, *The Golden Ass, or Metamorphoses*, intro. and transl. E.J. Kenney, Penguin, London, 1998, pp. 184-6.

23. Apuleius, *The Golden Ass*, pp. 70-1.

24. Ibid., p. 71.

25. Ibid., p. 133.

26. The theme of a jealous speaker/hero in competition for a woman whose husband or fiancé has died is repeated throughout Pushkin's *œuvre*, from the early poem 'To a Young Widow' ('K molodoi vdove', 1817) to such mature works as *Boris Godunov* (1824-5) (the Pretender vying with the 'ghost' of the murdered Tsarevich for the affections of Marina Mniszek), *The Stone Guest* (1830) (Juan trying to seduce Doña Anna in the presence of the statue of the murdered Comendador), *The Blizzard* (1830) (the original and destined-to-die bridegroom Vladimir getting bizarrely lost on the way to his wedding while his bride Maria Gavrilovna is married, without her knowing it, to the stranger Burmin), and *Evgenii Onegin* (in the drafts Lenskii's shade may be aware that his beloved Olga has with unseemly haste fallen in love after his death with a handsome ulan officer). See *Pss*, I, pp. 214-15; V, pp. 242-3; V, p. 343; and V, p. 453. All of these instances may be summed up psychologically with Pushkin's own words, when he contemplates marrying the beautiful Natalie and then at some point in the future leaving her a widow: 'God is my witness', he writes to his future mother-in-law on 5 April 1830, 'that I am ready to die for her, but that I should die to leave a dazzling widow, free to choose a new husband tomorrow - this idea is hell'. Alexander Pushkin, *The Letters of Alexander Pushkin, Three Volumes in One*, intro. and transl. J. Thomas Shaw, University of Wisconsin Press, Madison, 1967, pp. 405-6; *Pss*, X, pp. 217-18.

27. Apuleius, *The Golden Ass*, p. 135.

28. Ibid., pp. 73-4.

29. Ibid., p. 74.

30. Ibid., p. 75.

31. Ibid., p. 78.

32. Loc. cit. For the sake of consistency in narration, I am rendering all the verbs in this passage and the ones to follow in the present tense.

33. Ibid., p. 83.

34. Ibid., p. 84.

35. Ibid., p. 86.

36. Ibid., p. 88.

37. Loc. cit.

38. Ibid., p. 90.

39. See ibid., pp. xxvi, 104, 203. Lucius, for example, suffers from 'ill-starred curiosity' ('curiositas improspera').

40. Again, this is strongly reminiscent of the scene in *Ruslan and Liudmila* when the heroine falls into a death-like sleep.

41. Sisters of course in the Psyche myth.

42. *Pss*, V, pp. 50-1: 'Татьяна слушала с досадой / Такие сплетни; но тайком / с неизъяснимою отрадой / Невольно думала о том; / И в сердце дума заронилась; / Пора пришла, она влюбилась; / Так в землю падшее зерно / Весны огнем оживлено. / Давно ее воображенье, / Сгорая негой и тоской, / Алкало пищи роковой; / Давно сердечное томленье / Теснило ей младую грудь; / Душа ждала … кого-нибудь, / И дождалась … Открылись очи; / Она сказала: это он!'

43. *Pss*, V, pp. 61-2: 'Другой! … Нет, никому на свете / Не отдала бы сердца я! / То в вышнем суждено совете … / То воля неба: я твоя; / Вся жизнь моя была залогом / Свиданья верного с тобой; / Я знаю, ты мне послан богом, / До гроба ты хранитель мой … / Ты в сновиденьях мне являлся, / Незримый, ты мне был уж мил, / Твой чудный взгляд меня томил, / В душе твой голос раздавался / Давно … нет, это был не сон! / Ты чуть вошел, я вмиг узнала, / Вся обомлела, запылала / И в мыслях молвила: вот он! / Не правда ль? я тебя слыхала: / Ты говорил со мной в тиши, / Когда я бедным помогала / Или молитвой услаждала / Тоску волнуемой души? / И в это самое мгновенье, / Не ты ли, милое виденье, / В прозрачной темноте мелькнул, / Приникнул тихо к изголвью? / Не ты ль, с отрадой и любовью, / Слова надежды мне шепнул? / Кто ты, мой ангел ли хранитель, / Или коварный искуситель: / Мои сомненья разреши.'

44. See, for example, Iu.M. Lotman, *Roman A.S. Pushkina 'Evgenii Onegin': Kommentarii*, 'Prosveshchenie', Leningrad, 1980, pp. 219-20, 230-31. See also chapter 1 of the companion volume (*Two Hundred Years of Pushkin*, volume I) for discussion of this point.

45. Apuleius, *The Golden Ass*, pp. 88-9.

46. When Psyche first steps foot in Cupid's pleasure-house she sees 'walls … covered in embossed silver, with wild beasts and other animals confronting the visitor on entering'; and later, when she travels to the underworld to visit Proserpine, she is met at the palace threshold by a 'huge dog [Cerberus] with three enormous heads, a monstrous and fearsome brute, barking thunderously' (ibid., pp. 77, 103).

47. For a discussion of this theme in Pushkin and, especially, the writers who came after him, see chapter 1 in the companion volume (see note 44 above).

48. *Pss*, V, p. 128: 'Сперва ей было не до них, / Но показался выбор их / Ей странен. Чтенью предалася / Татьяна жадною душой; / И ей открылся мир иной.'

49. See Lotman, *Roman A.S. Pushkina 'Evgenii Onegin'*, pp. 314-20.

50. *Pss*, V, p. 129: 'Хранили многие страницы / Отметку резкую ногтей; / Глаза внимательной девицы / Устремлены на них живей. / Татьяна видит с трепетаньем, / Какою мыслью, замечаньем / Бывал Онегин поражен, / В чем молча соглашался он. / На них полях она встречает / Черты его карандаша. / Везде Онегина душа / Себя невольно выражает / То кратким словом, то крестом, / То вопросительным крючком.'

51. *Pss*, V, pp. 129-30: 'И начинает понемногу / Моя Татьяна понимать / Теперь яснее - слава богу - / Того, по ком она вздыхать / Осуждена судьбою властной: / Чудак печальный и опасный, / Созданье ада иль небес, / Сей ангел, сей надменный бес, / Что ж он? Ужели подражанье, / Ничтожный призрак, иль еще / Москвич в Гарольдовом плаще, / Чужих причуд истолкованье, / Слов модных полный лексикон? ... / Уж не пародия ли он?'

52. *Pss*, VI, p. 99: 'Во всех ты, Душенька, нарядах хороша' reads the epigraph from Bogdanovich to *Peasant-Lady*.

53. Much of my argument about Tatiana's creative abilities in this essay has benefitted from the excellent discussion in Olga Peters Hasty, *Pushkin's Tatiana*, Madison, University of Wisconsin Press, 1999.

La Beatrice Nuova: The Process of Tatiana's Beatification in Evgenii Onegin

by

MARGUERITE PALMER

Ma dimmi: al tempo d'i dolci sospiri,
a che e come concedette amore
che conosceste i dubbiosi disiri?

Inferno, V: 118-20

([T]ell me, in the time of your sweet sighing
how and by what occasion did love grant you
to know your uncertain desires?)[1]

Pushkin originally intended to use these verses from Canto V of Dante's *Inferno* as an epigraph to chapter 3 or 4 of *Evgenii Onegin*. They form part of the most famous encounter of Dante and Virgil in the Inferno, their meeting and conversation with the shade of Francesca da Rimini. By using the verses from Canto V as an epigraph, Pushkin would be in danger of losing control of Tatiana's image. The references to Francesca juxtaposed with the name of Tatiana must colour our view of what is further told to us by Pushkin; realizing this he finally chose other epigraphs entirely. References to Canto V bring a powerful subtext in their wake, and the exclusion provides evidence that Pushkin was aware of a broader *Commedia*. Thus Tatiana was to be linked to Dante's *Inferno*, but twice Pushkin removed the infernal epigraph before printing. So, although the verses were superficially a good choice, there was the problem that the episode of Francesca and Paolo brings too much in its train. There are indeed many points of similarity between Francesca and Tatiana, and had Pushkin left the epigraph in place comparisons would have been bound to have been drawn. Despite my conviction that Tatiana is no Francesca, these women have, however, many concordant features. Both Tatiana and Francesca are identified with stormy weather. The infernal lovers are closely associated with the noise of a torrent and adverse weather[2] - Tatiana herself is associated with winter, and the wintry scene described in her dream contains many stark infernal elements. They are both specifically described as distinct among the crowd. Francesca has the honour to be the first 'alive and real woman of modern times',[3] and Tatiana may lay claim to this position in Russian literature. The other point of reference is that these two young women were brought to love 'by the book'. Francesca claims her love was fired by her reading of the romance of Launcelot and Guinevere. Tatiana's behaviour finds a parallel in her reading. In Canto V Dante goes on to criticize the role of the romance in popular culture of the times; Pushkin addresses this point in his development of Tatiana.

In the place of the one pointed reference to Francesca, likely to overbalance the whole process of characterization, Pushkin relies on the equally pertinent examples of Delphine, Julie and Clarissa. Tatiana is patently none of these characters, yet in each a small part of her make-up may be discerned. The necessary distance from these models is apparent in the reading of the source material. This reading material that Pushkin gives her is shaped and interpreted by her and must be viewed with her eyes, not with those of the sophisticated critic; a Dantean epigraph on the other hand is outside her sphere of influence and denotes the author's choice above that of his characters. The distinction between Francesca and Tatiana is crucial because whereas the former is doomed and defiant in her misery, almost taking pride in her perverted love,[4] Tatiana is among the virtuous redeemed.

It seems clear that various libraries circulate around the text of *Evgenii Onegin*: there is the old-fashioned Larin library; Lenskii's library, Onegin's libraries and Pushkin's library. Tatiana gains access to Onegin's country library; in it she discovers what Pushkin allows her to discover about Evgenii. The object of Tatiana's reading, though it has been written about and analysed in great depth,[5] in some ways functions in large measure as a device for differentiating a young, alienated, and highly receptive girl, from the reader who no longer undiscriminatingly suspends her disbelief. Her reading provides her with a paradigm of behaviour which she may choose to follow; but only by outgrowing the paradigm is her behaviour allowed to blossom beyond that of her predecessors. Princess N. is a highly self-contained, self-reliant woman who is sufficiently grounded to make the right moral choices for herself, regardless of the love that she admits that she still feels for Onegin. She will behave in a fashion that is dictated by her conscience. She is, however, excluded from his initial reading, and has outgrown this mode of discovery in chapter 8. All these sources of reading material add to the depth of the work, and the boundaries between the various libraries are by no means distinct. Pushkin covertly informs us that he reads Dante via numerous echoes, and this is evidenced in his use of Dantean imagery, philosophy, and direct quotes. The characterization of his novel as a novel-in-verse may also have a precedent in Dante, ambiguously relating to *La Vita Nuova* or, much more daringly, to the *Commedia*. In Ginguené's fifteen volume *Histoire Littéraire d'Italie*, which Pushkin in part possessed, there is a brief, and misleading, description of *La Vita Nuova*. Discussing Dante's poetry he says: '[The poems] of his earliest youth are inserted into a kind of novel which he wrote a little while after the death of Beatrice, and which was titled The New Life, *Vita Nuova*: this is where he tells of all the circumstances of their loves'.[6] In Pushkin's letters where he mentions his new novel-in-verse some of these ideas are echoed: first, the idea of poetry and the form of a novel are connected; secondly the idea that the novel will be about the love of a couple; (this might follow the inaccurate statement that *Vita Nuova* is somehow the story of their love, that is, Dante's and Beatrice's). Ginguené's brief statement also introduces the idea of the death of the heroine, one of Pushkin's early ideas for the plot development of *Onegin*. These ideas present at the genesis of *Onegin,* coupled with Pushkin's perfunctory and second-hand knowledge of Dante's œuvre at this time in his life, credibly support the thesis for the early, tentative introduction of Dante into the work and the growing subtlety and development of the Dantean motifs during Pushkin's apprenticeship and maturation into a world-class writer. While she develops into a creature analogous to Dante's Muse, Tatiana is not simply an anachronistic rendition of Beatrice. She is a product of her time, and of the prevailing fashion, albeit initially lagging slightly behind the vanguard as becomes a provincial Miss. Her part in the novel-in-verse has a certain freedom and Pushkin encourages this fiction about the autonomy of his characters, by expressing surprise at their actions. If we can agree that in chapter 8 Tatiana does indeed mirror her literary predecessor Beatrice - she is the young, beautiful, chaste woman; married yet pure, an ideal of courtly love; elevated to the position of Muse; exclusive and unobtainable, and what is more, beatified - this paper seeks to describe the process.

The original Tatiana was a virgin martyr of third-century Rome, venerated only in the Eastern Church. She was killed in the amphitheatre by unspecified wild beasts, under the jurisdiction of Alexander Severus.[7] Tatiana had achieved high office in the Church; at the time of her martyrdom she was a deaconess. She died on 12 January, 230, hence the association with winter. It is the strong link with winter, among other things, that she bestows on her latter-day counterpart.[8] The beasts represent her mode of translation to Heaven. The imposition of a bear, in our heroine's dream, for the unspecified beasts seems wholly credible. Bears are a common attribute of the saints generally,[9] and are also a peculiarly Russian icon. The bear, where it appears, has been tamed or is actively helpful or deferential rather than threatening (although the mere fact of its size adds a frisson to the image). Just as these beasts are not autonomous, being pawns of their keeper, so Pushkin's bear acts in accordance with his wishes, symbolizing the power and will of its keeper. Chizhevskii notes Tatiana's unusual characterization finding a hagiographical echo both in her introduction and later in her dream.[10] She herself would presumably be aware of the biographical details of the deaconess, as far as they existed, and the linking of the Church, martyrdom, death by exposure to wild beasts, and her status as deaconess would provide one source of imagery suitable for a dream and perhaps a subconscious model of behaviour. The bear helps Tatiana to make the crossing of the water, a common marker of the threshold between life and death, and one figuring largely in the *Commedia*. In this light the appearance of the bear is significant as a symbol of the mode of her translation.

Tatiana's ostensible models are Clarissa, Julie and Delphine, but each literary reference is of some significance. The theme of a love which is out of the control of the lovers and therefore mistakenly imbued with some kind of divine blessing, is just the kind of love that both Dante and Pushkin are challenging. Love affairs which are carried on by means of reading and writing are rationalized in the eyes of the protagonists; some claim an intrinsic goodness to their love which must convince all those around them merely because their love exists with such power and energy. In *Purgatorio* Dante is instructed by Virgil on the two different kinds of love: natural love, always without error, and love of the mind which 'may err through a wrong object or through excess or defect of vigour'.[11] Guiding the love of the mind there is innate in each person a faculty which gives counsel, and which must occupy the threshold of consent. Thus, Virgil concludes, even if we grant that all love which is kindled arises through necessity, the power to control it lies in you.[12]

Following the writing of the letter and her rejection by Onegin we next see Tatiana about to engage in the ritual of divination on the eve of the name-day celebrations. The divination sets the scene for the prophetic dream. There is a Russian proverb which says 'A prophetic dream does not deceive' and that Pushkin subscribed to this proverbial wisdom is borne out in his diary.[13] The muddle of iconography from the impending name day celebrations, the associated custom of divination, and the imagery from the emotional turmoil of the recent past are irreconcilably intertwined to produce a startling dream. The prophetic aspect of Tatiana's dream could be viewed as a Dantean marker. All three dreams of the *Commedia* occur in *Purgatorio*; they are also deemed morning dreams, and are attributed as prophetic dreams. Tatiana's dream may be classed as a morning dream too.

Tatiana eventually settles down to sleep, her dream opens on to a nocturnal, wintry scene. There is a clear correspondence between the description of the weather around the infernal lovers and the opening description of the location of Tatiana's dream. The darkness, noise, and danger threatened in the initial description are belied by the repetitive use of the word brook to describe the water that Tatiana must now cross. It is Tatiana's determination to cross despite the bear which she accepts as a necessary part of the process. The fact that two arms can straddle the breadth of the torrent also denotes a narrow body of water. The potential threat of the landscape has for the present retreated into the background and Tatiana, far from being paralysed by fear, 'Как на досадную разлуку, / ... ропщет на ручей' ('As at a vexing separation / ... grumbles at the brook': 5: XII, 1-2.) which seems to express minor inconvenience rather than threat at this juncture. She might be at the threshold of the inferno itself, in the wild wood. The bear, despite the terror he now induces in Tatiana, turns out to be relatively benign, and his careful carrying of her has none of the ambiguity of Onegin's actions later in the dream. The bear has the metonymic markers of Pushkin himself as well as the same penchant for the well-turned foot. The unmanageable fur and the sharp-clawed paw advertise Pushkin's presence via two of his most distinguishing features: his unruly hair and notoriously long fingernails. Some of the physical features of the bear caricature descriptions of Pushkin himself found in memoirs and letters of his friends and acquaintances, for example, the grunting breaths.[14] Dante too wrote of forcing his attentions on a reluctant woman as a bear in one of his later poems.[15] This monstrous husband to whom she will be given is indeed something from a fictitious character's prophetic nightmare. At first Tatiana is not afraid to approach the bear and accept his help; it is only when perhaps an inkling of his future designs on her filter through that she attempts to widen the gap between them. It is in the dark wood that she finally is captured by the bear. The bear's generous first gesture is to deposit his prize at the threshold of his friend's house. This act of generosity Pushkin comes to reverse in chapter 8.

Following her dream, the prophecy is seen to unfold. The first event to follow the dream is the name-day ball. After the events at the ball we are left with two of Tatiana's clear impressions of Onegin as the process of separation begins. This process takes place over a period of time and not as soon as she wakes. Her development marks a growth in character and is not an immature knee-jerk reaction to her dream. She notices her jealousy in Olga's conquest of her hero; and she notes with certainty that happiness with Onegin is not for her. He will only lead her to death, which is in a sense true, but not in the melodramatic fashion that that thought could imply: "'Погибну", Таня говорит, / "Но гибель от него любезна. / Я не ропщу: зачем роптать? / Не может он мне счастья дать.'" ("'I shall die", Tania says, / 'But death from him is pleasing. / I do not grumble: Why grumble? / He can't give me happiness'": 6: III, 11-14.) The old Tania dies and gradually someone else is born in her place, someone the same yet infinitely different. This is the regeneration of Tatiana, or Princess N. as Pushkin's Beatrice - a separate individual from the girl of the rural countryside. The 'non-use' of the verb to grumble echoes Tatiana at the edge of the chasm in which the stream is flowing. In her dream she 'ропщет' ('grumbles') at the edge of the point of translation.[16] The interesting point after the name-day ball is that she decides consciously not to grumble, but merely uses the idea to remind us of her dream, and including the metaphorical chasm to further strengthen the association.[17] She knows that her future does not lie with Onegin. It has been predicted that both she and her sister are destined to be the wives of military men. So acceptance is at a beginning and it is by this process that she develops into the self-possessed woman of St Petersburg society and given the role of наставница ('moral teacher') by Pushkin the poet.[18]

The next stage of the prophecy comes true and this might be used as a marker for the reader to gauge the reliability of Tatiana's status as prophetess.

Lenskii is read as slain by Onegin, as the usual interpretation of events goes -
from the point of view of the characters in the novel, and various of the critics
too[19] - although Lenskii is actually slain by the skilled and carefully controlled
pen of the better poet. Lenskii is deliberately limited in his characterization. In
his role as poet representing an old order, Lenskii could be viewed as a parody
of Virgil, allowing Onegin to adopt the role of Dante. The difference in their
ages reflects, almost exactly, that of their predecessors.[20] Just as Virgil teaches
Dante of moral responsibility in *Purgatorio*, Lenskii is found to be no subscriber
to predestination.[21] Virgil as Dante's guide is severely limited in his role; and
just as Lenskii will not see the triumph of Tatiana in St Petersburg, neither may
Virgil enter into the Earthly Paradise to see his pupil's rebirth after the baptism
by fire nor witness the unveiling of Beatrice there. Lenskii modelled the
idealistic lover for Onegin, but Evgenii proved a poor pupil.[22] The curious thing
is not that Onegin did not avoid killing Lenskii but that Pushkin narrated the
events in the way that he did. The proximity of the wedding, notwithstanding
Pushkin's slight mismanagement of dates, was tantamount to declaring Lenskii
one of the family and hence Onegin has effectively killed Tatiana's brother,
which cannot be lightly forgiven by Tatiana. Following the duel Onegin leaves
the country to embark (presumably) on his wanderings. This chapter might be
viewed as a description of Onegin's infernal journey during the period after the
duel and before his arrival finally in St Petersburg. The infernal markers of
Onegin's Journey have been described by Gasparov.[23] The action once again
reverts to Tatiana.

It is in Onegin's library that Tatiana receives confirmation of her
assessment of him through the medium of her dream. Far from her having the
answer all that is now clear is that this man is not one to whom one should
entrust one's fate, whatever one's feelings. The list of possibilities is a wild and
improbable one. Onegin has none of the energy of the literary heroes in whose
role Tatiana may have attempted to cast him. There always lurks in the
background the problem of definition regarding Onegin. He begs to be labelled
but defies all attempts at categorization. Onegin's position at the end of the novel
is left open much as it is in real life, the closure of 'happily ever after' being
reserved for fairy tales. That the account of the journey hovers around the
finished text is a curious detail. It might be viewed as a description of Onegin's
activities during the period after the duel and before his arrival finally in St
Petersburg. That he goes on to better things is hinted at in various ways: the
projected participation in the Decembrist uprising, his forced attention to the
words and admonition of Tatiana - surely she does not speak in vain.

Tatiana's reading of Onegin's library shows us at least one more thing
about Onegin. That is, despite the insinuations of the narrator, Onegin was a
careful reader; this contradiction of the implied word of the narrator may lead
us to make other judgements about the eponymous hero in the face of the
contrary information provided by the narrator. It is true that Onegin was no poet:

the letter that he produces at the end, while never singled out for inclusion in the anthologies of Russian verse, is nevertheless a word for word rendition of Onegin's own letter, and not something translated - and versified - as in the case of Tatiana's letter. Pushkin nevertheless almost too frequently alludes to this fact, that is, that Onegin is less than appreciative of poetry despite his efforts, while bringing him to the brink of creativity more than once. Pushkin insinuates to us that Onegin did not read - he does; does not write - he does; he is even capable of falling in love which we find surprising in the light of the information Pushkin has divulged regarding his creation. Pushkin seems to be teasing Onegin and, of course, the readers; the role of poet is offered to Onegin and at the last moment snatched away.

Tatiana's entry into Moscow is heralded by a confusion of impressions for her, and this muddle is reminiscent of the disorder of her dream now revisited in a kind of flashback. The descriptions of the bustle and clamour of the social engagements are clearly infernal, and this list is interrupted by stanza LII, only to be continued in the following one. Infernal motifs are very much in evidence here: the whirl of the waltzing couples is reminiscent of the situation of Francesca and Paolo in Canto V. The undifferentiated group of Muscovite women represent the crowd that Tatiana stands in contradistinction to, despite occupying the same space; to the outward observer it is clear that Tatiana stands head and shoulders above them in every respect. Pushkin's descriptions of her clearly indicate his new feeling towards her as the epitome of femininity. Stanza LII is replete with Dantean imagery, but not infernal, and is the point at which the new heroine emerges. In this stanza are present the clear markers of the old Tatiana, that is, the night, the moon, now brought together with Dantean markers that Pushkin has used before: the adjective 'величавый' ('majestic'),[24] and the attention to her gaze. The idea that as moon among the stars, with proper celestial pride, Tatiana is rightfully located, is a clear reference to the sphere of the moon of *Paradiso*. Tatiana has come to represent the ideal that men such as Onegin and indeed Pushkin himself aspire to love reciprocally, in that she represents constancy but from a stance of informed responsibility and not the epitome of hedonistic unrestraint that the stereotypical male loves to idealize in a mistress.

In chapter 8 Onegin and Tatiana are brought together after a long separation, although at first Onegin fails to recognize Tatiana, and might deserve the rebuke that he had forgotten her. This meeting takes place in quite another location from their first meeting, just as Beatrice is first mentioned to Dante in the wild wood and then the next time she appears to him is in the Earthly Paradise, Onegin and Tatiana meet in a rural setting, 'в пустыне' ('in the wilderness'), a code name for the dark wood,[25] and then in the diametric opposite - a Petersburg salon. At their first meeting after the gap of years Tatiana is described by Onegin as the one in the 'малиновый берет' ('crimson beret': 8: XVII, 9). For Pushkin the merest hint of the requisite colour suffices and is delicately introduced, camouflaged as the height of fashion. Nabokov writes at length about the exact shade of Tatiana's beret but whatever the subtle variations evoked by translation the colour is a striking red; this is the colour of Beatrice's dress at the first meeting of Dante and Beatrice when she was eight and he was nine.[26] This too marks Onegin's first sight of the renewed Tatiana. From this moment Onegin is powerfully attracted to this new woman, termed the Neva's inaccessible goddess. Dante in *La Vita Nuova* becomes physically unwell because of the violence of his love, and turns to writing and more specifically poetry. Onegin tries hard in the intervening time to elevate himself. He too becomes ill, and even tries to become a poet but fails. This is the point which marks the limit of Onegin's development. Pushkin as narrator offers his creation an opportunity for growth, he is given a place for quiet contemplation, and meditation, but as a shade his blossoming is as unlikely as Lenskii's.

This period of Onegin's hibernation can be likened to the time that Dante and Virgil spend on the fourth terrace of Mount Purgatory, where the purgation of slothfulness takes place. Approaching the terrace Dante admits to a feeling of physical weakness. Sloth is linked to the related offence of too much thinking in place of action, and the penance is marked by the frenetic single-minded activity of those gladly in pursuit of atonement. According to Virgil the error may enter the processes of reasoning, weighing, judging, choosing in one of three ways: 'Through a wrong object, / Or through excess or defect of vigour'.[27] It is on the count of excess of vigour that Onegin stands accused, and his rush to Tatiana's house with no thought but to confront her stands as evidence. Onegin has roused himself from his hibernation far from having understood the subtextual message, and rushes to the good with more zeal than he ought. Instead, failing to learn the distinction in the two different kinds of love (the lesson of this terrace), he rushes off in pursuit of the object of his love.

When Onegin goes to Tatiana's home she is sitting pale and unadorned - almost unveiled. Tatiana, responding to his arrival in her rooms, keeps her eyes on him. She has already been noted as crying over some kind of letter, and this attention to her eyes highlights a metonymic reminiscence of Beatrice. In his letter Onegin had referred to the loss of Lenskii, 'Еще одно нас разлучило ... / Несчастной жертвой Ленский пал ... ' ('Still one thing separates us ... / Lenskii fell an unlucky victim': 8:XXXII, 29-30), but his light gloss over this painful fact is a direct contradiction to the long lament of Dante on perceiving the loss of Virgil. Obviously this pairing of Lenskii as Virgil is a parody or even a travesty of the original. Virgil is the admired and respected predecessor of Dante and when Tatiana fails to address the death of Lenskii she produces a similar effect as her model, Beatrice. Prickett succinctly describes the analogous situation in the Earthly Paradise - Onegin might well regard any location in the presence of Tatiana as an acceptable variant of the Earthly Paradise; he is soon disabused. Using Buber's idea of confirmation as the ideal of humanity,[28] Prickett explores the conceptual opposite of disconfirmation, where what one is being is not recognized. He cites the major example of disconfirmation: the meeting of Beatrice and Dante in the Earthly Paradise - where before Beatrice in the Earthly Paradise Dante describes his grief and confusion at the loss of his guide:

> The disturbing power of the scene, lies in the fact that we find this tension unacceptable and yet unresolvable ... Beatrice's rebuke gains weight not merely by the tangential nature of her response in *not* speaking to his immediate condition ... but also by challenging him at a different level.[29]

Analogously Tatiana notices Onegin's suffering and makes brief allusion to his condition. The tone of this completely diminishes the force of the imperative and skates over Onegin's primary reason for being in her house, his feelings at that moment. Tatiana passes over the death of Lenskii without comment producing the same effect as her model Beatrice. After her cursory acknowledgement of his condition she abruptly launches into her admonitory speech in which she reveals his nature to him and reduces his passions to a 'bagatelle'. She speaks as somebody who knows Onegin as well or even better than he knows himself. In the analogous situation in the Earthly Paradise Beatrice, contrary to our expectations, swiftly moves on from the disappearance of Virgil and then goes on to the real business: 'She charges him with infidelity, and in a public act of humiliation reduces him ... to tears ... [and continues with] a sustained systematic destruction of every shred of his self-respect'.[30] Tatiana in her speech also uses the traditional epithet of Dante, 'суровый' ('stern'), in relation to Onegin as if to highlight his position as she goes on to demonstrate the pathetic nature of his feeling but is not later embarrassed to delineate her own 'Я вас люблю' ('I love you': 8: XLVII, 12). In this way Tatiana alludes to the concept of the two kinds of love, allowing the reader to compare her statement with her assessment of his version of love. Onegin, like Dante, does not reply but where the choir intervenes in the Earthly Paradise, ('Lady, why dost thou so shame him?'[31]) Onegin's support is heralded by the 'clink' of Prince N.'s spurs.

   The tentative pairing of Virgil and Lenskii prompts the search for Dante. This role is mockingly given to Onegin and then withdrawn. It is tempting to cast Onegin as a poet - not only because Pushkin denies it so strenuously, even if just as a figure of parody. The idea that Onegin is not a poet is often cited as emanating from Pushkin. But there are many instances of tongue-in-cheek in the novel which are best treated with care. Of course, Onegin is not Dante, any more than he is Napoleon or a Quaker; he has merely tried the cloak on for size - and just as no other persona is apt, this too fails adequately to describe him. Onegin may have moved on now to be able to appreciate Tatiana, but he is only at a point where he can appreciate something outside himself - something which makes him feel real. His suffering is a step forward from the numbness of boredom. He now looks to Tatiana to rescue him but she will not be his guide through his Inferno - he must make that journey without her. She is merely there to inspire him.

It is here that Pushkin the author re-enters the story to depose Onegin from his false position as Dante in the narrative. Onegin is a chimera to distract us from the real man, the true Muscovite in Harold's mantle, to whom Tatiana has been given. Onegin's posturing as Dante is unconvincing and he has to be rejected by Tatiana, despite the 'intonations, the heaving breast, the broken speech, the anguished poignant, palpitating, enchanting, almost voluptuous, almost alluring enjambments'.[32] She is distraught; because as a fictional character of unlimited potential all avenues are open, but she is to be given as Muse to the author - wedded to a real person, removed beyond the text. Maybe Viazemskii acted as the pander, and perhaps the letter she is reading while crying in her private rooms is from Pushkin himself and not from Onegin at all. Maybe it is a poem from the real descendant of Dante, and not the feeble imitation which is the limit of Onegin's talents. Onegin tried, he even attempted the descent into the inferno, but although he seems to have been improved by his wanderings, he is finally knocked aside as a suitable recipient of the favours of the Muse. This is Pushkin's role as narrator, as author too perhaps, and not Onegin the potential poet's. It is for himself that Pushkin retains the energy of Tatiana. Pushkin is the Muscovite parading in Harold's mantle and this unconvincing disguise is finally discarded and the true suitor for Tatiana is revealed. The juxtaposition of the names of Byron and Dante occurs in Pushkin's poem of 1825, *André Chénier*; but it is an immodest step up from assuming the guise of Byron to presuming to wear Dante's crown.[33] She has been given to another and to him she will be faithful for life. Tatiana's transition from one state to another is nearing completion, the last vestige of regret is still felt, but does not draw her to act contrary to the general good. She has been elevated to Muse, poet's Muse: that is Pushkin's Muse. There is only one poet; Pushkin is at pains to remind us that Onegin could never even pretend to that title. We cannot even push Lenskii forward as a contender; he was cruelly killed as much by the narrator as by the named perpetrator. The rivalry between Onegin and Pushkin is at an end, Tatiana in her own words refuses Onegin and this leaves the way clear for Pushkin to take possession of his Muse. For Dante to be united with his Beatrice.

NOTES

1. All translations from Dante's *La Divina Commedia* from J.D. Sinclair, *The Divine Comedy of Dante Alighieri: vol I, Inferno; vol. II, Purgatorio; vol. III, Paradiso*, The Bodley Head, London, 1939 unless stated. References use volume and page number.

2. 'I came to a place where all light was mute and where was bellowing as of a sea in tempest that is beaten by conflicting winds' (Sinclair, I , 75). These verses are reproduced in French translation with the original Italian as a footnote in P.L. Ginguené, *Histoire Littéraire d'Italie*, in ten volumes, Michaud, Paris, 1811, (II, 43).

3. Francesco De Sanctis in P. Dronke, 'Francesca and Héloïse',*Comparative Literature*, XXXVII, 2, Spring 1975, pp. 113-35 (p. 117).

4. That is perverted in the Dantean sense whereby all the sins of the upper levels of the inferno are sins of perverted love and are reflected in the correct form in the other demesnes of the *Commedia*.

5. See *Eugene Onegin, A Novel in Verse by Aleksandr Pushkin*, Translated from the Russian, with a commentary, by Vladimir Nabokov in four volumes, Routledge & Kegan Paul, London, 1964 (pp. 338-48); Stanley Mitchell, 'Tatiana's Reading' *Forum for Modern Language Studies*, IV, 1, Jan. 1968, pp. 1-21; J. Douglas Clayton, *Ice and Flame*, University of Toronto Press, Toronto, 1985, chapter 4, goes into some detail about the less often researched books in Tatiana's library, for example, *The Trials of Werther*. On this subject, see also chapter 1 of the companion volume.

6. Ginguené, I, p. 466, my translation.

7. Pushkin was so fond of puns and word associations that this coincidence of initials and first name would not have been missed by him.

8. There is a palpable mediæval thread running through the text of *Onegin*, which gathers together the intertextual reference to the original Héloïse, and her consort Abélard, which in turn sheds light on the references to the mediæval and the monastic (which are numerous), and the term 'starina/y', which Nabokov gives as 'ancientry'. Pushkin made reference to his choice of name in one of his own notes to the text (note 13), where he makes a point of lining up old-fashioned Greek names that he considers agreeable and indicates their relegation to the peasant class. 'The most sweet-sounding Greek names, such as, for example: Agafon, Filat, Theodora, Fekla, and so on, are used by us only among the peasants', in Pushkin, *Polnoe sobranie sochinenii*, seventeen volume academic edition, Izdatel'stvo Akademii Nauk SSSR, Leningrad, 1937, (VI, p. 192), henceforth *Pss* with volume and page number. References to the text of *Onegin* will be given as chapter, verse, and line.

9. Helen Roeder, *Saints and their Attributes*, Longmans, Green and Co., London, New York, Toronto, 1955.

10. A.S. Pushkin, *Evgenij Onegin: A Novel in Verse, the Russian Text*, edited with introduction and commentary by Dmitry Chizhevskii, Harvard University Press, Cambridge, Mass., 1967, pp. 229 and 258. Also, Pushchin in his memoirs remembers Pushkin having a volume of the Saints' lives to hand when he visited him at his Mikhailovskoe estate in January 1825: see Tatiana Wolff, *Pushkin on Literature,* selected, translated and edited by Wolff, Methuen and Co. Ltd, London, 1971, pp. 101-2.

11. Sinclair, II, p. 225.

12. Dronke, p. 117 and passim.

13. Pushkin's diary entry 7 January, 1834 in Michael R. Katz, *Dreams and the Unconscious in Nineteenth-Century Russian Fiction*, University Press of New England, Hanover and London, 1984, p. 38.

14. Komovskii recalls, '"Pushkin was so sensual that at the age of fifteen or sixteen, the mere touch of his partner's hand at a school ball ... and his breath would quicken and whistle like the

snorting of a fiery steed in a herd of fillies." Yakovlev took exception only to the form …
without denying the facts.' in Henri Troyat, *Pushkin*, translated by Nancy Amphoux, Allen and
Unwin, London, 1974, p. 79.

15. 'Così nel mio parlar voglio esser aspro' ('In my speech I wish to be as harsh') in *The Penguin Book of Italian Verse*, introduced and edited by George Kay, Penguin, Harmondsworth, 1965, p. 91.

16. *Oxford English Dictionary*, 2nd ed., Clarendon Press, Oxford, 1989, XVIII, p. 409: 'To carry or convey to heaven without death' and used in this sense by Coleridge in 'Fears in Solitude'. Pushkin is recorded as reading various works by Coleridge.

17. Compare *Onegin*, 5: XII, 1-2 and 6: III, 11-14.

18. This role of teacher is picked up in the Dantean fragment of Pushkin also written at Boldino in 1830, 'В начале жизни школу помню я' ('At the start of life I remember school'), first published after Pushkin's death and titled by the editor *Подражание Данте* (*Imitation of Dante*).

19. See especially A.D.P. Briggs, *Alexander Pushkin's 'Eugene Onegin'*, Cambridge University Press, Cambridge, 1992, who refers to Onegin as the 'monster who has just murdered Lenskii', and the circumstances of the duel as cheating, in Onegin's favour, p. 107 and passim.

20. This is according to Nabokov's chronology. At the time of their deaths Virgil was 51, born B.C. 70, died B.C. 19; Dante died seven years older at 58, born 1165, died 1223; and in the various illustrations, for example, Doré, Flaxman, Virgil is depicted as the younger classical model of beauty while Dante is shown as the older, less well-proportioned figure.

21. Ralph E. Matlaw, 'The Dream in Yevgeniy Onegin, with a Note on *Gore ot Uma*', *Slavonic and East European Review*, XXXVII, 1959, pp. 487-503 (492).

22. There is no hint of fault in Lenskii's character; it is merely by virtue of being born at the wrong time that Virgil is excluded from the Earthly Paradise and Heaven. Notwithstanding the gloss put on the whole sequence of events leading to the duel by Lotman here is an area where, ostensibly, a great deal of the blame belongs at the door of Evgenii. He sees Onegin as an automaton caught up in the cycle of events and quite unable to think rationally at any point in the proceedings about how the affair might honourably be otherwise resolved. (See Iu.M. Lotman, 'Roman A.S. Pushkina "Evgenii Onegin". Komentarii' in Iu.M. Lotman, *Pushkin*, "Iskusstvo-SPB", St Petersburg, 1995, pp. 472-762 [537]). It is interesting to note that despite the number of duels we are given the impression that Pushkin himself was involved in, he was unhurt throughout, until his duel with d'Anthès, and he does not seem to have inflicted any serious injuries on his 'enemies' either. That there were fatalities in these combats is self-evident: to remember Pushkin and Lermontov is sufficient. It is evident from Pushkin's biography that many of the projected fights were averted only by the common sense of the seconds. For details of two averted duels involving Pushkin see Troyat (pp. 82 and 327). That Evgenii is culpable in choosing the wrong man for the job is made plain; that Lenskii was too hot-headed and young to choose judiciously is one of 'life's' tragedies and a matter of literary necessity.

23. Boris Gasparov, 'Funktsii reminitsentsii iz Dante v poezii Pushkina' *Russian Literature*, XIV, 1983, pp. 317-50 (322-3).

24. The use of this adjective as a Dantean marker, a translation of the Latin *superbo*, is described in detail by Gasparov, op. cit., pp. 331-2.

25. See Gasparov, p. 330.

26. 'She was dressed in a very noble colour, a decorous and delicate crimson'. All translations from *La Vita Nuova* are from Barbara Reynolds, *La Vita Nuova: poems of youth*, Penguin, Harmondsworth, 1969, p. 29.

27. Sinclair, II, p. 225.

28. 'The basis of man's life with man is twofold, and it is the wish of every man to be confirmed

as what he is, even as what he can become, by men.' Martin Buber in S. Prickett, 'Dante, Beatrice, and M. C. Escher: Disconfirmation as a Metaphor', *Journal of European Studies*, II, 4, December 1972, 333-51 (333).

29. Prickett, p. 337.

30. Ibid., p. 336.

31. Sinclair, II, p. 397.

32. Nabokov, III, p. 241

33. Pushkin did in fact draw himself wearing laurels, but it is, of course, a humorous caricature of himself. The sketch is entitled, 'Il gran'padre A.P.'

Sovereign Rapture: The Enigma of Pushkin's Cleopatra

by

LEON BURNETT

Late in 1824, shortly after returning to Mikhailovskoe from his Southern exile, Pushkin composed a 70-line poem, entitled *Cleopatra*.[1] This is the first indication we have of the poet's interest in this historical figure, an interest that was to culminate in the fragmentary poetic improvisation that concludes the far more widely known *Egyptian Nights* of 1835. The author's elaboration of the Cleopatra theme, as it has been called, extended across the most productive decade of his short life and coincided with his exploration of the potentialities of lyric poetry and imaginative prose as well as his experimentation in the composition of hybrid forms such as the novel in verse.

In *Pushkin's 'Egyptian Nights': The Biography of a Work*, Leslie O'Bell traces the evolution of the Cleopatra theme in Pushkin's works, and examines carefully the circumstances surrounding the appearance of each of Pushkin's three so-called Cleopatra poems - in 1824, in 1828 and in 1835 - and their relation to allied themes and motifs in his writing. In her own words, she sets out to follow the 'creative history' of *Egyptian Nights* by way of 'Pushkin's artistic work and thought', adopting an approach that 'makes use of a flexible notion of synonymy or equivalencies', which takes into account, for example, characters who 'play an analogous role' to those in *Egyptian Nights* and poems that explore related topics.[2]

This approach yields useful insights into Pushkin's Cleopatra. Yet his representation fits into a larger, diachronic picture that begins in history and ends in legend, in which the meaning of Cleopatra is constantly under revision. Whether we confine ourselves to the texts that Pushkin offers us or adopt a wider perspective in looking at the myth to which they contribute, a consensus, or agreed reading, fails to emerge. This resistance to closure accounts, to a great extent, for Cleopatra's enduring appeal. We need only glance at the diverse ways in which the image of the Queen of Egypt, who came to the throne in 51 B.C., has been projected in order to accept that the term *enigma* is an appropriate designation for her.[3]

Yet the enigma of Cleopatra is not the focal point of this paper. What I want to address is, more specifically, the enigma of *Pushkin's* Cleopatra. Although, in what follows, I shall concentrate on the 1824 version of Pushkin's poem *Cleopatra*, in which a radically new motif was introduced into the Cleopatra myth, I want to range beyond the confines of this text to consider some possible grounds for the poet's initial interest in the Cleopatra theme. To illustrate the diversity of response to Pushkin's composition, I shall also look at two later interpretations, proposed by Dostoevskii and Briusov, and conclude with some tentative remarks upon the significance of the *fabula*, the story, for readers at the end of the twentieth century and the beginning of the twenty-first.

The textual inspiration for *Cleopatra*, it is generally agreed, was Pushkin's reading of an anecdotal remark attributed to Sextus Aurelius Victor, a fourth-century Latin historian: 'Haec tantae libidinis fuit, ut saepe prostiterit: tantae pulchritudinis ut multi noctem illius morte emirent' ('This woman was so lustful that she often offered herself as a prostitute, so beautiful that many bought one of her nights with death').[4] 'From this single sentence', Lucy Hughes-Hallett remarks, '(which for all its sensationalism, and despite the fact that the text was available and several times published, lay ignored for fifteen hundred years) sprang all the Romantic killer-Cleopatras, of which Pushkin's was the first'.[5] An obvious question that this statement provokes one to ask is what attracted Pushkin to the idea of elaborating upon the Latin anecdote at the expense of the intermediate images of Petrarch, Shakespeare, Corneille and numerous lesser writers,[6] not forgetting artists ranging from Michelangelo to Tiepolo and Regnault in order to create what amounted to an image of 'eroticized violence' that inaugurated a Romantic tradition of cruel Cleopatras?[7]

Any answer to this question must involve the investigator in an enquiry into the plans and preoccupations that engrossed Pushkin at the time of composition late in 1824, for it is clear that the sensory substratum for this poem included more than just a chance encounter with Sextus Aurelius' text. Popular accounts of Pushkin's life make great play of the fact that the poet gained invaluable information from his former nanny during his lonely stay at Mikhailovskoe, but we must, on this occasion, be permitted to doubt whether her supply of Russian folk-tales was quite suited to put the poet in mind of the transactions of Eros that the Cleopatra theme discloses.[8] Not that ethnic folk material lacks an element of cruelty! More likely to be of significance is the fact that, in all probability, Pushkin had come to recognize that he had brought his cycle of Southern poems to a close. With *The Gypsies*, composed earlier in 1824, he had said all that he had to say about the matter. Conceivably, Byron's death in April 1824 would have strengthened his resolve to abandon the Russian Byronic. Pushkin was at a cross-roads in his career. Or, perhaps, not so much a cross-roads as a post station, where he could change horses in readiness for setting off on a new journey. He had already started *Eugene Onegin*, and this had met with initial success, although he could not have known at the time that it was to become his *chef d'œuvre*, or that it was to give rise - and meaning - to the type that was later to be identified, following Turgenev's coinage, as the superfluous man. He was also dallying with the idea of another type, that of the Demon, which, arguably, had a bearing on the genesis of *Cleopatra*. In 1823, Pushkin wrote a poem (purportedly describing Aleksander Raevskii) that received some unwelcome critical attention. Intending to respond to this criticism anonymously, he drafted a reply, in which (referring to himself in the third person) he commented on the poem's moral aim:

> At the best time of one's life the heart, as yet unchilled by experience, is responsive to beauty. It is credulous and tender. Gradually the endless contradictions of existence breed doubts, a painful but fleeting (непродолжительное) condition. It disappears, having destroyed for ever the finest hopes and poetic preconceptions of the soul. No wonder that that great man Goethe calls the eternal enemy of mankind *the spirit of negation*. And did not Pushkin wish to embody in his demon this spirit of *negation or doubt* and in this compact picture sketch its distinctive features and its unhappy influence on the morals of our age?[9]

Pushkin had written *The Demon* in 1823. In 1825, he was still brooding over the central idea - that of *negation or doubt* - and lamenting its 'unhappy influence on the morals of our age'.[10] In the interim, he had composed *Cleopatra*, a poem which closes with an image of a heart that may properly be described as being 'unchilled by experience', and yet which is fully 'responsive to beauty ... credulous and tender (легковерно и нежно)'. The ending of *Cleopatra*, it has been claimed, is its *raison d'être*. In his analysis of the poem, Tomashevskii wrote that the conflict

> consists in the fact that the brazen, cold challenge of Cleopatra is to some extent defeated by the love of the youth ... Cleopatra is all but won over by the youth's love. This is the concluding psychological situation of the elegy. And Pushkin, evidently, in no way intended to continue the elegy and describe Cleopatra's nights since such a continuation could not enrich the psychological characterization of Cleopatra.[11]

Or, in O'Bell's more summary assessment: 'One might even say that the poem was written for the sake of its significant breaking-off point'.[12] While this may overstate the case, it identifies the psychological *Schwerpunkt*. The *gravitas* of the poem is located in the image and the idea of youthful passion. It is in obedience to the constructive principle of 'Cleopatra' that Pushkin decided first to introduce two other claimants for a night of love, the soldier Aquila and the pleasure-seeker Crito, before he mentions the unnamed youth. The poem terminates in such a way as to preserve the aspirations, the hopes and the finest preconceptions of the soul, yet, in the Pushkinian - as in the Keatsian - aesthetic, the 'still unravished' moment, however admirable it may seem, is to be construed as a limited one.[13]

In his draft note on *The Demon*, Pushkin referred to 'the morals of our age'. One appeal of Sextus Aurelius' anecdote for Pushkin was that it had remained untouched for fifteen hundred years. The distance between the contemporary world and that of antiquity was accentuated by the fact that no text existed to mediate between the source and its rewriting. In *Cleopatra*, Pushkin was able to measure the morals of the modern world against those of the ancient without having to take account of the intervention of other ages. He had created the type of the modern man in *Evgenii Onegin*. The anonymous youth, who belongs to the world of antiquity (and also to the future insofar as he is unnamed), might be considered to be Onegin's anti-mask.

By 1825, Pushkin had experimented in his creative laboratory with two contrasting images of the male psyche. One was cold, disillusioned, negative; the other tender, devout, positive.[14] Soon, within the pages of *Evgenii Onegin*, these two types were to meet each other and engage in a duel. In the outcome of that confrontation, Pushkin was to deliver his verdict as to which one was fitter to survive in the contemporary world.[15] The type that the defeated male character represented, however, did not disappear from Russian literature with the death of his fictional embodiment in Pushkin's novel in verse. He resurfaced in the realist prose of the next generation and in the lyrical verse of the generation after that, always in the company, always in the shadow, of a dominant and eroticized woman. I shall return later in this paper to avatars of the Pushkinian prototype of the virtuous - or tender - Russian hero, but first I want to trace the subsequent development of the woman who made him what he was. To do so, I shall consider the interpretations offered by Dostoevskii, a fantastic-realist novelist from the succeeding generation, and Briusov, a decadent-symbolist poet of the *fin de siècle*.

How, then, did Dostoevskii respond to Pushkin's image of Cleopatra? Above all, he was absorbed by the psychology of the scene. Dostoevskii saw in her a *femme fatale*, who, among other attractions, possessed the characteristics of a reptilian, cannibalistic vampire. This is the crux of Dostoevskii's far from neutral paraphrase of *Cleopatra*:

> The queen has conceived a desire to astound all these guests by her challenge; she wants to enjoy her contempt for them ... But the thought has already taken complete possession of her soul ... Now she would like them to accept her monstrous challenge! ... What demonic happiness to kiss her victim, to love it, to become its slave for a few hours, to quench its every desire with all the mysteries of the kiss ... and at the same time to know every minute that this victim, this momentary lord and master will pay with his life for this love and for the proud insolence of his momentary dominion over her. ... Mad cruelty has long since warped this divine soul and often already reduced it to the likeness of a beast ... In her beautiful body is

concealed the soul of a darkly fantastical horrible reptile; it is the soul of a spider who, they say, eats her mate at the moment of their union.[16]

But Dostoevskii did not stop there. The ending - the reference to the 'anonymous youth on whom Cleopatra fixes her gaze in admiration' - detained him, for it hints at the idea of tender compassion, the condition expressed in the Russian word 'умиление' - a state of openness to others that both Pushkin and Dostoevskii depicted in their writings.[17] One must add the cautionary note, however, that while an interest in 'умиление' may be regarded as representing a point of contact between the two authors, Dostoevskii subjected Pushkin's enigmatic ending to a religious interpretation that is difficult to reconcile with an original *intentio*. Dostoevskii's commentary (in O'Bell's translation) continues:

> But the soul of the poet could not bear this picture; would not end it with Cleopatra the hyena, and for one instant he made her human ... for a moment the human being awakened and the queen looked with compassion on the youth. She could still feel compassion! ... But only for a moment... You understand to what kind of people our Divine Redeemer then came.

The colourful account that Dostoevskii gives of Cleopatra recalls aspects of the sexual personae depicted in his own works. One thinks, for example, of the conception of Nastasia Filippovna's psyche in *The Idiot*, that 'strong soul' filled with 'spiteful irony', who casts a bundle of one hundred thousand roubles into the fire as a 'monstrous challenge' to test her male admirers,[18] or the fantastic symbolism of the reptilian form in Ippolit's hideous dream (from the same novel), where 'образ' is transformed into its opposite - 'безобразие'.

Dostoevskii offers a 'Dostoevskian' interpretation of Pushkin's *Cleopatra* in a critical article. Briusov went further. He took it upon himself to complete Pushkin's elegiac fragment. Zhirmunskii, in his Formalist essay 'Valerii Briusov's *Egyptian Nights*', calculated that of the 662 lines of the new *Egyptian Nights*, about 111 belonged to Pushkin and the remaining 551 to Briusov.[19] There was plenty of opportunity, then, for Briusov to incorporate into the revised version what Zhirmunskii referred to trenchantly as 'exotic accessories'. Taking the fundamental theme of *Egyptian Nights* to be *passion* and *death*,[20] Briusov succeeded - again in Zhirmunskii's words - in transposing 'Pushkin's classically severe and precise art into the romantic style of erotic ballads'.[21]

In evidence, once more, are close similarities between the way in which Pushkin's composition is understood by a later author and the artistic construction of that writer's own literary works. One may, for example, point to a series of poems written by Briusov at the turn of the century about such figures as Circe, Medea and even Cleopatra herself, figures who 'drain frenzied passion to the last drop'.[22] According to Briusov, Cleopatra seemed to personify the 'cult of the flesh' that he regarded as the basis of the world-view of antiquity, a cult that embraced two fundamental ideas: 'наслаждение' and 'смерть' (pleasure and death).[23] For Briusov, the ideal of physical beauty and man's apotheosis of woman were incarnated in Cleopatra:

> Beauty and pleasure are gifts of the gods. To conceal beauty and to hide its charms is to commit a sin against God ... The ancient world knew holy prostitution in its temples. Woman, selling herself for money, was fulfilling a service to a god. Among the ranks of such temple prostitutes Cleopatra was to be found.[24]

Zhirmunskii concluded that Dostoevskii presented a 'moral condemnation of satanic depths', whereas Briusov managed to fashion from Pushkin's fragment a 'doctrine of the strained and dazzling beauty of earthly love'.[25] This verdict on the two readings that I have discussed seems fully justified. As Hughes-Hallett observes in the introduction to her book on Cleopatra, 'Each image of Cleopatra ... provides clues to the nature of the culture which produced it, in particular to its sexual politics, its racial prejudices, its neuroses and its fantasies'.[26]

To adopt the word that Hughes-Hallett employs to refer to this revisionary practice, it may be said without fear of contradiction that Dostoevskii and Briusov both distorted Pushkin's Cleopatra in their reading of his poem.[27] One should, however, acknowledge that this is exactly what Pushkin himself did with his subject. Each new poem, by definition, distorts, that is to say modifies or transforms, the material upon which it is based. This tenet is central to the definition of 'остранение' or 'making strange'. Indeed, in the Formalist view, distortion is what makes art.

One significant effect of this was noted by T.S. Eliot in his essay 'Tradition and the Individual Talent', when he stated that 'what happens when a new work of art is created is something that happens simultaneously to all the works of art which preceded it.' He goes on to maintain that '[w]hoever has approved this idea of order ... will not find it preposterous that *the past should be altered by the present* as much as the present is directed by the past'.[28] This principle of æsthetic criticism applied in Pushkin's time as much as it does in ours. When Pushkin lived, the prevailing literary mode in Russia, as in the rest of Europe, was what we now define as 'Romantic'. Pushkin could not but be affected by this fact, just as we cannot but read him through the perspective of post-romanticism tinged, if ever so slightly, with the reticulations of post-modernism. At present, it seems to be as difficult for the literary critic to disengage the image of Cleopatra from the tag of 'Orientalism', as it is for the popular mind to disassociate it from the cinematic extravagance of Elizabeth Taylor.

Greenleaf, for example, asks the question: 'What would this poem [*Cleopatra*] have conveyed to a reader in 1824?'[29] Her answer involves her in using the word 'Oriental' five times in less than three pages of commentary.[30] Such an emphasis on the Orient re-situates the last of the Macedonian rulers of Egypt in the Ptolomeic line of succession that went back to 323 B.C., following the death of Alexander, in a cultural and historical setting that is not so much as mentioned in the poem. As O'Bell notes, more judiciously, the 'classical decoration of the poem … in 1824 and 1828 had never been specifically Egyptian. Not until the 1835 reworking would Pushkin elaborate an Egyptian setting for Cleopatra, cosmopolitan Alexandria, Alexander's city of hellenized Egypt, breathing the generalized atmosphere of late antiquity'.[31] There are, then, distortions and distortions. We cannot construe the meaning of Pushkin's poem entirely independently of the readings practised by Dostoevskii, Briusov and others. Work on Cleopatra continues as it has done in the past, transforming her from public benefactor and scholar to barbaric voluptuary and mighty queen.[32] This work, in Bakhtinian terms, forms part of a continuing dialogue.

Tynianov drew attention to the inevitability of distortion when he proposed the Formalist dictum that the *dynamism* of a literary work 'reveals itself … in the concept of the constructive principle'. He proceeded to make the fundamental claim that:

> Not all factors of a word are equivalent. Dynamic form is not generated by means of combination or merger (the often-used concept of 'correspondence'), but by means of interaction, and, consequently, the pushing forward of one group of factors at the expense of another. In so doing, the advanced factor deforms the subordinate ones.[33]

Art lives by means of this interaction and struggle.[34] The 'constructive factor', which possesses the power to 'deform' other functions in order to bring about the 'correlation and integration' of the text, was known to the Formalists as the 'dominant' (*dominanta*).

What I want to propose is that in Pushkin's *Cleopatra* the *dominanta* is the idea of *sovereign rapture*, to which, in their idiosyncratic readings, both Dostoevskii and Briusov responded. At the heart of their distortions, then, there was a grain - or two - of truth. It is these grains that make up the nucleus of Pushkin's poem, which itself, by definition, since it's a work of art, a classically severe and precise art, distorts - or deforms - the material upon which it draws. That material, as I suggested at the start of this paper, is part history, part legend. We do not need to go very far into any historical account of Cleopatra to discover evidence of the grains that are preserved in the extreme readings of a Dostoevskii or a Briusov. Jack Lindsay, for example, in the first paragraph of the Author's Introduction to his book *Cleopatra*, referring to his predecessor, the Greek historian, Plutarch, notes that:

His account has many qualities of genuine penetration and poetic insight; and though elements of the hostile [Roman] tradition are mingled in it, it yet manages to convey a strong feeling of Cleopatra's *charm and force*, her distinct personality.[35]

Here we have it: charm and force. These are the distinct qualities of Cleopatra's personality that run through a multitude of literary and artistic re-creations in different languages and cultures in the course of two thousand years. Dostoevskii chose to accentuate *force*, Briusov *charm*, in their respective re-workings.

Pushkin placed equal stress on each of these two aspects that had been suggested to him by the epigrammatic balance between the 'tantae libidinis' and 'tantae pulchritudinis' of Sextus Aurelius' formulation.[36] It is this balanced distribution, I would suggest, that allows his Cleopatra to remain enigmatic. And it is this dual emphasis that I want to explore by taking up some of the implications of the two words in my title: *sovereign rapture*.

On a narrative level, we may distinguish between the guests at the feast, who constitute the backdrop to the central action, and the four main *dramatis personae*: Cleopatra and her three doomed lovers, an archetypal constellation of 1 plus 3. If we consider Cleopatra as embodying *force* and *charm* in equal (and indissoluble) measure, then Aquila, the soldier, may be regarded as the male counterpart who serves to accentuate the former attribute and Crito, the pleasure-lover, as complementing the latter.[37] What place, then, for the 'anonymous youth'? The fact that he is not named may suggest that he corresponds to an undefined quality in Cleopatra, her past perhaps, her 'salad days' when, in Shakespeare's words, she was 'green in judgement'- the youthful aspect that lives on in the mature woman, belonging to a less constrained time before she became the Egyptian sovereign in her eighteenth year and, in all probability, married her younger brother. Yet, in the formulation of *sovereign rapture*, the youth is the unnamed remainder, the surplus, the excess, who freely determines his own disappearance from this world at the threshold of dawn.

He is, however one wishes to construe it, the male enigma, who confirms a discontinuity between sovereignty and rapture, just as Cleopatra, in contrast, confirms the unity of the two for the female. Pushkin's poem takes the form of a fragment. A fragment is a piece broken off from a larger whole. In this case, what seems to be missing is the ending, since there is no indication that anything of interest might precede the beginning.[38] Indeed, the very first word of *Cleopatra* (in the 1824 version) 'Царица' - sovereign - announces the first component of the poem's thematic. And if the notion of *sovereignty* is invoked in the opening word, then it is only at the very end of the poem, where the reader - like the crowd at the feast - is left silent in expectation, that the complementary idea of *rapture* is addressed: 'Он Клеопатрою, казалося, дышал, / И молча долго им царица любовалась'. ('He was, it seemed, all imbued with Cleopatra, / And long and silently the sovereign gazed at him admiringly'.)

The penultimate word of the poem is also 'царица', thus bringing us round full circle to the start of the poem.[39] Yet, in order to generate the open structure of a poetic fragment and to establish the enigma of its narrative theme, Pushkin allows the composition to linger on for one final word, the longest in the last line.

As I have already noted, the poem's gravitational pull is all towards the ending, where the youth appears. When Pushkin revised the poem in 1828, one of the most striking changes had to do with the depiction of the youth. The 'fire of love' ('Огонь любви') that blazed in his eyes in the first version is no longer mentioned. The image of *fire* has been replaced by that of *rapture* - 'Восторг в очах его сиял' ('Rapture shone in his eyes') - just as *love*, in the next line, has been replaced by *passion*.[40] This new configuration is symptomatic of a change in the poem's inner image, which marks a *rapprochement* of executioner and victim (as well as the development of a prose thematic). Indeed, one might speculate, had the poem continued, what might have occurred would have been not so much a rapprochement as a reversal of roles whereby the youth makes rapture and passion his own and the signs of tenderness ('умиление') that Dostoevskii detected in Cleopatra's character are confirmed by her actions. But, of course, the poem does not continue. Pushkin is more circumspect. He contrives to give a sense of finality to the fragment by means of an alteration in the verb that ends the poem. In place of 'любовалась' (admired), he substitutes 'остановила' (rested).

In the 1828 version, the new line that contains an explicit reference to *rapture* - Восторг в очах его сиял - commences with an alliterative effect (marked by underlining). Earlier in the poem (in a line present in the 1824 composition and retained in 1828), we encounter a similar phonic duplication of the first syllable: Кто к торгу страстному приступит? (Who will venture upon passionate barter?) The repetition of the phonic device, combined with the disclosure of a concealed link between 'торг' and 'восторг', invites us, however subliminally, to make a connection between the two lines. When we make this connection, we discover that the link is conceptual as well as acoustic. The common denominator between 'торг' and 'восторг' has to do with *passion*.

Cleopatra asks, 'Who will venture upon *passionate* barter?' In this context, *barter* would seem to be the right word to translate *торг* into English, rather than, say 'bargain' or the more neutral 'trade'. There is an excitement or thrill about the act of bartering that is absent from bargaining, which calls for a cooler head and more protracted negotiations. What is more, to barter is to exchange goods of equivalent value, whereas to bargain carries the implication of an attempt to get the better of an opponent. One might also say that the act of barter conveys more powerfully the sense that each side has something of direct interest to offer to the other. Earlier in the poem, Cleopatra had spoken of '*equality* (*равенство*) between us' (my italics).

'Торг' can be as passionate as 'восторг'. In *The Queen of Spades*, Pushkin was to tell the story of a man whose downfall came as the result of his abandoning a prudent, calculating *modus vivendi* (necessary 'bargaining') for the sake of a rash pursuit of fortune (superfluous 'barter'). When Hermann sits down at the gaming table and elects to play faro (thus determining his fate in the presence of yet another awe-struck, Pushkinian crowd), he has an even chance of winning or losing the game. In 1824, Pushkin had not yet hit upon this means of objectifying the thematic choice that presents itself to the self-destructive psyche of the *amateur*. Instead of exploiting a narrative plot that centred on a game of chance and leaving the reader in doubt as to the meaning of a playing card, having to decide between the possibility of supernatural intervention and psychological derangement, the author himself drew a queen from the pack of history.

There is, however, a work contemporary with the inception of the Cleopatra theme in Pushkin's writing, which attests more immediately to the dialectic between 'торг' and 'восторг' that informs *Cleopatra*. It is *The Conversation of a Bookseller and a Poet*. In this poem, binary oppositions proliferate. They range from the bookseller's crude contrast between bank-notes and the leaves of the poet's verse[41] introduced in his opening gambit - 'Стихи любимца муз и граций / Мы вмиг рублями заменим / И в пук наличных ассигнаций / Листочки ваши обратим' ('In an instant we will exchange for rubles / Verses by the favourite of Muses and Graces / And we will turn your pages / Into a bundle of ready cash') - to the distinction between inspiration and manuscripts (the beginning and the end of the poetic process, as it were) in his closing remarks: 'Позвольте просто вам сказать: / Не продается вдохновенье, / Но можно рукопись продать'. ('Allow me simply to tell you: / Inspiration is not for sale, / but a manuscript can be sold'.) It is to the poet's response, however, that we must turn to encounter an explicit opposition between 'торг' and 'восторг':

Тогда, в безмолвии трудов,
Делиться не был я готов
С толпою пламенным восторгом
И музы сладостных даров
Не унижал постыдным торгом.

('Then in the silence of my labours / I was not prepared to share / With the crowd my burning rapture / Nor the sweet gifts of the Muses / Did I degrade with shameful barter'.)

What we are presented with here, in the pointed opposition between *flame* and *shame* (the flame of rapture and the shame of mercantile trade), is an early affirmation of the credo of an Olympian poet whose voice will be heard in a series of powerful lyric utterances from 1827 to 1830, declaring the poet to be an acolyte of Apollo rather than a devotee of Dionysus.[42] The latter role is more akin to the part played by the unnamed youth of *Cleopatra* and to Hermann as revealed in the unfolding plot of *The Queen of Spades*. If it is an Apollonian credo of *purity* that is articulated in *The Conversation of a Bookseller and a Poet* ('Кого восторгом чистых дум / Боготворить не устыдился'['Whom he was not ashamed to worship / With the rapture of chaste thoughts']), then the one glimpse we are vouchsafed of the Dionysian comes in the poet's question: 'Вся жизнь, одна ли, две ли ночи?'(' What is all life, one night or two?')

In *The Conversation of a Bookseller and a Poet*, the bookseller promotes a form of 'торг' that demands (for the poet) a shameful, or impure, courting of public adulation, whereas the poet, who respects the purity of 'восторг', embodies (for the bookseller) a sterile and profitless denial of fame and money. The bookseller's code of practice is based upon a simple, accumulative premise: 'Нам нужно злата, злата, злата: / Копите злато до конца!' ('We need gold, gold, gold: / Hoard up gold until the end!') There is no likelihood of a resolution between the diametrically opposed viewpoints expressed by the artist and the entrepreneur. Although, in the end, the poet agrees a deal with the bookseller in order to get rid of him, he does so in prose. The self-definition offered at the start of his first utterance remains unaffected: 'Поэт беспечный, я писал / Из вдохновенья, не из платы'. ('A carefree poet, I wrote / From inspiration, not for pay'.)

In *Cleopatra*, however, the circumstances (and the stakes) are different. If, as Georges Bataille has claimed, it is the 'aura of death' that 'denotes passion',[43] then the price one has to pay for its consummation is life itself. In this case, rapture does not lead to poetic inspiration since the 'tender' youth is no poet. He is a lover, for whom rapture is predicated upon an experience that is potentially both erotically sublime and squalidly commercial. Sextus Aurelius' 'morte emirent' must be weighed against his 'prostiterit'. Bliss is for sale, but the irony that Pushkin's poem insists upon is that the nature of the transaction is such that it must be at once mercenary and self-sacrificing.[44] The presence of the crowd ensures that the basest of interpretations will be put on the night's proceedings once the feasting is over. To appreciate the distinction between the rapture of the lover and the rapture of the poet, we need to turn to a draft note that Pushkin wrote in response to two articles that Küchelbecker published in *Mnemozina* in June and October 1824, that is to say at the time when Pushkin was engaged in composing *Cleopatra*. In his note, Pushkin cites with approval Küchelbecker's claim that 'strength' ('сила'), 'freedom' ('свобода') and 'inspiration' ('вдохновение') are the three essentials of all poetry. The first two qualities seem unproblematic to Pushkin. It's the third one that detains him, and calls for a gloss (since he believes that вдохновение and восторг have been confused). In Pushkin's view:

rapture excludes *calm*, which is an absolute condition for *beauty*. Rapture does not require any intellectual power capable of relating the parts to the whole. Rapture is fleeting, inconstant, and consequently incapable of creating anything which is truly great and perfect (without which there can be no lyric poetry).

Rapture is a heightened state of the imagination alone. One can have inspiration without rapture, but rapture cannot exist without inspiration.[45]

In Keats, with whom I have already compared Pushkin, one finds a similar contrast between the inspired poet and the rapturous lover (or, to use Keats' word, the *fanatic*), in that only the former proceeds from *rapture* to *inspiration*. At the start of *The Fall of Hyperion*, Keats writes that 'Fanatics have their dreams':

> But bare of laurel they live, dream and die;
> For Poesy alone can tell her dreams,
> With the fine spell of words alone can save
> Imagination from the sable charm
> And dumb enchantment.

Cleopatra and the tender youth, we might say, are *equal* in *rapture*, but embody different archetypes. Cleopatra's is a rapture that comes from a passion for exercising the sovereignty that she possesses (power, dominion); the youth's is a rapture that bestows sovereignty upon him (freedom, autonomy). He *acquires* sovereignty, sovereignty as selfhood, in which rapture, as Pushkin noted, is 'fleeting, inconstant' ('непродолжителен', 'непостоянен'). Unlike Aquila or Crito, his character is not yet fixed. Unnamed and inexperienced, he remains mobile.

There is a congruity between the triadic configuration of soldier, pleasure-lover and tender youth in *Cleopatra* and that of *strength, freedom* and *inspiration* in Küchelbecker's identification of the three essential qualities of all poetry. In both instances, the apparent instability of the third constituent was what interested Pushkin. We even find an echo of this in the situation that Pushkin presents at the end of *The Queen of Spades*, where it's the indeterminacy of the third card's identity (queen or ace) that undoes - destabilizes - Hermann: 'The old woman!' he cried in horror.

Taking up this motif of the instability of the third component, I should like to return, in conclusion, to the meaning of the central figure, Cleopatra, for today's reader, a meaning as much determined by the system of ideas that the poem evinces as the imagery that it incorporates. For Pushkin, the figure of Cleopatra functioned as an objective correlative for values belonging to a past that no longer existed in a world that had become indifferent. She represented a positive force in a sceptical age. For us, as we enter a new millennium, Pushkin's Cleopatra and those that followed in her wake - Gautier's *Une Nuit de Cléopatre*, most immediately - have now taken on that correlative function of remoteness (as have, in a sense, their authors). That is to say, we measure ourselves by them, and in so doing effect an alteration in them. The *femme fatale* of the nineteenth century embodies a vitality that is largely absent in our millenarian outlook that offers hastily constructed exhibitions (or, as we have been encouraged to call them, 'experiences') and equally hastily constructed optimism.

Do we, then, still discover an inclination in contemporary literature to explore the theme of sovereign rapture in which the ceaseless contest between Eros and Thanatos is enacted? To answer that question in the affirmative I should like to end by quoting in full a poem that gives an alternative name - 'Hunger' - to the force that drove the unnamed youth to sacrifice himself for the 'sable charm' of a night with Cleopatra (and, indeed, Cleopatra to offer herself in the first place). There is in this poem, as far as the constellation of the four main characters and the nocturnal outcome that is implied, a dramatic tension that is strangely reminiscent of Pushkin's treatment of the same theme.[46] Readers of the poem may recognize in the archetypal situation a re-enactment of the triadic structure depicted in Pushkin's fragment, that is to say, a dramatic scene that once again ends in an equivocation or, alternatively, they may acknowledge the enigma of a myth that has the power to transform each and every daughter of whatever century into a Cleopatra ... for one night, or two.

Hunger

On their way home
from the war
three soldiers stop
at a border farm.

Food is scarce,
but their host makes them
welcome, and his daughter
cooks an enormous *tortilla*
which she serves with yam.

When night comes she knows
that other hunger will need
feeding. She brings with her
to bed the knife used
for slaughtering pigs.

The first soldier
reeks of leather
and horse shit.
The second scrapes
her face with stubble.

The skin of the third
is smooth. She cannot find it
in her heart to kill him
and he, being young,
is hungriest of all.

NOTES

1. Leslie O'Bell, *Pushkin's 'Egyptian Nights': The Biography of a Work*, Ardis, Ann Arbor, 1984, (hereafter O'Bell), p. 132, gives the date of composition as: ll. 1-58 (between 2 and 9 October); ll. 59-63 (between 10 and 15 October); and ll. 64-70 (around 1 November). Monika Greenleaf, *Pushkin and Romantic Fashion: Fragment, Elegy, Orient, Irony*, Stanford University Press, Stanford, Cal., 1994), (hereafter Greenleaf), writes that *Cleopatra* was 'written between November 1 and 10 or 15, 1824, four months after Pushkin's arrival in Mikhailovskoe' (p. 289).

2. O'Bell, op. cit., p. 4.

3. Implicit in this categorization is a distinction between a problem, which may be solved, and an enigma that resists any adequate resolution.

4. Text and translation in O'Bell, p. 14. Greenleaf states that 'in Pushkin's time' the sentence was 'still falsely attributed' to Sextus Aurelius, p. 299. Compare Alexander Pushkin, *Complete Prose Fiction*; transl. Paul Debreczeny, Stanford University Press, Stanford, Cal., 1983, p. 521.

5. Lucy Hughes-Hallett, *Cleopatra: Histories, Dreams and Distortions*, Bloomsbury Publishing, London, 1990, (hereafter Hughes-Hallett), p. 233.

6. Petrarch's lines from his *Trionfi* ('She triumphs over him [i.e. Julius Caesar]: and right it is / That he who conquered the world should be conquered in his turn', quoted in Hughes-Hallett, op. cit., p. 298) could just as readily have served Pushkin as a subtextual inspiration for a (very different) poem on Cleopatra. Shakespeare's *Antony and Cleopatra* (1607) and Corneille's *Rodogune* (1644) could also have served Pushkin as a source.

7. See Hughes-Hallett, op. cit., pp. 225-6.

8. Greenleaf (p. 290) writes: 'It was during the climactic two weeks of [a] family crisis that Pushkin composed "Kleopatra". On November 19 his family left for St Petersburg, abandoning Pushkin to solitude, provincial society, and the company of his nanny'. In a letter to his brother, which Thomas Shaw assigns to the first half of November 1824, Pushkin wrote: 'In the evening I listen to fairy tales, and thereby I am compensating for the insufficiencies of my accursed upbringing. How charming these fairy tales are! Each is a poem!' (*The Letters of Alexander Pushkin*, I, translated by J. Thomas Shaw, Indiana University Press, Bloomington, 1963, pp. 188-9).

9. Tatiana Wolff, ed. and transl., *Pushkin on Literature*, Methuen, London, 1971, p. 129, (translation modified). For the original, see A.S. Pushkin, *Sobranie sochinenii v desiati tomakh*, VI, *Kritika i publisistika*, Khudozhestvennaia literatura, Moscow, 1976, p. 233.

10. Goethe's evocation of the *spirit of negation* comes in part one of *Faust*. It is perhaps worth noting Hans Blumenberg's remark, made in reference to Goethe, that 'That which destroys is secretly the creative': *Work on Myth*, translated by Robert M. Wallace, MIT, Cambridge, Mass., 1990, p. 448. In Pushkin's *Cleopatra*, the sexual polarity that we find in the relationship between Faust and Margarita is reversed.

11. Quoted in O'Bell, op. cit., p. 32.

12. Ibid., p. 29.

13. As O'Bell observes, 'These moments of feeling, these flashes, have always impressed readers of Pushkin' (loc. cit.).

14. The two are juxtaposed in the poem *The Angel*, which O'Bell cites, op. cit., pp. 29-30.

15. Chapter 6 of *Evgenii Onegin*, in which the death of Lenskii is recounted, was composed in 1826.

16. This is O'Bell's translation (p. 33) of a passage from an article ('Otvet *Russkomu vestniku*') that Dostoevskii wrote in 1861. For the original, see F.M Dostoevskii, *Polnoe sobranie sochinenii v tridtsati tomakh*, ed. G.M. Fridlender, XIX, *Stat'i i zametki 1861*, Nauka,

Leningrad, 1979, pp. 119-39 (136-7), and for an account of the 'Tolmacheva affair' that provoked Dostoevskii to write his article, see Paul Debreczeny, *Social Functions of Literature: Alexander Pushkin and Russian Culture*, Stanford University Press, Stanford, Cal., 1997, pp. 209-15. To set a more objective account against Dostoevskii's subjective reading, I cite O'Bell's synopsis of the plot: 'The poem presents Cleopatra presiding over a feast where she has fallen into a reverie. From this reverie she rouses herself in order to issue a challenge by which she offers a night of her love to any man who will agree to forfeit his life on the morning after. Amid the general consternation of the guests, three accept Cleopatra's terms. Cleopatra swears a solemn oath to fulfill her bargain, and the lots of the three lovers are drawn from the urn one by one. First comes the soldier, Aquila, then the pleasure-seeker Crito, and last an anonymous youth on whom Cleopatra fixes her gaze in admiration. On this the poem closes' (O'Bell, op. cit., p. 11).

17. Compare O'Bell, op. cit., pp. 29-34.

18. Hughes-Hallett (op. cit., p. 233) indicates a subtextual reference to *Egyptian Nights* in *The Idiot*.

19. '"Egipetskie Nochi" Valeriia Briusova' [hereafter Zhirmunskii] is chapter 2 (pp. 52-86) of V. Zhirmunskii, *Valerii Briusov i nasledie Pushkina: Opyt sravnitel'no-stilisticheskogo issledovaniia*, El'zevir, Petersburg, 1922, repr. Letchworth, Prideaux Press, 1972. Translations from this essay are mine.

20. Zhirmunskii, op. cit., p. 59.

21. Ibid., p. 58.

22. For *Circe* (1899), *Medea* (1903, 1904), and *Cleopatra* (1899), see Valerii Briusov, *Sobranie sochinenii v semi tomakh*, ed. E. Malinina, I, *Stikhotvoreniia i poemy 1892-1909*, Khudozhestvennaia literatura, Moscow, 1973, pp. 148, 387-38, and 153 respectively. The expression quoted comes from *Circe*.

23. *Pleasure* in the sense of physical gratification. Hazlitt had already commented in 1817 (about Shakespeare's dramatization) that 'Cleopatra's whole character is the triumph of the voluptuous, of the love of pleasure and the power of giving it, over every other consideration'. Quoted in Hughes-Hallett, op. cit., p. 209.

24. Zhirmunskii, op. cit., p. 59.

25. Ibid., p. 58.

26. Hughes-Hallett, op. cit., p. 2.

27. The subtitle of Hughes-Hallett's book is *Histories, Dreams and Distortions*. Isaiah Berlin, in characterizing Dostoevskii as a hedgehog, indicts him on the count of distortion: 'Dostoevsky who is nothing if not a hedgehog ... transforms, indeed distorts, Pushkin into a dedicated prophet, a bearer of a single, universal message which was indeed the centre of Dostoevsky's own universe' ('The Hedgehog and the Fox', in Henry Hardy and Aileen Kelly, eds, *Russian Thinkers*, Penguin, Harmondsworth, 1979, p. 23). Yet, 'distortions' of this kind have a beneficial side-effect in that they encourage us to re-assess, if only to re-assert, our understanding of the original text.

28. T.S. Eliot, 'Tradition and the Individual Talent', in *The Sacred Wood: Essays on Poetry and Criticism*, Methuen, London, 1920, (repr. 1934), pp. 47-59 (49-50; italics added).

29. Greenleaf, op. cit., p. 301.

30. 'Oriental tyranny', 'Oriental society' (both on p. 301), 'Oriental potentate', 'Oriental luxury and satiation', two nouns for the price of one! (both on p. 306) and 'the homogeneous Oriental throng' (p. 307).

31. According to O'Bell (op. cit., p. 57), the 'Egyptian motif' first appeared in the creative history of the 'Cleopatra tales' in 1830.

32. Plutarch wrote that 'she could pass from one language to another' and Flavius Philostratus, in the first century A.D., stated that she derived 'a positively sensuous pleasure from literature'. See Hughes-Hallett, op. cit., pp. 73-4. Some indication of the many twists and turns in the evolution of Cleopatra's image may be given simply by listing Hughes-Hallett's chapter headings (in part two of her book): The Suicide, The Lover, The Woman, The Queen, The Foreigner, The Killer (which includes Pushkin's construction), and The Child. The last chapter, 'Cleopatra winks', examines the 'camp' Cleopatras of the twentieth century.

33. Yuri Tynianov, *The Problems of Verse Language*, ed. and transl. Michael Sosa and Brent Harvey, Ardis, Ann Arbor, 1981 (Russian original, 1924) p. 33.

34. Ibid., p. 33.

35. Jack Lindsay, *Cleopatra*, Folio Society, London,1998 (first published, 1971), xix [my italics]).

36. Pushkin's amplification of Sextus Aurelius' observation, of course, does not preclude the view that there is charm in force, and force in charm.

37. Alternatively, these two claimants could be said, in Pushkin's poetic economy, to stand in for the two lovers of Cleopatra that history acknowledges - Julius Caesar the military commander and Mark Antony the pleasure-lover, respectively. If we take this view, the poem demonstrates that Cleopatra is a match for all men of force and for all men of charm. Compare the suggestion made in endnote 6 above.

38. O'Bell takes a somewhat different view. She notes that the two lines Pushkin added to the start of the poem in 1828 ('The palace shone. Singers thundered in chorus / To the sound of flute and lyre.') 'add more than a setting. The insistent presence of the guests and the chorus, of the audience, now punctuates the poem' (p. 34). This shift 'leads into the future development of the same themes in prose' (p. 34). Her observation is consistent with the Formalist propositions, enunciated by Tynianov, that *'The laws of the development of plot in verse are different than in prose'* and that *'The perspective of verse refracts the plotting perspective'* (*The Problem of Verse Language*, p. 131; italics in the original), but an investigation of this topic falls outside the present scrutiny.

39. Similarly, the word 'царица', in its syllabic structure, ends as it begins.

40. The love that 'was expressed in every feature' becomes the 'inexperienced force of passion' that 'seethed in the young heart'.

41. The bookseller's crude contrast is to be distinguished from the poet's (that is, Pushkin's) ironic juxtaposition (ассигнации / Листочки) and playful rhyme (граций - ассигнаций).

42. From *Поэт* (1827) to *Поэту* (1830).

43. Georges Bataille, *Eroticism*, translated by Mary Dalwood, Marion Boyars, London, 1987, p. 20. In a later formulation, he writes:'Eroticism opens the way to death. Death opens the way to the denial of our individual lives' (p. 24).

44. Or, as Hughes-Hallett puts it laconically: 'Although she may not be known, she can be had'. Cleopatra conforms here to the type of the Foreigner: 'An object of wonder, not a person to be loved and understood, she becomes both superficial and profoundly mysterious, a surface so dazzling that one cannot think of looking beyond it. So the viewer is absolved of responsibility for her ... A foreigner, and a sight for seeing, she is nothing to do with us' (op. cit., p. 213).

45. The translation, by Tatiana Wolff, appears in *Pushkin on Literature*, pp. 169-70. For the original, see A.S. Pushkin, *Sobranie sochinenii*, VI, op. cit., p. 239. David Bethea, commenting on the contemporary association between 'sublime' восторг and the genre of the ode, makes the significant observation that, after 1825, восторг enters a different semantic field in Pushkin's lexicon, namely that of the 'misplaced sublime' in post-Decembrist Russia. See his detailed discussion of восторг (which he prefers to translate as *ecstasy*) in David M. Bethea, *Realizing Metaphors: Alexander Pushkin and the Life of the Poet*, University of Wisconsin Press, Madison, 1998, pp. 180-8. This shift of emphasis is consistent with the Egyptian trappings and prose setting that Cleopatra acquires after her first appearance in 1824. Compare,

in the light of Bethea's analysis, the association of rapture with the crowd in *Поэту*: 'Восторженных похвал пройдет минутный шум' ('The momentary noise of rapturous praises will pass').

46. *Hunger*, by Celia de Fréine, is included in *Of Cabbages and Queens*, a collection of poems which shared first prize in the 1998-99 translation competition, sponsored by the British Comparative Literature Association and the British Centre for Literary Translation. It is translated from the Irish by the author.

Don-Juanism and Stylistic Code in Pushkin's
The Stone Guest

by

ANDRE G.F. VAN HOLK

1   PRELIMINARIES[1]

In this chapter I intend to highlight a number of supposedly salient aspects of Don-Juanism and its role in the stylistic code of Romanticism in Pushkin's *The Stone Guest*. This 'little tragedy' stands out as one of the jewels among Pushkin's œuvre,[2] mostly perhaps by the compactness and intensity of its poetic evocation. Moreover, the figure of Don Juan has through the centuries aroused vivid interest among historians of European culture.[3]

   The fascination with Don Juan might well originate in those properties which led Jung to admit this character among his 'archetypes'.[4] It is not my intention (and indeed lies outside my competence) to venture into the psychoanalytic aspects of Don-Juanism; instead, I take it that the text of *The Stone Guest* confronts us with a literary hero as the product of artistic creation, and hence as a possible object of literary and text-linguistic enquiry. Accordingly, the programme of this chapter will comprise the following issues:

(1)   the thematics of the 'story' (in Chatman's sense);[5]

(2)   the stylistic code of the text, in particular the devices by which the ideological sphere of the text is conjured up;

(3)   the thematic structure of Don Juan's character.[6]

2   THEMATICS OF THE STORY IN *THE STONE GUEST*

2.1

The endeavour to describe a complex cultural reality by means of a limited array of minimally structured 'elements' has a long tradition.[7] Using Chatman's convenient survey of the basic units of literary meaning, the present attempt will lead to a description of the form of content of a story in terms of certain recurrent semantic patterns, covering events (actions and happenings) and existents (characters and settings), while the discourse will include the structure of narrative transmission and its verbal manifestation, for instance, the expression side of the text, as the result of the stylistic devices and code.[8]

From the story we first extract the *static* semantic material underlying events and existents, which in the text-linguistic frame of a literary work appear as recurrent clusters of meanings, each attached to a syntactic construction; the latter carries an invariant content, for which I use the term *theme*. The ultimate constituents of such clusters are dubbed *elementary thematic constructions* (ECs); these each contribute a likewise invariant categorial content (such as 'plurality', 'location', 'motion', 'reciprocity' etc.).

A crucial part of the thematics of *The Stone Guest* appears to be pivoted about a particular variety of masculine-feminine interaction, with Don Juan as the main male actor and Doña Anna as his female antagonist. This interaction is, in Lotman's words, 'rehearsed' in the episode with Laura, while in both, moreover, the thematic component of rivalry - first with Don Carlos and then with the Comendador - strongly contributes to the 'event' aspect of the story; this aspect is further enhanced by the fatal presence of the Statue coming to life towards the end of the narrative string. Don Juan's character of defiant die-hard, courageously ('I fear No other soul in all Madrid beside'), yet egotistically pursuing his amorous overtures[9] and challenging the Statue, provides a uniting principle, presumably to be described by a special brand of what I have in earlier work proposed to call 'character themes': this issue is taken up in section 4.[10]

2.2

Turning now to the thematics of the narrative core, the 'story' of *The Stone Guest*,[11] the following components (or subthemes) may be readily distinguished:

(1)   an opposition between the two locations of 'exile' and 'capital';[12]

(2)   a second binary opposition - running parallel to the former - between the 'real' world of Don Juan's actions and the 'unreal' world of the living statue, which intermittently flows over into the former.

The two opposed locations (1) will be each represented by a LOCATIVE construction (in Fillmore's sense) of the form (3) with its transformations, and exemplified by expressions from the text such as the ones quoted below.[13]

(3)

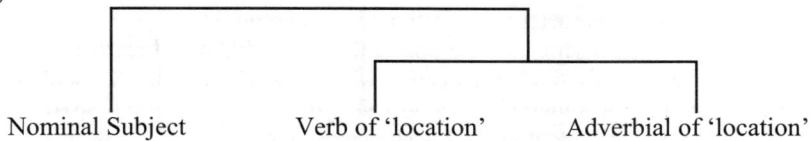

Nominal Subject   Verb of 'location'   Adverbial of 'location'

(4)   Examples:

LOC I /exile/	LOC II /capital/
	Ах, наконец Достигли мы ворот Мадрита!
Что Дон Гуан из ссылки	самовольно В Мадрит явился
Сидели б вы себе спокойно там.	… это место Знакомо нам
Я едва-едва не умер там со скуки Что за люди, / Что за земля!	Теперь которую в Мадрите / Отыскивать мы будем?
Я стою / За городом, в проклятой венте	Я Лауры / Пришел искать в Мадрите.
	And so at last / We've reached the portals of Madrid.
Without authority returned from exile	That Don Juan is in Madrid again
If only you had stayed there quietly	We seem to know this place; you recognize it?
I all but died of boredom there. What people! And what a land!	And now what lady in Madrid Shall we be seeking out?
I am lodging outside the city in a wretched tavern.	For Laura's sake I'm visiting Madrid.

The second opposition (2) consists of two ECs, termed REAL, the internal make-up of which is, however, a good deal more complex than that of the

Locative, as their construction is to cover at least certain expressions for the 'real' v. 'unreal' character of the referenced situation.

The underlying construction of the REAL EC will therefore contain a second-level ('qualitative') predication which bears on the full 'tensed' clause embedded in the personal subject noun (NPe_0 in 5), and the source (So) of which is included in that same nominal, as shown in (5).[14]

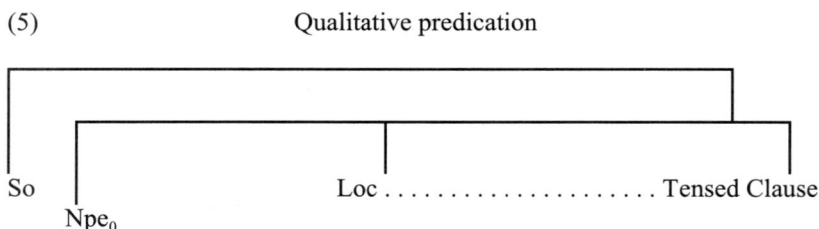

(5)   Qualitative predication

```
  ┌───────────────────────────────────────────────────────┐
  │        ┌───────────────────┬──────────────────────────┐│
So│        │                   │                          ││
  │Npe₀    Loc.................. Tensed Clause
```

So │   Loc . . . . Tensed Clause
     Npe_0

Thus the 'unreal' status of the Comendador's statue is expressed in its barest form by sentences such as

(6)   second-level predication

Кажется,   на вас она глядит и сердится
It seems   as though it's looking at you angrily

The following sample sentences may exemplify the 'real' v. 'unreal' of the opposition at issue (7).

(7)

REAL I   REAL II
                                         Дон Гуан
                                                    Дона Анна
                                         Де Сольва! как! супруга командора
                                         Убитого ... не помню кем?
                    Дон Гуан   Дон Гуан
             Так, я не монах   ... отшельником смиренном
                                         Я скрылся здесь
                    Дона Анна   Дон Гуан
                                         Диего де Кальвадо

REAL I	REAL II

REAL I

Как вас зовут?

REAL II

Дон Гуан
(*статуе*) Я, командор, прошу тебя прийти
К твоей вдове, где завтра буду я,
И стать на стороже в дверях.
Что? будешь?
Статуя кивает опять.

Don Juan: Doña Anna / De Solva? What? The wife of the Comendador / Slain by ... the name I can't recall ...?

Don Juan: I am no monk.

... in humble hermit's guise / I've taken refuge here.

Doña Anna: What's your name?

Don Juan: Diego de Salvado. (*To the statue.*) Comendador, I do herewith bid you come / Unto your widow's house, where I shall be tomorrow, / And keep watch before the door. / Well, will you? (*The statue nods again.*)

2.3

The two binary opposites (1) and (2) are each compounded with a thematic subtheme of triangular form representing the situations of encounter and rivalry between the main characters (8).

(8)

Don Juan _____ Laura		Don Juan _____ Doña Anna
Don Carlos	&	the Comendador

As the diagram indicates, the participants of each triad do not stand on a par: in each case, the relation between Don Juan and his beloved is disturbed by the presence of a rival - first Don Carlos, then Don Alvaro. Before going into the implementation of the triads in terms of ECs it should be pointed out that Don Carlos' rivalry is unsuccessful, and ends in his being slain, whereas the Comendador's is successful to the point of destroying Don Juan; his is indeed a destructive power, as remarked by Jakobson, who also speaks of 'the myth of the destructive statue'.[15]

Let us now turn to the crucial question as to what thematic elements are to be substituted for the terminal points of the two triads in (8). First of all, we notice that the relations which make up each triangle are love-relations. This holds primarily for Don Juan, while on the female side we have, first, the playful flirtation in which Laura indulges; Doña Anna's role is more complex, inasmuch as she at first tries to remain faithful to her deceased husband's memory:

(9)   мне вас любить нельзя,
        Вдова должна и гробу быть верна.

        It is forbidden to love you: / E'en to the grave a widow must be faithful.

This is indeed a duty (долг), as she confesses having been married by her mother, to escape from poverty, and rather against her will:

(10)

                        Дон Гуан
                Я не должен ревновать,
        Он вами выбран был.
                        Дона Анна
                                Нет, мать моя
        Велела мне дать руку Дон Альвару,
        Мы были бедны, Дон Альвар богат

Don Juan: I ought not to be jealous, / For he was your own choice.
Doña Anna: Oh no; my mother / Commanded me to marry Don Alvaro,
For we were poor and Don Alvaro rich.

Finally she succumbs to Don Juan's passionate rhetoric, and even grants him a kiss. Doña Anna indeed answers Don Juan's impetuous declaration of love, so that, she too, figures as the subject of a love-relation.

Now for the third relation-terminal in each triad. Don Carlos is evidently in love with Laura, and much more seriously than even Don Juan.

Nevertheless, his love for Laura comes as an external disturbing factor, since Laura and Don Juan apparently knew each other before the appearance of Don Carlos, and Laura certainly feels a more intimate affinity with Don Juan, whose songs she knows by heart. In the case of the Comendador we have an even more one-sided love-relation, since Anna's feeling for him is imposed by duty, though she pretends to be loved by him:

(11)   Когда бы знали вы, как Дон Альвар
         Меня любил! ...

         If only you could know how Don Alvaro / Did love me!

Despite the alleged sincerity of Don Alvaro's love it becomes a disturbing factor of rivalry at least from the moment Doña Anna has confessed her love for Don Juan.

As to the nature of the thematic construction best suited to implement the six end-points of the triadic love-relations, I confine myself here - by-passing the technical linguistic details - to a simplified representation (12), which shows the internal make-up of the construction termed 'experiential'.[16]

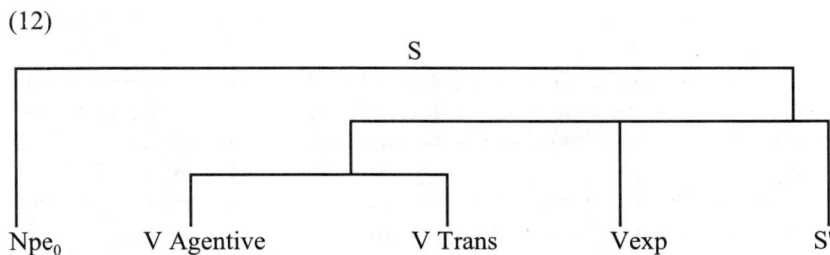

(12)

$$S$$

NPe_0 V Agentive   V Trans   Vexp   S'

Key: $NPe_0 \rightarrow$ personal noun in subject position; VExp $\rightarrow$ verb of experience (say, see, hear, think, feel ... etc.); S' $\rightarrow$ embedded sentence as object clause.

A verb of 'experience' may take either a clause or a verbal noun as its object: *She felt he might come back* or *She feels love for him*. One instance of this complex construction is the 'donative', with indirect object, which transforms into an indirect passive with nominative subject, for example, 'Он дал ей розы' ('He gave her roses'), and 'Чувствуется [вам], что ребенок любознателен' ('You feel that the child is fond of knowledge'); 'Он рад' ('He is glad') and 'Ему радостно' ('He feels glad'). This is indeed the mood expressed by Don Juan when in love: 'Я счастлив! / Я петь готов, я рад весь мир обнять' ('I am happy! / I'm ready to sing, I'd love to embrace the whole world').

We conclude from this brief discussion that each terminal point of the two triadic love-relations is to be represented by a construction of the experiential class. This gives us for the total compound theme of the narrative core of the poem the following structure (13):

(13)   LOC   REAL
                    EXP   EXP   EXP   EXP
                         EXP   &   EXP
              LOC   REAL

The triangular love-relations evoke a three-person speech situation underlying a three-dimensional model of signification - semantic, syntactic, pragmatic - as proposed by Bocheński.[17] The rival outsiders (Don Carlos, Don Alvaro) occupy the position of a third person, which is either 'personal' or 'impersonal', i.e. *he/she* v. *it*); insofar as this third person is the absolutely unmarked member of the three-person system, it stands for the entire triangle, which consequently may be taken to represent the combination of the first, second and third person characteristics of a *deity*: indeed, the statue is compared by Jakobson with the *lekan* of Siberian folklore.[18] Curiously enough, a supernatural agent of this sort (including personified Nature) in some languages is expressed by a feminine pronoun: thus *It is raining* is translated into Welsh by *Y mae hi yn bwrw glaw* (lit. 'She is throwing rain'); cf. also the feminine form of the Russian 'нелегкая' (devil).

In order to prepare the integration of the thematic core of the text into what will presently be identified as a Romantic world-view, this thematics may be verbalized as something like *the adoration of womanhood* (Laura, Doña Anna) *in conjunction with the rejection of social reality in search of the dangerous confrontation with the supernatural embodied in the statue.* Further details of this synoptic formula follow below.

3   ON THE STYLISTIC CODE OF ROMANTICISM IN *THE STONE GUEST*

3.1

Basing myself on the work of a number of logicians, linguists and semiologists[19] I shall adopt a conception of culture as a three-dimensional space occupied by some community using signs to store and transmit meaning; it is for cultural space in this sense that I use, following Lotman, the term *semiosphere*.[20] If it is agreed that the semiosphere through the intermediary of the speakers brings forth linguistic systems and texts, it will accordingly be possible to distinguish a number of *subspheres* on the basis of the linguistic material produced by it. Thus the material sphere of artefacts will be responsible for the most rigid, lexico-morphologic elements of language: roots, stems, words and set phrases.[21] The sphere of social intercourse, using a conversational style, naturally generates the stock of propositions with their relatively loose organization: free phrase order, the insertion of particles, and the use of intonation profiles to convey, for example, conditional modality, as in the Russian 'Послушать, так его мизинец умнее всех ...' ('To listen to him one would think that his little finger was cleverer than anybody ... ')[22] with falling pitch of about one fifth on the infinitive. Finally the *ideosphere* will produce the largest suprasentential structures, such as proverbs, anecdotes, narratives and arguments, with their linguistically least codified arrangement of components.

Within the semiosphere as a whole a crucial role is to be attributed to the cultural 'surface' (a term modelled after the 'surface' of a text), especially the boundary separating the material and social spheres from the ideosphere. In order to incorporate into this still unspecific model the stylistic devices of *The Stone Guest* I propose to assess the following two issues: (i) the degree of semantic coherence, and (ii) indicators of dynamics, such as intonational semantics and the use of verbs of fast or violent motion. The following brief discussion concentrates on the delimitation of these devices from those of adjacent style periods (in particular Rationalism).

3.2

What is meant here by 'semantic coherence' may be exemplified as follows. In contrast to, say, a simple enumeration of successive events in a newspaper report, in literature the artistic creation is prominent, and this entails, as we know from Jakobson, a 'set towards the message'.[23] The semantics of a poetic text differs from the zero-degree of literariness (литературность) of a prototypical newspaper report by a factor of *repetition* of semantic traits (figurae, semes) such that a vocabulary of perhaps several thousand items may be represented by a few dozen semes. Thus, referring to the opening lines of Scene I, the words дождаться (wait for) and ночь (night) both contain the feature 'time' (T), recurring in скоро (soon) and наконец (at last); similarly, the items достичь (reach), ворота (gate), Мадрит (Madrid), здесь (here) and улицу (street) repeat the seme 'location' (L), while достичь (reach) and полететь (fly; hurry) repeat the seme 'motion' (M); also characteristic of this passage (and the immediately subsequent ones) is the seme of 'secrecy' or 'incognito', contained in закрыть усы, брови (hide one's moustache and eyebrows) as well as, once the larger context is considered, in ночь (night) and, of course, in узнать (find out), признать (recognize), знакомы (well-known). The climax of this first passage is reached in 'Я никого в Мадрите не боюсь' ('I don't fear anyone in Madrid'), with the seme of 'danger' (P), 'caution', and the corresponding seme of 'courage' (denial of danger, challenge). To be sure, a good deal more can be said on this issue if the entire text is considered; for the present purpose, the few examples given may suffice to illustrate the notion of coherence.

3.3

Let us now look at the two passages adduced in (14).

(14)

(i)

Дон Гуан
Я завтра весь к твоим услугам.
Дон Карлос
                                                            Нет!

Теперь - сейчас ...
Дон Карлос
                                        Я жду. Ну что ж,
Ведь ты при шпаге.
Дон Гуан
                                        Ежели тебе
Не терпится, изволь.
(*Бьются*)

Don Juan: To-morrow I am at your service.
Don Carlos: No! / Not then - at once ...
I'm waiting. Well? / Your sword is at your side.
Don Juan: Oh, if you / Have no patience, Very well.

(*They fight*)

(ii)

Дон Гуан
Когда ж опять увидимся?
Дона Анна
                                        Не знаю.
Когда-нибудь.
Дон Гуан
А завтра?
Дона Анна
                                Где же?
Дон Гуан
                                                            Здесь.

Don Juan: When shall we meet again?
Doña Anna: I do not know. / Some time.

> *Don Juan*: To-morrow?
> *Doña Anna*: Where, then?
> *Don Juan*: Here.

The peculiar stylistic devices of sharp intonational contrasts together with a rapid succession of speakers and situations, and dialogues ending in violent action, though not limited to any particular style period, stand out as Romantic in contrast with certain Rationalist devices displayed by moralistic adages and proverbs in, say, Fonvizin's or Fredro's comedies.[24] In proverbs of the prototypical form '*Whoever* + verb phrase VP, (*he*) + verb phrase VP', the interrogative *Who* ...? is superseded by the dependent clause structure of *Whoever* + VP. The fable, characteristic of Russian Classicism (Sumarokov, Krylov, up to and including the proverbial insertions in Griboedov's *Woe from Wit*) is to some extent a text-size elaboration of a proverb.

Thus the Rationalist devices lead to the extraction of intonational semantics from the total text, and its subsequent integration into the ideosphere in the shape of proverbial sentence constructions. Under this process the material basis of the text is enriched by the storage of certain recurrent themes like 'nepotism', 'bribery', 'profitable marriage', and so on, which betray their origin in the sphere of social intercourse. In sharp contrast to this, the Romantic devices realize an inverse process of discharge of intonational material into the social sphere, and may end in the physical confrontation of a duel (for example, the *They fight* stage direction in example 14 [i]). Considering Romanticism as a body of typologically Romantic texts - or even a single supertext - it stands to reason that the onflow of intonational semantics, when transposed to the scale of a period's content, leads to a discharge of emotional ideology from the ideosphere into social action, increasing its intensity into rebellious or even revolutionary behaviour.[25]

3.4

The dynamic thrust behind Don Juan's behaviour - attested by verbs of motion and rapid violent action - may possibly be viewed as due to a collision of two antagonistic trends in the Romantic's world-view. Inspired by Thom's semiotic analysis of transitive constructions,[26] I propose to identify one trend of Romantic stylistics as the agent's orientation towards a goal or object (a 'pregnance' in Thom's terms), the other as the orientation from object or goal back to the agent, resulting in a state of 'satisfaction' or, in the case of failure, of 'dissatisfaction' (for example, by loss of the beloved object). The resultant of these colliding trends may then be identified as the egomaniac's pursuit of love attributed by several authors to Don Juan,[27] which culminates in the adoration of womanhood as a deity of sorts:

(15)   *Дон Гуан*
                              Если б
            Я прежде вас узнал, с каким восторгом
            Мой сан, мои богатсгва, всё бы отдал,
            Все за единый благосклонный взгляд;
            Я был бы рад священной вашей воли …

> *Don Juan*: If I / Had known you first, with utter rapture / I'd have
> bestowed on you my rank, my wealth, / All, everything, for but one
> gentle glance! / Your slave, I would have held your wishes sacred …

It seems worth noting that the antagonistic trends discerned above both operate
in what the anthropologist Leroi-Gourhan calls an 'itinerant' society,[28] whereas
the resultant adoration rather reflects a 'radial' society with its search for
protection, a sheltered life in the maternal enclosure of the house, much as in
Rousseau's idealized 'Clarens'.[29] In other words: Rousseau's Romanticism is the
outcome of the two antagonistic trends of Romantic ideology.

4   ON THE STRUCTURE OF DON JUAN'S CHARACTER

The picture of the semiosphere which generates Pushkin's *The Stone Guest*
would be patently incomplete without an account of the character of its main
hero, Don Juan. This issue has been assessed by many scholars from many
different angles; in what follows I must confine myself to a few remarks on the
text-linguistic aspects of this character.

    In my previous work I have attempted an approach to character analysis
in terms of thematic constructions of a particular type, consisting of a basic
skeleton of 'actions' (headed by the Agentive EC) and point-like 'situations'
(represented by Nominative ECs).[30] So, for instance, a duel will be represented
by a triad of phases such as 'offence-fight-satisfaction', each phase being in turn
enacted by an 'action' involving the hero, his adversary and his weapon as points
or entities in a 'situation'.[3]

    In order to obtain the salient features of Don-Juanism it seems
appropriate to distinguish within a character of this type a superficial layer of
'macho' behaviour, such as is shared by many members of a military aristocratic
élite (including, for example, Pechorin), and oppose this to the deepest layers of
the character at issue, such as were described by Jakobson as the 'dead
impotence' issuing from the statue.[32] This component may be dissected into a
number of subcomponents, to wit: (i) killing the Comendador, (ii) killing his
brother Don Carlos; (iii) being killed by the Statue; these are held together by a

fourth subcomponent, the pursuit of 'fatal causality' (by challenging danger and death).

A second component of Don-Juanism in our text may be termed the 'double motion', which externally leads from exile back into the capital, and internally away from the facile conquest of Laura towards the more and more seriously longed-for Doña Anna.[33] The actual driving force of Don-Juanism as presented in our text may be identified as the cluster of offended honour, rivalry and vengeance. This component is exemplified by such expressions as 'You think he [the Comendador] will be jealous?'; 'Don Diego, are you jealous then?'; 'I ought not to be jealous', which turn up throughout the course of events. Don Juan's alertness in defence of his honour is also implied by Don Carlos' challenge: 'I'm waiting. Well? Your sword is at your side'. The subcomponents are five in number: (i) the subject's offended state; (ii) the subject's affective relation to the instrument of revenge (sword, poison); (iii) the offender; (iv) the state of satisfaction (sometimes associated with a trophy, as in Hebbel's drama *Judith*, 1841); finally (v) the role of the vengeful hero. The deepest layer of Don-Juanism under the present analysis accommodates what may be termed its destructive power; this in turn deploys itself in the subcomponents of 'potent action' and the exertion of 'power' over Laura and Anna, and culminates in the challenge of the Comendador and the fatal response by the statue. In conclusion, I might add in this context that the character type of Don Juan, like that of Pechorin, especially as regards their die-hard cynicism and egomania, crucially set off Romanticism from the adjacent style-periods of Rationalism and Sentimentalism.

REFERENCES

Bayley, John, *Pushkin. A Comparative Commentary*, Cambridge University Press, Cambridge, 1971.

Beckermann, B., *Dynamics of Drama: Theory and Method of Analysis*, Knopf New York, 1970.

Briggs, A.D.P., *Alexander Pushkin: A Critical Survey*, Croom Helm, London and Canberra, 1983.

Brouwer, Sander, *Character in the Short Prose of Ivan Sergeevič Turgenev*, Rodopi, Amsterdam-Atlanta, 1996.

Chatman, Seymour, *Story and Discourse: Narrative Structure in Fiction and Film*, Cornell University Press, Ithaca and London, 1998.

Costello, D.P., ed., *A.S. Griboedov, Gore ot uma*, Clarendon Press, Oxford, 1963.

Elam, Keir, *The Semiotics of Theatre and Drama*, Methuen, London and New York, 1980.

Fillmore, Charles J., 'The Case for Case', in Emmon Bach and Robert T. Harms, eds., *Universals in Linguistic Theory*, Holt, Reinhart and Winston, New York, 1968, pp. 1-88.

Gerlinghoff, P., *Frauengestalten und Liebesproblematik bei M.J. Lermontov*, Hain, Meisenheim a. Glan, 1967.

Jakobson, Roman O., 'The Statue in Pushkin's Poetic Mythology' (1937), in id., *Selected Writings*, V, Mouton, The Hague, 1979, pp. 237-80.

Jakobson, Roman O., 'Linguistics and Poetics', in id., *Selected Writings*, III, Mouton, The Hague, 1981, pp.18-51.

Jung, Carl G., *Archetypen (Archetypes)*. Translated from the German *Von den Wurzeln des Bewusstseins* by Elisabeth Camerling, Servire, Wassenaar, 1977.

Levey, Michael, *Rococo to Revolution: Major Trends in Eighteenth-Century Painting*, Thames and Hudson, London, 1979.

Lotman, Yuri M., *Universe of the Mind: A Semiotic Theory of Culture*, translated by Ann Shukman, I.B. Tauris & Co., London-New York, 1990.

Margolin, Uri, 'Structuralist Approaches to Character in Narrative: The State of the Art', *Semiotica* LXXV, 1/2, 1989, pp. 1-24.

Mersereau Jr., John, 'The Nineteenth Century: Romanticism 1820-40', in Charles A. Moser, ed., *The Cambridge History of Russian Literature*, second revised edition, Cambridge University Press, Cambridge, 1992, pp. 136-88.

Moskey, S.T., *Semantic Structures and Relations in Dutch: An Introduction to Case Grammar*, Georgetown University Press, Washington, 1979.

Oerlemans, Jacques W., *Rousseau en de privatisering van het bewustzijn: Carrierisme en cultuur in de achttiende eeuw*, Wolters-Noordhoff, Groningen, 1988.

Pushkin, A.S., *Polnoe sobranie sochinenii v desiati tomakh*, izd. 4-oe, Nauka, Leningrad 1977, V, pp. 316-50.

Souriau, Étienne, *Les deux cent mille situations dramatiques*, Flammarion, Paris, 1950.

Staiger, Emil, *Grundbegriffe der Poetik*, Atlantis, Zürich, (1946) 1951.

Thom, René, *Esquisse d'une Sémiophysique: Physique aristotélicienne et Théorie des Catastrophes*, Inter Éditions, Paris, 1988.

Tokarev S.S., ed., *Mify narodov mira, v dvukh tomakh*, T.I (A-K), T.II (K-Ia), Entsiklopediia, Moscow, 1982.

van Holk, A.G.F., 'Character in Text Linguistics. On the Deep Structure of Pechorin', in G.B. Bercoff et al., eds., *Filologia e letteratura nei paesi slavi. Studi in onore di Sante Graciotti*, Carucci editore, Roma, 1990, pp. 891-903.

van Holk, A.G.F., 'O glubinnoi strukture Pechorina', *Russian Literature* XXXI, 4, 1992, pp. 545-54.

van Holk, A.G.F., *Theme and Space. Text-Linguistic Studies in Russian and Polish Drama. With an Outline of Text Linguistics*, Rodopi, Amsterdam-Atlanta, 1996.

Yarmolinsky, Avrahm, ed., *The Poems, Prose and Plays of Alexander Pushkin*, The Modern Library, New York [1936] 1964.

Zaslavskii, O.B., 'Personazhi i siuzhet "Kamennogo gostia"', *Russian Literature*, XXXIV, 3, 1993, pp. 403-10.

NOTES

1. Translations from A.F.B. Clark, in Yarmolinsky, 1964, pp. 438-63.

2. As one of the few who do not share the overall admiration I mention Briggs, *Alexander Pushkin*, 1983, pp. 177 ff., who also for good reasons rejects Bayley's supposition that Don Juan disappears together with Anna into the hereafter, instead of with the Comendador; see Bayley, *Pushkin*, 1971, p. 199.

3. A summary test revealed over 18,000 publications concerning Don Juan on the internet!

4. Cf. Jung, *Archetypes*, 1977, p. 90: ' ... with Don-Juanism the mother is being subconsciously sought for "in every woman". The effects of the mother-complex become manifest in the ideology of the Kybele-Attis-type: self-castration, madness, and early death'. As a matter of fact Jung's archetypal traits apply fairly well to Pushkin's Don Juan, witness his alleged madness - 'you are out of your mind', says Anna of him - and his shaking hands with the Comendador's statue, which comes close to an act of self-castration.

5. Chatman, 1978, pp. 19 ff.

6. The problem of character in literary analysis so far has not received due attention; see, however, Margolin's paper on structuralist approaches to character (1989) and the clear and concise survey of the problem in Brouwer (1996).

7. One well-known example is Souriau's attempt to describe 'dramatic situations' in terms of a limited array of elementary units; cf. Souriau, *Les deux cent mille situations dramatiques*, discussion by Elam, *The Semiotics of Theatre and Drama*, pp. 127-31. Another, more fundamental treatment of this issue is found in Thom, *Sémiophysique*, pp. 17-20, who distinguishes 'salliances' (salient points of a situation) and 'prégnances' (connecting vectors between those points).

8. Chatman, op. cit., p. 26.

9. See Mersereau, 1973, p. 175.

10. Van Holk, 1996, pp. 15-21.

11. In the present analysis I stick to the traditional reading of the story of our text, despite the tempting suggestions in Zaslavskii, 'Personazhi i siuzhet v "Kamennom goste"', *Russian Literature,* 1993, who argues that Don Alvaro is to be identified as Ineza's deceased husband; this leads not only to a striking symmetry of interpersonal relations, but also would seem to offer a novel ground for explaining Don Juan's provocation of the Statue (p. 405). As Zaslavskii himself adds (p. 408), his reading does not interfere with the familiar ones, and, in any case, the text-linguistic approach proposed here leaves room for both readings.

12. Cf. Jakobson on the role of the Capital in Pushkin's world-view: 1979, p. 245.

13. Fillmore, 1968, pp. 25 ff.

14. It may be recalled in passing that the 'real/unreal' opposition is the thematic origin of *negation* in language, and on the scale of entire texts accounts for such prototypical traits of romantic ideology as the 'Dichtung und Wahrheit' antinomy in Goethe and the view of social reality as a masquerade in Lermontov's play of this name.

15. Jakobson, op. cit., pp. 242 and 247.

16. See Moskey, 1979, pp. 48-62.

17. Bocheński, 1954, p. 39.

18. Jakobson, op. cit., p. 241.

19. For example, Beckermann, 1970, p. 14.

20. Lotman, 1990, pp. 223 ff.

21. Staiger (1951, p. 208) for this very reason associates this subsphere with epic poetry in the style of Homer's *Iliad*.
22. Costello, ed., 1963, p. xxiii.
23. Jakobson, 1981, p. 25.
24. See van Holk, 1996, pp. 153-4.
25. On this see especially Levey, 1979, p. 9.
26. Thom, 1988, pp. 39-40.
27. For example, Mersereau, op. cit., p. 175.
28. See Tokarev, I, 1982, pp. 341-2.
29. See Oerlemans, 1988.
30. See van Holk, 1990, p. 233.
31. Cf. Thom's 'saillances': Thom, op. cit., pp. 17-20.
32. Jakobson, 1979, p. 241.
33. Don Juan shows striking resemblance here with Pechorin's situation of 'a man between two women': Gerlinghoff 1967, p. 115.

The *Alter Ego* and the Stone Guest: Doubling and Redoubling Hermann in *The Queen of Spades*

by

ROBIN AIZLEWOOD

Interpretations of *The Queen of Spades* through card playing, the card game and the particular cards have been many and varied, from Iurii Lotman's account of the semiotics of card playing in Russian culture of the time to the numerology of Lauren Leighton.[1] Indeed Pushkin, characteristically, gets in first with his epigraph to the story itself, said to be from the 'latest' fortune telling book: 'The queen of spades signifies secret malevolence'.[2] This epigraph is no less characteristic for its irony and ambiguity and, one might say, does not wish one well in pursuit of a key to the story's meaning. In this spirit Caryl Emerson has suggested that all interpretations of *The Queen of Spades* aimed at a solution of the mystery, at a system, are undermined by the story itself, but she too draws a parallel to cards. For Emerson, the story's codes are not designed to build any single system, and it is the passion of the reader to explain the whole that is the target of Pushkin's parody: here the parallel with the cards is that the ultimate essence of gambling is that there is no system.[3]

Among such interpretations some, though much less, attention has also been paid to the actual mechanics, the purely compositional aspect of the game at the centre of the story, namely faro. There can be considerably more to this than an explanatory technical aid to reading, as some recent studies have demonstrated. For example, Sergei Davydov, with his insight into the hidden ace (туз with its final consonant devoiced) in Hermann's invocation 'вот что утроиТ, УСемерит мой капитал' ('that's what will triple my capital, multiply it seven-fold' [p. 235]), reveals how this reproduces the hidden, face-down card between the two that are dealt.[4] More generally, the binary aspect of the game, the dealing of two cards, is realized, as Wolf Schmid has most effectively shown, in the story's dualities, ambivalences, competing discourses and interpretations (realistic/fantastic etc.);[5] it is a dominant of both the game and the story.

The compositional aspect of the game which I would like to highlight is doubling. In fact, doubling is present in the game in two ways, one primary, the other secondary. First, what is going on in faro is a version of the game of snap, the juxtaposition and, if successful, matching of cards, a play for doubles: this is the primary aspect of doubling. Translated into the composition of the story, the most direct parallel lies in characters as doubles. The secondary aspect lies in the betting, in which a key, though optional, feature is again doubling. The sequence of progressive doubling of a stake can generate winnings equivalent to the numbers one, three and seven, though this is not, as Davydov points out, the same order as the cards.[6] But I would like to emphasize simply the function in operation here, that is, doubling. A certain flexibility is quite in order in translating this second aspect of doubling to the story's composition, rather than seeking a precise parallel to a mathematical series; but what this aspect of doubling also brings into play is the motif of generating an open-ended sequence.

Taken together, then, these two aspects of the card game carry a clear orientation towards doubling. When translated into the composition of the story, such doubling may operate in a number of ways. It could certainly be incorporated into the broad domain of duality and the binary in the story. It can also be related to patterns of juxtaposition, repetition, parallelism, overlapping (and discontinuity) that can be found at various levels.[7] This includes, for example, the relation of the two temporal planes of the story;[8] or there is the possible repetition of Lizaveta's story in that of her ward which is prompted by the text's conclusion;[9] and beyond that there is the relation of textual and extratextual realities (starting from matching the Countess with a real life prototype in Princess Golitsyna).[10]

Above all, however, in keeping with the primary compositional aspect of the game, that is, matching cards, doubling relates to the configuration of characters in the story. In the main body of this study I will focus on the two key manifestations of doubling in relation to Hermann. The identification of such doubles adds a further dimension to the well-established duality of Hermann's character and develops the existing, more or less scattered remarks on doubling in the story. But it is important to emphasize that matching, overlapping and alternatives can be seen as a pervasive and open-ended feature of the configuration of characters in the story, just as doubling in the betting can generate an open-ended sequence. This feature can be applied, for example, to the Countess and Lizaveta, perhaps also to Hermann and Lizaveta, Hermann and the Countess and so on; certainly there is a whole web of connections amongst the male characters.[11] On the other hand, it is no less important to recognize that the opposite may apply too: not matching, but its absence, and also difference; after all, the card game cautions that not all pairs match, and the final formula in the story presents both matching and difference as Hermann endlessly repeats 'Three, seven, ace! Three, seven, queen!...' (p. 252). Equally, the exposition of a configuration of doubling does not contravene Emerson's (and indeed Pushkin's) admonition concerning a key to the story's meaning, for doubling is a constructive principle, a key to *how* the story works; moreover, as we shall see, doubling works in different ways. As such, it does not especially privilege one line of overarching interpretation over others, but may variously engage with some or all of such interpretations: psychological or psychoanalytical, fantastic or supernatural, socio-cultural, ludic and so on. Finally, all this can then be related to Pushkin's ongoing engagement and disengagement with genre expectations and romantic - in the case of doubles, particularly Hoffmannesque -

poetics.[12] With his characteristic genius for inhabiting forms, Pushkin's use of doubling in *The Queen of Spades* transcends the models he draws on.

Before proceeding to Pushkin's doubling and redoubling of Hermann, it is worth noting that the matching of character or appearance is embedded in the story in a different way too, at the level of the characters' perception. Just as with the cards, there are three such instances, each featuring the same word 'сходство' (resemblance/likeness/similarity), and all three instances involve Hermann. The first is at the ball, where the stereotypical romantic portrait of Hermann idly sketched by Tomskii for social chit-chat 'resembled' Lizaveta's own idea of Hermann formed under the influence of her reading: a 'hackneyed figure', as the narrator comments (p. 244). The dismissive thrust of the comment applies equally to the naïveté of perception that forms the basis for the matching. The second such matching again involves Lizaveta and Hermann, shortly afterwards, when Hermann is in her room. Here it is a physical pose, not a mental portrait. The frowning Hermann seated by the window recalls a portrait of Napoleon: 'This likeness struck even Lizaveta Ivanovna' (245). With these words the narrator seems to give objective authority to the likeness, albeit specifically in this pose, but the force of 'even' is ambiguous: in the previous instance Lizaveta has been only too quick to match images, while now, repentant and with tears in her eyes, she is slow to do so and/or reluctant to recognize an image that may or may not be objective but is certainly also of her own making. Again, as with the first instance, the interest lies as much in the creation and perception of the image as in what it may tell us about Hermann. The third instance, in compositional emphasis of the significance of doubling, coincides with the third play of the cards at the story's climax. Now, as in the card game, the tables are turned: Hermann is no longer the object in the process of matching images but the perceiver (or, perhaps, agent). Ironically his mistake or failure in the game is followed by his successful recognition of the Countess in the card, the moment which marks his descent into madness: 'An unusual likeness struck him …' (p. 251).

The motif of doubling is set up in the opening chapter. Whereas the epigraph to the story as a whole invokes the symbolic significance of the cards, the verse epigraph to the first chapter can be seen, among other things, to foreground doubling as a compositional function.[13] The first numbers encountered in the story provide no grist to the numerological mill; instead they introduce the motif of doubling, and purely as a function: 'They used to double their stakes - God forgive them! - / From fifty / To a hundred' (p. 227). Moreover the word 'гнули', which refers to the action of bending the corner of the card used to signify doubling, is highlighted here by hypermetrical stress at the start of the anapaestic dimeter 'Гнули - Бог их прости!'[14] The motif of doubling is present again in the repetition of the opening 'And on gloomy days' in 'So on gloomy days' in the epigraph's conclusion, and it is echoed, with subtle variation and difference, in the parallelism, rhyming and sound play

throughout: 'А в ненастные дни / Собирались они / Часто; / Гнули - Бог
их прости! - / От пятидесяти / На сто, / И выигрывали / И отписывали
/ Мелом./ Так, в ненастные дни, / Занимались они / Делом' (p. 227). Two
examples will have to suffice. First, there is the sound repetition in the trio
неНАС(Т)ны -НА СТо - неНАС(Т)ные which links the negative 'gloomy'
with the doubled number 'hundred'. Second, there is the subtle play on the
presence or echo of rhyme and the stressed vowel и in the anapaestic dimeters:
thus, while 'дни'- 'они' rhymes, the next pair 'прости'- 'пятидесяти' only
echoes rhyme since the stressed 'и' in 'пятидесяти' is in the middle not at the
end, and so on.

The motif of doubling is then reinforced in the rest of the chapter. Most
significantly, in the only explicit mention of the word itself in the story, the
audience 'doubles' its attention to Tomskii's story about his grandmother and
Saint-Germain precisely at the crucial moment when a secret is first mentioned
and Tomskii, the skilful story-teller, pauses to light his pipe: 'At this point he
revealed a secret to her, a secret for which any one of us would give dearly ...
The young gamblers doubled their attention' (p. 229). The juxtaposition of
'secret' and 'doubling' not only serves to associate these two motifs, but also,
metapoetically, it points to juxtaposition and association and by extension
metonymy as key semantic functions in the story (and, as noted earlier,
juxtaposition is the way faro works too). Tomskii's story itself takes double
form: first the Saint-Germain story, then the Chaplitskii one. Finally, as has of
course been noted, there is an obvious doubling in the names Saint-Germain and
Hermann;[15] they are also both described as 'remarkable' by Tomskii (pp. 228,
243), an epithet which draws attention to them but offers no substantial link
between the two. Chaplitskii, through the suggestion that the secret can be
repeated for the benefit of a young man, seems rather an obvious double for
Hermann as well. Pushkin, as we know, is not afraid of being obvious, but he
rarely settles for it.

These are not the doubles which I wish to explore. Instead, especially
in the case of Saint-Germain, the role or status of a double in the text within the
text can serve a different function. Firstly, as a number of studies seek to show,
Saint-Germain may stand not as a double but as something 'other' in relation to
Hermann. Thus, in two more recent psychoanalytic interpretations, Gary
Rosenshield relates Saint-Germain to a Lacanian Other as the object of
Hermann's desire, while for Alfred Thomas, also in Lacanian terms, he
metonymically represents the absent authority of the Name-of-the-Father. In a
different vein, Wolf Schmid proposes a line of master story-tellers from Saint-
Germain and Casanova to Tomskii and Pushkin in contradistinction to those,
foremost among them Hermann, who cannot orientate in discourse (one might
see a realization here of the literal meaning 'mute' in the root of the Russian
word for 'German' - 'НЕМец').[16] Secondly, Saint-Germain prompts the
problematic intersection - overlapping and discontinuity - of textual and

extratextual realities, made more problematic still by the fact that his presence is in the text within the text, not to mention the grey area of his biography.[17] Thirdly, and for the purposes of this study most importantly, the very obviousness, in *name*, of his doubling of Hermann points to Saint-Germain not as a double but as an emblematic sign of doubling in the story. This function is also embodied in his name itself, which signifies kinship: in French *germain* means 'cousin', while in the original Latin it means 'brother'/'sister' (it also means 'German'). In keeping with this function, he serves not just as emblem but also as compositional node for the configuration of doubling. But there is a further dimension to this doubling of names. The correspondence is not full: Hermann does not have the prefix 'Saint' (according to some versions, a fabrication on the part of the historical Saint-Germain, which is anyway belied by both his occult interests and worldliness). On the one hand, Hermann is thereby metonymically associated with lack or absence, which he seeks to make good through pursuit of the secret.[18] On the other hand, the absence of the specific prefix 'Saint' links to questions of the demonic, of good and evil,[19] both at the level of interpretations of Hermann and at a deeper level, which includes the question of whether there is such a metaphysical dimension to the story at all.

Of the two doubles I want to look at, one works intratextually, the other works both intra- and intertextually. I am going to start with the first of these, although in the story he comes last. This is Chekalinskii. Links between Chekalinskii and the Saint-Germain story can be - and have been - identified or constructed. Briefly, Chekalinskii is 60 and so is linked to the time of the original anecdote; literally or symbolically, he could be the son of Saint-Germain and the Countess, as has also been suggested of Chaplitskii, who can be linked to Chekalinskii through paranomastic association of their names. [20] Chekalinskii is directly linked to Saint-Germain through (almost) identical description: Saint-Germain has a 'very respectable appearance', Chekalinskii a 'most respectable appearance' (pp. 228, 250). By association, Hermann too can be placed in this series. But the doubling of Hermann and Chekalinskii does not work only by association, it can also be established quite directly, characterologically.

First, however, it is worth noting that the motif of doubling is repeated, subtly and paradoxically, at the start of the final chapter, in which Chekalinskii appears. The epigraph, like the epigraph to the first chapter, features verbal repetition, here of '*attendez*' given in Russian transcription (p. 249). But it is the unusual aphoristic first sentence, in itself a kind of displaced or repeat epigraph, that is of particular interest. It alludes to doubling negatively, by asserting that 'Two fixed ideas cannot exist together in the mind [literally: moral nature], just as two bodies cannot occupy one and the same place in the physical world' (p. 249). In terms of what happens, this turns out to be both the case and not the case. This is then followed by an account of Hermann's fixation with the cards which leads him to make associations (pairings) between them and people or objects in the outside world. Another striking feature of this chapter is that, after the opening paragraph, which shows how the inner and outer worlds are no longer distinguished by Hermann so that the outer is a projection of the inner, we learn nothing about what is going on inside him. Instead, the focus is on Chekalinskii.

In two introductory paragraphs we get a surprisingly detailed description of Chekalinskii and his appearance, and then in the sparse, factual account of the card game it is principally Chekalinskii's (and the spectators') reactions that are recorded. At Hermann's second win 'Chekalinskii was visibly shaken', and before the third game he is pale, still smiling, but his hands shake as he deals (p. 251). All we know of Hermann's reactions until after he loses is that he takes his second winnings 'coolly' (p. 251), although in reality he is by now deep in the antithetical realm of his 'fiery imagination' (p. 235). The description of Chekalinskii's appearance in the second of the two introductory paragraphs establishes the association with Saint-Germain already mentioned. But it is the account of Chekalinskii's life and character in the first of these paragraphs that subtly yet precisely establishes him as Hermann's *alter ego*. Quite specifically, he is the embodiment of the three qualities of 'calculation, moderation and hard work' which Hermann earlier calls his 'three reliable cards' that will increase his capital 'triple, seven-fold' (p. 235). As well as representing his own perception of himself, these qualities can be inferred from the narrator's brief background description and from Hermann's behaviour, and so have a certain objective status in defining his character too. But either way - or both ways - they are embodied in Chekalinskii. Chekalinskii has become famous and wealthy (in Russian an 'ace') by virtue of calculation, moderation and hard work: he has only ever lost what he can afford, accepting IOUs but paying losses in cash; he has built up trust through his 'long experience'; and in his calculating way he works hard on his public, what with his 'famous chef' and his charming or ingratiating manner (p. 249). In terms of such outward manifestations of manner, however, as exemplified in his 'constant smile' (p. 250), he is the opposite of Hermann. This character sketch and potted biography is then confirmed by the concrete instance: the same qualities are apparent in the way he conducts the long card game, in which he works hard, takes care over calculating sums, and has a measured, polite manner in handling gamblers, especially when they 'inadvertently' bend over a corner to double the stake (p. 250). In this way, therefore, Hermann is playing against himself, whether objectively or subjectively constructed. By extension, the description of Chekalinskii's appearance not only links him to Saint-Germain but also, antithetically, draws attention to the absence of any apparent description of the inner world; there is an ironic echo of the Countess here, in whose eyes 'was depicted a complete absence of thought' (p. 240). This absence could be interpreted as negatively indicative of Hermann losing his mind. But, beyond this, the point is that the dissolution of the boundary between the inner and outer worlds described in the opening paragraph continues in the rest of the chapter.

In this connection, it is interesting that, when Narumov 'introduces' Hermann to Chekalinskii, this is the same verb представлять(ся)/представить(ся) as has just been used in its reflexive form to describe the appearance of the seven and ace in Hermann's dreams as 'gothic gates' and a 'huge spider' (pp. 249-50).[21] Chekalinskii is an aspect of Hermann's inner world: he is Hermann's rational *alter ego* which has given way to the other side of his personality, and the confrontation between them is taking place simultaneously in the two worlds, just as the aphoristic opening sentence sets up. The physical world mirrors the mental, and although there are two bodies and two personae, they are also one but can no longer co-exist. Hermann, in playing against himself, must go mad, but we also see the final stages of the process from the outside looking in.[22]

Let us now turn, or in the story's order, return to my other double. This is the doubling of Hermann with another of the possible 'aces' in the story, namely the Countess' husband. It works to an altogether different effect from the doubling of Hermann and Chekalinskii, which, as we have seen, endorses and substantiates a psychological reading. This doubling adds to such a reading too, but primarily it engages with the symbolic and ludic, and also intertextual and contextual, dimensions of the text. The Countess' husband appears twice in the story. First of all he appears in Tomskii's anecdote, where he is presented as an alternative to Saint-Germain: explicitly, in terms of solving the problem of the Countess' debt, and explicitly/implicitly in terms of the denying or giving of sexual favour. The Countess, having started to undress in front of her husband as she tells him of her loss (Tomskii titillates), then excludes him from her bed when he refuses to bail her out (p. 228). More generally, in terms of character, one can suppose that he is the very antithesis of all that Saint-Germain is or is rumoured to be, and the same could be said of Hermann. We know very little about the husband, but the details we do have link him to Hermann. Firstly, for all that he is an aristocrat, according to Tomskii he was treated by the Countess as a 'kind of butler' (p. 228), so that he is linked to Hermann through a variation on the motif of inferior social status. But much more significantly he is presented in a key situational rhyme with Hermann: they both witness the Countess undressing. The situations are the same but also inverted. The Countess undresses in front of her husband in order to get his agreement, whereas Hermann observes her undressing in order to get her agreement; on the other hand, in both cases the male figure is sexually subordinate or inadequate. The fact that this is a situational rhyme, and that Tomskii's account has no certain status in reality, points to the different significance of this double.

The other appearance of the Countess' husband is as a picture alongside one of the Countess which Hermann observes as he waits.[23] In other words, the husband has a presence throughout the ensuing scene between Hermann and his wife, a presence which can be related to the theme of the dead or inanimate coming to life. It is not only cards that can come to life, but also pictures;[24] and of course statues. Here, however, with the picture a presence, the opposite metamorphosis occurs. When Lizaveta and the Countess return, Hermann feels 'something akin to a pang of consience', but this falls silent and then: 'He turned to stone' (p. 240). The single sentence, in context, is enough to establish the link to *The Stone Guest*. It invokes the whole text and its context, which in itself is characteristic of Pushkin's open use of intertextual connections; and through this *The Queen of Spades* can be related to the theme or myth of the statue, with all its ramifications, in Pushkin.[25] In fact, from this single point of contact, the relation of the two texts is remarkably open and complex. Hermann, who should be and in a sense still is playing the role of Don Juan, *vis-à-vis* both Lizaveta and the Countess, is now also a Stone Guest. In this way the doubling is itself double: intratextually he is doubling as the dead husband, the ace from the painting; correspondingly, intertextually he is both Don Juan and the Comendador, who in Pushkin's version is the husband not the father. In this way too the character as double is reversed: whereas Chekalinskii was the double of Hermann, it is Hermann who is the double here.

At the level of names, one could suggest a linking, through paranomasia, of Don Juan and its variants, which in Russian is Don *G*uan, with Saint-Germain and Hermann (in Russian *G*ermann). Hermann as Don Juan links into the whole area of sexuality and sexual motivation and desire in the story. In his pursuit of Lizaveta he is playing the role of a Don Juan, but in this role he is false, a parody and failure. It is interesting that at the outset of the romance Hermann's appearance to Lizaveta, with his face covered by his collar and eyes flashing from beneath his hat (p. 234), echoes the clichéd disguise adopted by Don Juan on his return to Madrid (face covered with his cloak and hat down to his eyes).[26] Moreover, given that Hermann's real object is the Countess, he, like Don Juan, is in pursuit of a widow; yet in terms of the mapping of the female characters she is - or was - more of a Laura than an Anna. However, while Don Juan is the successful lover and swordsman, Hermann's pistol is unloaded, he is a sham as Lizaveta's suitor and the whole scene between him and the Countess parodies an encounter between lovers. His sexuality would seem to be atrophied, with perhaps just a shade or flicker of repressed sexual interest in the aged Countess undressing or the vulnerable Lizaveta.[27] Or at least that is how it appears until the suggestive passage after he has left Lizaveta, when he stares for a long time at the dead Countess and then descends the 'dark staircase, excited [or: agitated] by strange feelings' and thinking of her former lovers (p. 245). It is here, in the knotty area of love/sex and death, with implications of necrophilia, that the story revisits in an unsettling way a theme explored throughout *The Stone Guest*: from Don Juan's memories of Inessa, with her 'deathly lips' (VII, p. 139), to the sex with Laura in the company of the dead body of the just killed Don Carlos, to the courtship of Doña Anna in the company of her dead husband (whether in his grave or as statue by the door). Even so, the difference between the two texts is striking. The exploration of this theme and taboo in *The Stone Guest* takes on a metaphysical dimension that would appear to be absent from

The Queen of Spades, although the topic of Hermann's dysfunctional sexuality is without doubt more compellingly weird.

The sexual motif continues in the doubling of Hermann as the husband, not just the Countess' husband (as already indicated) but also the Comendador. As Bethea notes, there is a 'deadly erotic play' in *The Stone Guest* on the statue and standing erect, especially in Don Juan's mocking invitation to 'come and stand on watch by the door' (VII, p. 160) while he is entertained by Doña Anna.[28] This location echoes the motif of inferior status that applies to both Hermann and the Countess' husband, while Hermann occupies a similar position to the statue as he voyeuristically observes the Countess undressing from behind the study door, just as he watches the card game in the opening scene. There is also an echo of Hermann as both the Comendador and Don Juan in the funeral oration, replete as it is with ironies. The Countess is depicted there as visited by the 'angel of death' as she waits for the 'midnight bridegroom' (p. 246). Hermann, the false Don Juan, brings retribution and death in his role as the double of the returning husband, the Stone Guest; yet, as we have seen, when he returns to the scene the role of a necrophiliac Don Juan (midnight bridegroom) is entertained.

In *The Stone Guest* the symbolic gesture which imparts the statue's retribution and Don Juan's damnation is the giving of the hand. This gesture is present in *The Queen of Spades* too, three times. In each case it involves Hermann, but its direction varies. After the Countess has collapsed to the floor, as happens at the end of *The Stone Guest*, Hermann takes her hand and only then realizes that she is dead (p. 242); the gesture of retribution is performed, albeit unwittingly and after the event. The Countess is only described as having 'turned to stone' (p. 243) subsequently, when Hermann returns through her room at the end of the next chapter. But this of course means that when she visits him after the funeral, at which he has inadvertently fallen to the ground, she may also be a Stone Guest. At this level, it does not matter whether the visitation is in his dream/imagination or a supernatural event; and if the boundary between death and life has already been symbolically crossed in Hermann, then the grounds for the visitation of the Countess have already been prepared. The Countess' retribution has to wait, but at the start of the card game Chekalinskii, who is already linked to Saint-Germain through his 'respectable appearance', 'screws up his eye' (p. 250) just as the dead Countess had seemed to do when Hermann bent over her coffin at the funeral. The second instance of hand contact occurs when Hermann takes his leave of Lizaveta, only her hand is 'cold and not responsive' (p. 245).[29] With Hermann here in the role of failed Don Juan, her cold, statue-like hand could carry her retribution. Finally, when Hermann arrives at the card game, Chekalinskii shakes his hand 'in a friendly manner' (p. 250), as is his wont: retribution with a smile. At this point, the psychological and symbolic doubling come together: Hermann's fate is first sealed symbolically and then enacted psychologically. At this point too the very first thing we learn about Hermann, which is that he has never 'taken cards into his hands' (p. 227), is about to be reversed.

The reworking of *The Stone Guest* in *The Queen of Spades* thus provokes questions of retribution, fate and hence, by extension, conscience, good and evil. The figure of Don Juan is that of an archetypal transgressor, beyond good and evil. He is described by the monk as 'debauched, without conscience, Godless' (VII, p. 141), words that are not so dissimilar to the epigraph to chapter 4 in *The Queen of Spades*, 'Homme sans moeurs et sans religion' (p. 243).[30] Indeed, the motifs of the demonic, of sin, evil and crimes on the conscience are all invoked, both about Hermann, as, for example, in Tomskii's idle words to Lizaveta at the ball, and by Hermann as he pleads, pulling out all the rhetorical stops, for the Countess to reveal her secret. But, like the epigraph, they have to be seen in context, and this context undermines any objective, let alone metaphysical, status. It is worth recalling too that the very first mention of doubling in the epigraph to chapter 1 is accompanied by the apparently frivolous 'God forgive them!' (p. 227). Furthermore, the narrator's references to Hermann's conscience, significantly placed either side of the meetings with the Countess and Lizaveta, are highly ambiguous and leave the issue open. The sentence preceding Hermann's metamorphosis into stone refers to 'something like a pang of conscience' (p. 240), while at the start of chapter 5 we read: 'Although he did not feel any remorse, he could not, however, completely drown the voice of conscience which told him: you are the old woman's murderer!' (p. 246). There is a significant gap between lack of remorse and the voice of conscience, so that it is not surprising that he is most influenced by a superstitious fear of her malign influence.

In general, then, the doubling of Don Juan and the Comendador in *The Queen of Spades* serves to reinforce the presence in the story of such themes as love/sex and death, retribution and good and evil, but at the same time they are placed in a context that tends to desacralize, to remove them from the transcendental to other, immanent planes. There is a ludic dimension too, since it is an open question as to how these themes are to be interpreted. In the final scene of *The Stone Guest*, Doña Anna may fear Don Juan as a 'demon' but cannot hate him, while he claims - whether genuinely, cynically or blindly - to be on the path to moral regeneration through love (VII, p. 168-9); and the retribution that awaits Don Juan is hell, although Pushkin ends before this. In *The Queen of Spades*, on the other hand, what awaits Hermann on the third evening - surely a travesty of Christ's passion - is not hell (or resurrection) but condemnation to the madhouse, while the Countess is so old that neither retribution nor redemption may have much meaning for her. In the same vein it is intriguing that Pushkin, whose concerns about his Don Juan past, his marriage and future cuckolding are all refracted in *The Stone Guest*,[31] entertains the prospect - or is it pretence? - of distant retribution for an erring wife in *The Queen of Spades* some four years later. If the Countess' words that 'it was a joke' (p. 241), words which Hermann angrily rejects, are taken by some commentators to provide the key to the story and its ludic orientation,[32] *The Stone Guest* traces the opposite trajectory: Don Juan's invitation to the statue turns from an inappropriate 'joke' (VII, p. 160), in Leporello's estimation, into something deadly serious.

Finally, in broader context, Pushkin's use of doubles as part of the configuration of characters in *The Queen of Spades* is enormously protean for subsequent variants of the Petersburg text, from Gogol to Dostoevskii and beyond. No less important, perhaps especially for Dostoevskii, are both the psychological grounding of the doubling (Chekalinskii) and the projection of doubling, however ambiguously, on to a background of metaphysical issues of good and evil; on the other hand, the possibility of a desacralized treatment is also introduced.[33] Beyond this, the variation on the statue myth in the story adds yet further to the ways in which *The Queen of Spades* links into some of Pushkin's most fundamental problematics and the problematics of the Petersburg text.

In this connection, in conclusion, I would like very briefly to draw attention to the presence of this motif in the text beyond Hermann's appearance as a Stone Guest. This is achieved by a recurrent association of Hermann with the motif of standing motionless (he is also, in classic Petersburg fashion, a wanderer).[34] When Lizaveta first catches sight of Hermann he is 'standing motionless' (p. 234), and this is his repeated pose as he woos her. When he is waiting for the Countess to return, he again takes up this pose, and when he appears before her we do not see him move into position: instead, all of a sudden, 'an unknown man stood before her' (p. 241). In the final round of the card game, 'the queen lay on the right, the ace on the left'; but when Hermann realizes that he has lost, he shudders, for 'instead of the ace he had the queen of spades standing there' (p. 251). In his final pose in this scene he then mirrors his queen: 'Hermann stood motionless' (p. 252).

NOTES

I am grateful to participants at the conference (Justin Doherty, Barbara Lönnqvist, Ann Shukman, Willem Weststeijn and others) and to Julian Graffy for their questions and comments.

1. Iu.M. Lotman, 'Tema kart i kartochnoi igry v russkoi literature nachala XIX veka', *Uchenye zapiski Tartuskogo gosudarstvennogo universiteta*, CCCLXV, *Trudy po znakovym sistemam*, 7, 1975, pp. 120-42; Lauren G. Leighton, 'Numbers and Numerology in "The Queen of Spades"', *Canadian Slavonic Papers*, XIX, 4, 1977, pp. 417-43; revised as 'Numbers and Numerology: "The Queen of Spades"' in his *The Esoteric Tradition in Russian Romantic Literature: Decembrism and Freemasonry*, Pennsylvania State University Press, University Park, Pennsylvania, 1994, pp. 131-52.

2. A.S. Pushkin, *Polnoe sobranie sochinenii*, ed. V.D. Bonch-Bruevich et al., Akademiia nauk, Moscow-Leningrad, 1937-59, VIII, part 1, 1948, p. 225; further references to the story are given in the text, citing page numbers only; translations are my own.

3. Caryl Emerson, '"The Queen of Spades" and the Open End' in David Bethea, ed., *Puškin Today*, Indiana University Press, Bloomington and Indianapolis, 1992, pp. 31-7 (pp. 35-6); the ludic character of the story is also highlighted, for example, in: Gareth Williams, 'Convention and Play in *Pikovaja dama*', *Russian Literature*, XXVI, 1989, pp. 523-38; and Justin Doherty, 'Fictional Paradigms in Pushkin's "Pikovaya dama"', *Essays in Poetics*, XVII, 1, 1992, pp. 49-66.

4. Sergei Davydov, 'The Ace in "The Queen of Spades"', *Slavic Review*, LVIII, 2, 1999, pp. 309-28 (p. 314); in Russian: 'Tuz v "Pikovoi dame"', *Novoe literaturnoe obozrenie*, XXXVII, 1999, pp. 110-28.

5. Vol'f Shmid (Wolf Schmid), '"Pikovaia dama" A.S. Pushkina (problemy poetiki)', *Russkaia literatura*, 3, 1997, pp. 6-28.

6. Davydov, op. cit., p. 311.

7. In his detailed stylistic analysis of *The Queen of Spades* Vinogradov shows how pervasive are the features of duality, alternatives, parallelism etc. (V.V. Vinogradov, 'Stil' "Pikovoi damy"' and '<O "Pikovoi dame"> iz knigi "Stil' Pushkina"' in his *O iazyke khudozhestvennoi prozy. Izbrannye trudy*, Nauka, Moscow, 1980, pp. 176-239; 256-83); on juxtaposition as a feature of the story's organization, see Heidi E. Faletti, 'Remarks on Style as Manifestation of Narrative Technique in "The Queen of Spades"', *Canadian-American Slavic Studies*, XI, 1, 1977, pp. 114-33.

8. See, for example, Vinogradov, '<O "Pikovoi dame">','Kritika i publitsistika', pp. 256-62; Williams, op. cit., pp. 528-30.

9. See Joseph T. Shaw, 'The Conclusion of Pushkin's *Queen of Spades*' in Zbigniew Folejewski et al., eds, *Studies in Russian and Polish Literature: In Honor of Wacław Lednicki*, The Hague, 1962, pp. 114-26; for a rereading of this conclusion as open in respect of Lizaveta, rather than finalizing closure, see Svetlana Grenier, '"Everyone Knew Her ..." or Did They? Rereading Pushkin's Lizaveta Ivanovna ("The Queen of Spades")', *Canadian Slavonic Papers*, XXXVIII, 1-2, 1996, pp. 93-107.

10. For an interesting gloss on Hermann's confusion of ace and queen and the gender ambiguity of the prototype Princess Golitsyna, see Davydov, op. cit., p. 324. In his study of *The Queen of Spades* in the context of the critical literature, Neil Cornwell charts an enduring tendency to adduce the extratextual in interpretations of the story (Neil Cornwell, *Pushkin's 'The Queen of Spades'*, Bristol Classical Press/Duckworth, London, 1993, passim).

11. See Paul Debreczeny, *The Other Pushkin: A Study of Alexander Pushkin's Prose Fiction*, Stanford University Press, Stanford, 1983, p. 234.

12. For a study of the story as a parody of Hoffmann (without, however, an identification of the doubling), see Roberta Reeder, '"The Queen of Spades": A Parody of the Hoffmann Tale' in George J. Gutsche and Lauren G. Leighton, eds, *New Perspectives on Nineteenth-Century Russian Prose*, Slavica, Columbus, Ohio, 1982, pp. 73-98.

13. On the epigraphs, with a reading of them as a 'single text' relating to Alexander I, see Gareth Williams, 'Otgoloski otnosheniia Pushkina k Aleksandru I v epigrafakh k "Pikovoi dame"', *Studia Slavica Academiae Scientiarum Hungaricae*, XXXVII, 1991-2, pp. 287-95; concerning the orientation towards society discourse prompted by the epigraphs, see Schmid, op. cit., pp. 14-15.

14. The verb 'гнуть', for 'bending'/'doubling' does not feature in the story other than in this special meaning, although the action of bowing or bending does: Hermann, for example, bows to the ground and then bends over the Countess's coffin, while Chekalinskii bows to Hermann before each of the first two games but, interestingly, this detail is omitted before the third and final game in which Hermann's sequence of stake-doubling wins comes to an end.

15. See, for example, Doherty, op. cit., p. 59; Shaw, op. cit., p. 125n.; Andrej Kodjak, '"The Queen of Spades" in the Context of the Faust Legend' in Andrej Kodjak and Kiril Taranovsky, eds, *Alexander Puškin: A Symposium on the 175th Anniversary of His Birth*, New York University Press, New York, 1976, pp. 87-118 (103-4); B.M. Gasparov, *Poeticheskii iazyk Pushkina kak fakt istorii russkogo literaturnogo iazyka*, Wiener Slawistischer Almanach, Sonderband XXVII, Gesellschaft zur Förderung slawistischer Studien, Vienna, 1992, p. 305.

16. Gary Rosenshield, 'Freud, Lacan, and Romantic Psychoanalysis: Three Psychoanalytic Approaches to Madness in Pushkin's *The Queen of Spades*', *Slavic and East European Journal*, XL, 1, 1996, pp. 1-26 (pp. 13-19); see also his 'Choosing the Right Card: Madness, Gambling and Imagination in Pushkin's "The Queen of Spades"', *PMLA*, CIX, 1994, pp. 995-1008; Alfred Thomas, 'A Russian Oedipus: Lacan and Puškin's "The Queen of Spades"' in A.A. Hansen-Löve, ed., *Psychopoetik*, Wiener Slawistischer Almanach, Sonderband XXXI, Gesellschaft zur Förderung slawistischer Studien, Vienna, 1992, pp. 47-59; Schmid, op. cit., pp. 21-8; and his 'Sen-Zhermen, Kazanova, Tomskii, Pushkin: Magi rasskazyvaniia', *Die Welt der Slaven*, XLIII, 1998, pp. 153-60.

17. For a brief summary of sources and information on Saint-Germain, with reference also to *The Queen of Spades*, see Cornwell, op. cit., pp. 87-90; see also Schmid, 'Sen-Zhermen, Kazanova, Tomskii, Pushkin'.

18. However, Hermann does have a double 'n' at the end of his name ... (for an interpretation of this form of the name, see V. Esipov, 'Istoricheskii podtekst v povesti Pushkina "Pikovaia dama"', *Voprosy literatury*, 4, 1989, pp. 193-205 [p. 203]).

19. See Kodjak, op. cit., pp. 103-4; Gasparov, op. cit., p. 305.

20. For a summary of such links/interpretations, see Davydov, op. cit., pp. 325-6; for her interpretation of an 'erotic cabal' of Saint-Germain, the Countess and Chaplitskii, see Diana Lewis Burgin, 'The Mystery of "Pikovaja dama": A New Interpretation' in Joachim T. Baer and Norman W. Ingham, eds, *Mnemozina: Studia litteraria russica in honorem Vsevolod Setchkarev*, Fink, Munich, 1974, pp. 46-56.

21. For an interpretation of the cards and these images, see Nathan Rosen, 'The Magic Cards in "The Queen of Spades"', *Slavic and East European Journal*, XIX, 3, 1975, pp. 255-75; see also Davydov, op. cit., pp. 315-20.

22. There is much, not just in the doubling in this scene but also in terms of doubling more generally, that could feed into psychoanalytical interpretations of the story, from the interrelation of ego, superego and id to repetition compulsion (see note 16 above for details of recent studies by Rosenshield and Thomas; earlier psychoanalytic interpretations include: Murray M. Schwarz and Albert Schwarz, '"The Queen of Spades": A Psychoanalytic Interpretation', *Texas Studies in Literature and Language*, XVII, 1975, pp. 275-88; Adele

Barker, 'Pushkin's "Queen of Spades": A Displaced Mother Figure', *American Imago*, XLI, 2, 1984, pp. 201-9).

23. Davydov has suggested the presence here of the fatal cards, queen and ace, whose juxtaposition contributes to Hermann's confusion and fatal mistake (Davydov, op. cit., p. 323).

24. The presence of this motif is noted by Michael Shapiro, 'Pushkin's Modus Significandi: A Semiotic Exploration' in Nils Åke Nilsson, ed., *Russian Romanticism: Studies in the Poetic Codes*, Almqvist and Wiksell, Stockholm, 1979, pp. 110-34 (124).

25. The most famous study of the statue in Pushkin (although without reference to *The Queen of Spades*) remains Roman Jakobson, *Puškin and His Sculptural Myth*, Mouton, The Hague, 1975; this myth, and Jakobson's treatment of it, have recently been revisited by David M. Bethea, *Realizing Metaphors. Alexander Pushkin and the Life of the Poet*, University of Wisconsin Press, Madison, Wisconsin, 1998, pp. 89-117 (again without reference to *The Queen of Spades*). In his study of card playing, and also of *The Stone Guest*, Lotman focuses on the opposition of inanimate/dead and living (Lotman, op. cit., pp. 136-7; Iu.M. Lotman, 'Iz razmyshlenii nad tvorcheskoi evoliutsiei Pushkina [1830 god]' in his *Pushkin. Biografiia pisatelia; Stat'i i zametki 1960-1990; 'Evgenii Onegin'. Kommentarii*, Iskusstvo-SPB, St Petersburg, 1995, pp. 300-16); he also posits a paradigmatic triangle in Pushkin made up of the rebellion of the elements, a statue and a person (Iu.M. Lotman, 'Zamysel stikhotvoreniia o poslednem dne Pompei' in ibid., pp. 293-9 [p. 298]). Neil Cornwell notes that this triangle could relate to *The Queen of Spades* in terms of Hermann, the Countess as statue and Lizaveta (Cornwell, op. cit., p. 70). Gasparov also briefly includes *The Queen of Spades* in the context of his study of the statue, but not directly in relation to it (Gasparov, op. cit., pp. 304-5).

26. Pushkin, *Polnoe sobranie sochinenii*, VII, p. 137; further references to *The Stone Guest* will be given in the text, citing volume and page numbers only.

27. Concerning Hermann's sexual interest in the Countess and/or Lizaveta, see, for example, Debreczeny, op. cit., pp. 223-8; 232-3; 238; Schmid, '"Pikovaia dama" A.S. Pushkina', pp. 18-20; Gareth Williams, 'The Obsessions and Madness of Germann in *Pikovaja dama*', *Russian Literature*, XIV, 1983, pp. 383-96 (389-91); A.D.P. Briggs, *Alexander Pushkin: A Critical Study*, Bristol Classical Press, Bristol, 1991, pp. 221-2.

28. Bethea, op. cit., p. 10.

29. Schmid links this metamorphosis of Lizaveta to the petrification of both Hermann and the Countess (Schmid, '"Pikovaia dama" A.S. Pushkina', p. 11).

30. On the source of this epigraph in Voltaire, see Williams, 'Otgoloski otnosheniia Pushkina k Aleksandru I', pp. 288-9.

31. For an eloquent treatment of this topic, see Bethea, op. cit., pp. 95-117.

32. See, for example, Emerson, op. cit., p. 36.

33. An extreme point in the reworking of *The Queen of Spades* is Kharms' *The Old Woman* (*Старуха*), in which a possible shift into the sacred comes against the background of the most far-reaching desacralization; Kharms' text also features overlapping and discontinuity of details (see Robin Aizlewood, '"Guilt without Guilt" in Kharms's Story "The Old Woman"', *Scottish Slavonic Review*, XIV, 1990, pp. 199-217).

34. This motif can of course be related to the whole treatment of posture in the story which incorporates sitting, bowing, kneeling, lying etc. too (on bowing, see note 14 above); concerning posture and gesture in Pushkin, see Alexandra Smith, 'Poetika vrazitel'nosti i nekotorye aspekty neverbal'noi kommunikatsii v poezii A.S. Pushkina', *Australian Slavonic and East European Studies*, XIII, 2, 1999, pp. 95-114.

The Bronze Horseman and the Tradition of Ekphrasis

by

TATIANA SMOLIAROVA

Architectural sites - not only descriptions of the Falconet statue, but also those of various buildings, towers, embankments, etc. - constitute an essential part of *The Bronze Horseman*. The main concern of this chapter is the dialogue between the language of these descriptions and their object.

We would like to begin not with the poem itself but at the 'meta-level': with the two most important articles ever written on *The Bronze Horseman*, which cannot be ignored whatever our approach to Pushkin's poetry. Both the articles we have in mind deal with description in *The Bronze Horseman*. One of them, 'The Statue in Pushkin's Poetic Mythology', by Roman Jakobson is very widely quoted;[1] the other, '*The Bronze Horseman* and the Poetic Tradition of the eighteenth century', unfortunately much less known, is by Lev Pumpianskii and deals with the survival of lyric genres of the eighteenth century inside the multi-level stylistic structure of *The Bronze Horseman*.[2] Although the approach to *The Bronze Horseman* is quite different in these two articles, both of them try to inscribe Pushkin's text into a wider poetic context and to consider it alongside other authors and literary traditions. Indeed the work's literary background is enhanced by approaches which view the Russian solemn ode of the previous century as of one of its possible sources, or consider it in relation to other statuary poems in the European poetic tradition. Such a *contextual* direction in literary studies was particularly developed by the Russian Formalists. Our present concern is to attempt a joint commentary on both Pumpianskii's and Jakobson's works.

In his various studies Pumpianskii argues that in early nineteenth-century Russian poetry the 'ode layer' (a certain set of images and motifs, high-flown words, etc.) is confined mostly (if not exclusively) to descriptions of buildings and monuments, generally speaking, to the *descriptive* mode of speech. Thus, the main point to be discussed here is why it is in this particular mode that the ode survives outside the framework of the system of genres in nineteenth-century poetry (while the text of the classical ode itself contains narration as well as description).

To approach a solution to this problem, we will first have to tackle one of the most important and, one may even say, exciting questions of literary theory: that of the biography of genre. We proceed from the following basic assertion: literary genres cannot disappear utterly, they do not vanish into thin air, but they can be transformed into other genres. There exist several possible ways in which such transmutations can take.[3]

We can distinguish between three main patterns: one of them, perhaps the most productive, is parody. *The English Ballad on the French Ode* (1695), the famous parody by Matthew Prior of Nicolas Boileau's *Ode on the Capture of Namur* (1693) (*Ode sur la Prise de Namur*) may serve as a perfect instance of such a metamorphosis. In eighteenth- and nineteenth-century Russia there existed a whole tradition of 'disguised' texts (typical examples of which were ode-into-fable or elegy-into-epigram).[4] Another type of transforming genre, characteristic of the avant-garde and modernist cultures, is the conscious amalgam of the most distant and disparate genres. The third mode, of particular interest for us here, is the natural mixture of close literary forms or genres, which appeared in the same or similar circumstances and were developed together. Depending on the given cultural context, they sometimes have the potential to replace each other or, at least, to exchange important intrinsic features. These genres can either exist simultaneously or, if one of them flourishes while the other is in temporary decline, the latter may hide itself inside the former. It may exist in latent form only to realize its potential some years (or even centuries) later and, probably, serve as a similar shelter for its 'fellow-genre' (or genres). Which genre functioned as such a companion to the ode?

Neither Jakobson nor Pumpianskii ever name it, although indirectly Jakobson evokes it on several occasions. He sees the poem about a statue as 'a sign of a sign', 'a verbal representation of a visual representation'. We have in front of us two precise definitions not of some random text, but of quite a concrete genre - that of *ekphrasis.*

The word 'ekphrasis' goes back to the Greek verb *ekfrazein* which means to 'describe in detail'. First applied to any description, this term is now restricted to the descriptions of works of art exclusively.[5]

Ekphrasis takes the form of a separate genre within the Neo-Sophist school and is associated with three representatives of this philosophical school: first and foremost, with Philostratus the Elder, but also with his disciples Philostratus the Younger and Callistratus.[6] The *Images* (*Eikones*) by Philostratus the Elder are considered to be the canon of the ekphrastic genre. It is a book describing in strict sequence 65 pictures brought together in a Fine Arts Gallery, supposedly situated in Naples in the second century A.D. Scholars still cannot say for sure whether this gallery ever existed, although at present the majority view is that it was imaginary. Callistratus, by contrast, described, in his *Ekphraseis,* statues which undoubtedly existed and were produced, at least some of them, by quite well-known sculptors.

The Neo-Sophist school developed ekphrasis not only as an isolated genre, but also as a rhetorical exercise, which constituted the core of *Progymnasmata* ('School Exercises') together with another important element of it, *basileukos logos* ('the eulogy of a ruler'), a genre directly related to that of the solemn ode.

The first common feature of ekphrasis and of the royal eulogy (be it an ode or a prose panegyric) is their laudatory character. This statement does not require further proofs with regard to the genre of ode; as for ekphrasis, some explanations are necessary. According to the Neo-Sophist theory and practice, ekphrasis never presupposes a neutral description; it is inevitably complimentary. To describe an object *in detail* (that is, to consider it to be worth describing), already means to valorize it. Another important intrinsic quality common to ekphrasis and eulogy lies in the essential mode of functioning of these two literary forms, which may be described as 'a point unrolling into a line'. This strange geometrical metaphor needs to be elucidated: the main aim of any ekphrasis is to inscribe the given moment into a sequence of moments, to reconstruct what precedes and what follows it. In transforming even the most stable and self-sufficient picture into an episode of a story, ekphrasis supplements it with a 'cinematographic' dimension. As for the ode, one of the best interpretations ever given to this genre, that by Paul Valéry, defined it as 'an exclamation expanded into a text'. Eulogy and ekphrasis also share other important generic attributes, but it is the two above-mentioned qualities which have determined their common trajectory in the history of world culture.

The revival of the Ode and ekphrasis took place at more or less the same time and in a common milieu. It is to French culture of the late Renaissance, that both genres owe their rebirth. While the name and heritage of Pindar, who embodied the genre of triumphal ode as such, were retrieved from oblivion by Ronsard and Du Bellay, Philostratus and his 'Images' were revived by Blaise de Vigenère, a contemporary of the Pléiade poets, just a few years younger than its two leaders.

Blaise de Vigenère (1527-1596) occupied a rather strange position at the court of Henry III. He was the Court Mythographer: his main duty consisted in the inscribing of the *historical present* of sixteenth-century France in the *mythological past* of Ancient Greece and Rome, as did Virgil, who traced the ancestry of the emperor Augustus directly to Jupiter.[7] During the period of her regency Catherine de'Medici charged Vigenère with various cultural missions, which he was supposed to accomplish in the course of his numerous journeys to different cities and countries. During his two trips to Italy, Vigenère had a very complicated and wide-ranging problem to solve: how to implant Italian visual culture in France, where, despite all the efforts of François I and his milieu, artists were still treated disdainfully, as artisans, whose work could hardly be regarded as creative. Vigenère decided that the first step was to translate into French Philostratus' *Images*, which he found in the library of the Villa d'Este, one of the most renowned Italian salons of the early sixteenth century, frequented by eminent poets and artists of the time. *Images* was translated into Latin in 1522 by the personal order of the Villa's mistress Isabella d'Este, the famous Italian humanist. The Latin version of the book by Philostratus was always available on the shelves of her widely visited library and served many artists as one of the main iconographic sources for paintings on mythological subjects.

Descriptions of imaginary paintings were thus transformed into programmes for the real ones. In the framework of this short chapter we cannot dwell upon the question of Vigenère's choice of Philostratus as the first author to be translated to counter the lack of respect for artistic culture in France: this question requires separate study. At present we shall only say that such a choice can be explained, at least partly, by the fact that the same Philostratus wrote *The Life of Apollonius of Tyana*, one of the earliest biographies of an artist, often considered to be a precursor of Vasari's *Lives*.

It is also important to mention that the Culture of Fontainebleau, to which both Vigenère and poets of the *Pléaide* belonged, made virtually no distinction between word and image, that is, the relationship between word and image during this period was much more intimate than that of a text and its illustration (or, conversely, of a picture and its interpretation). Whether they formed the *motto*, *pictura* and *subscriptio* of an emblem or were just an inscription on a triumphal arch erected on the occasion of a royal entry in a city, the verbal and the visual could never be separated. It was next to impossible to divorce these two elements without destroying not just their unity, but also the intrinsic entities of each. One of the main paradoxes of sixteenth-century France (especially of the second half of it) consisted in the fact that nothing was more serious than amusement. The crucial importance of court festivities for the establishment of the state ideology resided in their interactive combination of the verbal and the visual, which were able to fortify it and provide it with food for the imagination as long as they remained together.

For this reason during the regency of Catherine de'Medici Horace's famous maxim 'Ut pictura, poesis erit' ('As with painting so with verbal composition') with its apparent promise to eradicate all barriers between the arts, played a considerable role not only in the domain of æsthetics, but also in the ideological sphere.[8] That is why the ekphrastic genre, the main feature of which was this indivisible unit of Word and Image was of such an importance for Vigenère and his contemporaries.[9] This is why Vigenère did not want *Images*, first published in 1578, to be illustrated. He insisted on this prohibition on several occasions in his vast *Letter to Mr Barnabé Brisson* (*Epistre à Messire Barnabé Brisson*) with which he prefaced the translation of Philostratus.[10]

Present-day scholars sometimes define ekphrasis as a trope elevated to a status of a genre during certain epochs, favourable for tropes, for instance, the baroque. Such an interpretation correlates with what Iurii Lotman wrote in one of his works on the rhetoric and the theory of tropes: 'it is quite evident that wherever a trope is placed in any logical classification of figures, it always contains two elements, one of which is of verbal and the other, of a visual nature, even if this second element is thoroughly camouflaged'.[11] Any division of these elements puts an end to the trope. Any illustration cuts off an ekphrasis.[12]

As it progressed the seventeenth century in France became more rationalistic and less able to tolerate a mixture of semiotic codes, which had been so important for the baroque culture of the several previous decades.[13] Vigenère died in 1599. During the seventeenth century his work was republished eight times. All of these posthumous editions, beginning with that of 1614, were illustrated. Moreover each *Tableau* was accompanied not only by an engraving, but also by an edifying epigram summing up the contents of the image in a didactic manner, totally alien to Philostratus' original creation.

The well-known struggle against excessive use of tropes in lyric poetry, especially in the genre of the ode, represents the same negative attitude towards polysemy. The correlation between the will to isolate one and only one visual image from an ekphrastic text and the aspiration to reduce a word to a single, quasi-terminological meaning is confirmed by a simple fact: the most ardent adversaries of metaphors in poetic texts and the majority of those who insisted on the necessity of illustrating *Images* belonged to one and the same circle, that of the friends and disciples of Malherbe, such as Guillaume Du Vair or Antoine de Laval.

Ekphrasis gradually disappears from the literary space of the seventeenth century: by the end of it one is hard put to find either the word or the genre itself. The history of art with its neutral or critical judgements on pictures and statues came to replace ekphrastic delight, with its ability to develop isolated moments into coherent albeit polysemantic stories. In the learned treatises of Roger de Piles and the Abbé Du Bos, as well as in Diderot's salons of the 1760s, we deal with pure descriptions, clearly separate from the objects described.

It is therefore not surprising that in Russian literature of the eighteenth century we do not come across any direct references to the ekphrastic genre. At the same time, ekphrasis was too important to French culture of the previous century to be completely ignored, neglected or despised by the Russians, whose main aim was to catch up with Europe, in particular with France, and to reconstruct the western cultural situation as closely as possible.

For this reason we believe that ekphrasis did exist in eighteenth-century Russian culture in some latent, potential forms. One must suppose it was no accident that in his *Rhetoric* (1748) Lomonosov gave examples of an ideal, perfect *descriptio* from *Images*, namely, from Philostratus' famous description of the Cupids. The secret invasion of Russian literature by ekphrasis might have been reinforced by another important tendency: Byzantine influence on Russia in the eighteenth century. The ekphrastic genre was one of the most significant in Byzantine literature.[14] The distinctive feature of Byzantine *ekphraseis* in relation to Greek was their general architectural orientation. Buildings and their surroundings, temples and monuments usually served as objects of description.

For various reasons, the descriptive mode was of particular relevance for the burgeoning Russian poetry of the second half of the eighteenth century. Such a mode was first and foremost associated with the name of Gavriil Derzhavin.[15] 'Derzhavin and ekphrasis' is a separate subject, which includes a number of points beyond the scope of the present chapter. One of the most important, however, is that Derzhavin wrote many architectural odes, not only dedicated to the construction of new buildings, but also written 'on the occasion of the dismantling of the old Kremlin ...' (1770). It is in Derzhavin's poetry that ode and ekphrasis meet again and that description recovers its function of praise. To describe an object in detail means to judge it worthy of description. The great influence exerted by Derzhavin upon Pushkin is an axiom: this fact is so well known and widely studied that it does not require any further explanations. Pumpianskii speaks of architectural inspiration and vocabulary as the 'Derzhavin layer' of Russian poetry: 'It is the origin of the statuary theme in *The Bronze Horseman*', writes Pumpianskii, '(the very title of the poem belongs to Derzhavin's poetic language)'.[16]

At this point we are obliged to quit Russia for a while and return to France. As has already been said, in the eighteenth century ekphrasis is no longer relevant to painting. But, strange as it may seem, it remains highly active in the plastic arts, sculpture in particular. During this period Callistratus was very popular; he was translated several times and quite well-known, at least much more so than his great predecessor.[17] Already by the end of the seventeenth century he became one of those well known authors who were so familiar to the potential reader that they were never quoted or, at least, referred to. As Jean Seznec points out about the eminent textbooks of mythology, 'those books that everybody consults and keeps handy, are never, or nearly never, mentioned; for the very reason of their extreme popularity, they turn shortly into anonymous repertories : one would never quote a dictionary ...'[18]

Callistratus' *Ekphraseis* became a popular repertory of commonplaces for the description of statues after 1700, although such a use of his heritage goes back to the previous century.[19] The author of the famous Latin cento *The Painting of the Ancients* (1637) (*De Pictura Veterum*), Franciscus Julius, the secretary of Count d'Arundel, draws 70 percent of his quotations in what concerns sculpture from Callistratus. His contemporary, the Jesuit father Binet, also has constant recourse to this same source in his work *On the Right Way to Praise Sculptures* (*Sur la façon de louer les sculptures*) - part of the vast treatise *Essay on the Wonders of Nature and the Most Noble Works of Man* (*Essai des merveilles de nature et des plus nobles artifices*). The title alone witnesses to the fact that description of sculpture was not supposed to be neutral. So, how should we appraise a statue according to Father Binet or Callistratus?

The crucial notion, the key-word for such a description would be the Greek word *pneuma*, translated as 'life', 'breathing', 'spirit' or even 'inspiration', but usually left in its Greek original without translation. The first thing to emphasize is the animation of the statue in question. One should say that it is energetic as if it were alive; one should show that it is vivid, as if it has just jumped or will be jumping in the next few minutes. The barrier between life and its representation in the statue should be completely obliterated. Whether one is dealing with bronze or marble, it is necessary to speak of the material as something to be 'got over' or 'surmounted' by the sculptor. This is why the main rhetorical figure in this sort of writing is personification.

In his numerous observations on the art of Falconet, especially in the notes on Falconet's *Pygmalion*, Diderot develops a quite special style for the description of statues with a number of recurrent metaphorical constructions: on several occasions he says that 'marble is obedient' or that 'bronze facilitates'.[20] It is well known that Diderot and Falconet were close friends and that for years they were in an active and, one might say, profound, correspondence.[21] Diderot (as well as some other art critics - for instance, the passionate antiquitarian, the Count de Caylus)[22] exerted an obvious and considerable influence on the sculptor, who, in contradistinction to many others, left copious commentaries upon his own art.[23]

One can judge of Falconet's exceptional literary activity from the six volumes of his writings, published in Lausanne in 1781 and entitled *The Works of Etienne Falconet, Sculptor, Containing Several of His Writings on the Fine Arts, Some Already Published, Though in Defective Form, Others New* (*Œuvres d'Etienne Falconet, statuaire, contenant plusieurs écrits relatifs aux beaux-arts dont quelques uns ont déjà paru, mais fautifs, d'autres sont nouveaux*).[24] It is the first volume of this collection that attracts our attention at present, since we will find there the *Reflections on Sculpture* (*Réflections sur la sculpture*), the famous speech, delivered by Falconet at the Royal Academy of Painting and Sculpture in 1760 and supposed to have served as the basis for the article *Sculpture* in the *Encyclopedia*; the *Scheme of an Equestrian Statue* (*Projet d'une statue équestre*[p.55]), a small note which is of particular interest for us now; as well as the *Letter to a Blind Man* (*Lettre à une espèce d'aveugle* [p.145]), addressed to one of Falconet's compatriots who visited his studio in St Petersburg and saw there the model of the statue of Peter the Great; finally, in the same volume we will find the endless *Observations on the Statue of Marcus Aurelius* (*Observations sur la statue de Marc-Aurèle* [pp. 144-348]).

Some of these writings, as well as the excerpts from Falconet's correspondence with Diderot (especially those related to the statue of Peter the Great) were brought together and translated into English by a certain Mr Tooke, Chaplain to the Factory at St Petersburg. Tooke published them in London in 1777 in a rather sumptuous volume *in quarto*.[25] The translation was prefaced by Tooke's brief observations on Falconet and his art. Tooke admires the totality of Falconet's talents and each of them taken separately: 'The man capable of being one of the first Sculptors of his age, if he had employed his genius that way, would have become one of the first writers ... How much he is of a scholar, every one is sensible that has read pieces he has already published. His notes on the elder Pliny are sagacious and acute; and his remarks on the Statue of Marcus Aurelius will remain a literary monument of his taste ...'.[26]

Falconet left for Russia on September 12, 1766. From that point on the character of his correspondence with Diderot somewhat altered: their letters

were no longer sent from one side of the fireplace to the other, but travelled
between two distant countries. Naturally discussion of the ideal equestrian statue
for an Emperor was the main subject of these letters. Such a monument had been
embodied for centuries in a unique specimen, that is, the statue of Marcus
Aurelius on the Capitoline hill.[27]

This statue had served as a model to various sculptors charged with the
difficult task of immortalizing an emperor on a horse, whether the emperor in
question was Henri IV, Louis XIV, Louis XV (whose equestrian statue by Patte
was erected in Paris in 1765, just on the eve of Falconet's departure for Russia)
or Peter the Great himself. In the case of the latter, the commission was first
entrusted in the 1730s to Rastrelli who considered imitating Girardon's Louis
XIV but soon gave up the whole project. The new statue of Peter the Great was
conceived by Falconet as a complete antithesis of Marcus Aurelius and its
numerous derivatives. To oppose his own creation to the exemplary work of
classical antiquity was one of Falconet's main concerns throughout his work in
Saint-Petersburg.[28]

One might still be surprised by the violence of Falconet's judgements
on Marcus Aurelius evident in the aggressive tone of the *Observations*. Falconet
did detest this Roman statue, but his hatred, which might seem inappropriatly
directed at an object dating back to remote ages, was grounded on an entire
theory, mature and well developed, and not on pure æsthetic displeasure.
Falconet thought that the praise of Marcus Aurelius' statue was invariably based
not on direct observation but on the judgement which men of letters, from
classical antiquity onwards, had formulated with respect to the statue; the same
judgements, Falconet discovered, were quoted again and again. More dangerous
still, according to Falconet, was a further consequence of this tradition: the
conventional image and the conventional criteria which the tradition formed,
were imposed as norm and model upon the modern artist, who thus could not
follow his own ideas and imitate objects as nature offered them to the
unprejudiced eye of the creative genius.[29]

It was just one aspect of Falconet's overall view of mimesis in
Sculpture: 'The Mind of the Sculptor is not to dwell only on the famous statues
of antiquity …'[30] Whatever the imagination of the Sculptor can create of the
most majestic, of the most sublime, of the most uncommon, ought to be only
the expression of the possible *appearance* of Nature, of her effects, of her
sports, of her *accidents'* [my emphasis].[31] At the same time this impressionistic
approach to the object of imitation presupposes its long and meticulous analysis:
'Whatever the Sculptor takes for the object of his imitation, it ought to be the
continual subject of his Study'.[32] The lack of such a study was principally
to blame for the shortcomings of Marcus Aurelius' horse, to the presentation
of which Falconet deliberately limits his discussion of the statue on the
Capitoline hill.[33]

In Falconet's opinion, Marcus Aurelius' horse is ugly, both as a whole and in its details; its author failed to observe and to imitate the body of a real horse and completely ignored equine movement. Falconet argued that if this horse were to move, the statue would fall down, since the position of the legs was entirely unnatural: 'The horse is so made as to offend against all the laws of optics: his head is cold, harsh and is not expressive at all; as for its proportions and movements, this horse would have run on its back-legs alone without setting the front ones in motion'.[34] Falconet reproached his predecessors as well as his contemporaries for not going to the manège, and Diderot tried to defend, for instance, Bouchardon and to persuade Falconet that he did visit the manège and did study horses' movements thoroughly enough to reproduce them 'according to the effects of Nature'.[35] When Falconet was working on Peter the Great's horse, his main concern was to make future spectators and critics forget that they had just a piece of bronze in front of them and exclaim 'But it is alive, isn't it ?!'- to make them ask those questions which Callistratus usually addressed to statues : 'Whither do you rush? Where will you stop?' This result was achieved.

One of the numerous foreign travellers who visited Russia in the 1770s left these observations on Falconet's creation: 'One of the noblest monuments of the gratitude and veneration universally paid to Peter the First is that which her present majesty has ordered to be erected ... In his production he [Falconet] has united the greatest simplicity with the truest sublimity of conception ... This attitude has given him room to exert great anatomical beauty and skill in the muscles of the horse's hind thighs and hams, on which the whole weight of his body is necessarily sustained. The Tzar's figure is full of fire and spirit ...'[36] Diderot also praised the passion of the monument, especially its bestial, surging quality. In the most famous lines of the *Bronze Horseman* we read:

> The waves, rapacious, press around him
> And hiss and roar in spite. He knew
>
> The square, the horse, the lions two
> And him who towered, by murk surrounded,
> Above them all, detached and still,
> One who, Fate bowing to his will,
> The city on the sea has founded ...
> Enclosed by night, how fearful he!
> How deeply plunged in revery!
> In him what dreaded force is hidden!
> His horse, what fire in its eye!
> Where dost thou, steed, in frenzy fly,
> And where to halt wilt thou be bidden?[37]

Here Pushkin uses a device common to all the sculptural ekphraseis of the Callistratus tradition. In his article Jakobson enumerates similar places from various poets, Pushkin's contemporaries: 'It is a traditional image: "He has brought me to life in stone", says Derzhavin about the sculptor who moulded his bust, and Dashkov is constantly surprised in his inscriptions on statues that "Praxitel's chisel has given stone sensibility and life" (*K istukanu Niobi [To a Statue of Niobe]*) and that "the hero breathes in metal" (*Izvaianie Aleksandra [A Statue of Alexander]*). "Divine bronze! It seems to come to life," proclaims Benitskii'.[38] Such an enumeration can be continued. But in all these examples we will find some variants of the parenthetic clause 'it seems'. It goes back to the Greek particle ωσ in Callistratus's *Ekphraseis*, which means 'as', 'just as' and 'as if it were', that is, presupposes that in fact 'it is not'. Pushkin eliminates this particle in all its possible variants. In *The Bronze Horseman* we go from the metaphor back to the myth. Metaphors read and interpreted in the mode of myth constitute the basis of the art of surrealism. The Statue does not *seem* alive. It *is* alive. By introducing the motif of the madness of Evgenii, Pushkin turns this common ekphrastic device into the central point of the plot, on which the whole poem is sustained. The shifting point of these two modalities of perception is shown in the text: while in the first lines Evgenii just 'seems to hear' the Bronze Horseman following him, in the last few verses the rider does really pursue him:

> ... Across the empty square
> Yevgeny ran and seemed to hear
> Great, swelling, mighty peals of thunder,
> And feel the pavement shaking under
> A horse's heavy hoofs. For there,
> Behind him, to the darkness wedded,
> Lit by the moon's pale ray and slight,
> One hand in warning raised, the dreaded
> Bronze Horseman *galloped* through the night.
> Till morn, where'er Yevgeny frightened
> Did bend his steps and wander, mute,
> The fell Bronze Horseman *rode*, benighted,
> In *mad,* in thunderous pursuit.
> [my emphasis] [39]

Pushkin was probably not familiar with the theoretical views of Falconet, although we cannot completely exclude the possibility: according to the famous bibliographical description of Pushkin's Library by Boris Modzalevskii, in the edition of Diderot's correspondence, which belonged to Pushkin (*Memoirs, Correspondence and Unedited Works of Diderot, Based on Manuscripts Entrusted by the Dying Author to Grimm [Mémoires, correspondance et ouvrages inédits de Diderot, publiés d'après les manuscrits confiés, en mourant, par l'auteur, à Grimm*]), the only pages cut with a paper-knife in the third volume are those with Falconet's letters.[40]

As shown by Pumpianskii, it was mainly from Derzhavin's odes that Pushkin borrowed his descriptive vocabulary, but what is of particular interest to us is the chain of coincidences, through which the language of the description meets its object in *The Bronze Horseman*. It may be that such accidental encounters are, in fact, the most productive mechanisms in cultural history. At the same time this encounter may have had some direct literary sources.

There is an interesting problem which remains unresolved: not long before Pushkin started work on *The Bronze Horseman*, a new book appeared in his library. It was The Poetical Works of Coleridge, Shelley and Keats.[41] It is well known that by the end of the 1820s Pushkin had just began to study English, and at this time it was rather inadequate: the poet was not able to read the book through, but selected individual texts to analyse in detail. We find some pencil notes on the margins of Shelley's *Ozymandias*, a poem which has usually been considered to be one of the ideological sources of *The Bronze Horseman*. But what seems even more significant to us now, is that another text, carefully studied by Pushkin, was Keats's *Ode on a Grecian Urn*:

> Who are these coming to the sacrifice?
> To what green altar, O mysterious priest,
> Lead'st thou that heifer lowing at the skies,
> And all her silken flanks with garlands drest?
> What little town by river or sea shore,
> Or mountain-built with peaceful citadel,
> Is emptied of this folk, this pious morn?[42]

These and similar questions constitute the constructive principle of the composition of this ode which is traditionally regarded as the perfect example of ekphrasis in modern European poetry.[43]

NOTES

1. Roman Jakobson, 'The Statue in Pushkin's Poetic Mythology' in R. Jakobson, *Language and Literature*, Cambridge and London, 1987, pp. 318-67.

2. Lev Pumpianskii, 'Mednyi vsadnik i poeticheskaia traditsiia XVIII veka', *Pushkin: Vremennik pushkinskoi komissii*, Leningrad, 1939, IV-V, pp. 91-124.

3. Aaron Kibédi-Varga gave one of the most precise definitions to a rather vague domain of the history of rhetoric, considering as a sequence flourishing genres and those which are dying but tend to be transformed into new ones (see 'L'histoire de la rhétorique et la rhétorique des genres', *Rhetorica*, III, 1985, pp. 201-21).

4. These texts were brought together and thoroughly studied by Iurii Tynianov, who regarded Parody as the 'plenipotentiary' form of literary evolution. In 1931 he published a special collection: *Mnimaia Poeziia*, Academia, Leningrad, 1931.

5. See Ernst Robert Curtius, *European Literature and the Latin Middle Ages*, Bollingen Series XXXVI, Princeton University Press, Princeton, New Jersey, 1990, pp. 192 ff.

6. At a certain moment ekphrasis came into vogue and at present is one of the most widely studied topics on the interface of literary history and the history of the arts. The literature on the subject is thus quite extensive. Among the most recent studies are: James Heffernan, *Museum of Words. The Poetics of Ekphrasis from Homer to Ashbery*, The University of Chicago Press, Chicago, 1993; Michael Riffaterre, 'L'illusion d'ekphrasis' in G. Mathieu-Castellani, *Pensée de l'image. Signification et figuration dans le texte et dans la peinture*, Presses Universitaires de Vincennes, Paris, 1994.

7. Important articles on the biography and literary heritage of this most curious figure of his time can be found in a recent collection published by the Ecole Normale Supérieure: *Blaise de Vigenère poète et mythographe au temps de Henri III*, numéro 11 des Cahiers V.L. Saulnier, Spring, 1994.

8. Erica Harth, 'The "Ut Pictura Poesis" Representational System' in *Ideology and Culture in Seventeenth-Century France*, Cornell University Press, Ithaca and London, 1983, pp. 23-7.

9. Grant F. Scott, 'The Rhetoric of Dilation: Ekphrasis and Ideology', *Word and Image*, VII, 4, 1991, pp. 301-10.

10. I refer here to one of the latest and the best editions of the Vigenère's work: Françoise Graziani, ed., Philostrate l'Ancien, *Les Images ou les Tableaux de Platte Peinture, traduction de Blaise de Vigenère*, 2 volumes, Honoré Champion, Paris, 1995.

11. Iurii Lotman, 'Retorika kak mekhanism smisloporozhdenia' in id., *Vnutri misliashchikh mirov*, Iazyki russkoi kul'tury, Moscow, 1996, pp. 46-73 (48).

12. Vigenère had one more argument against illustrations: according to him, any illustration, even the best one, inevitably reduces the huge spectrum of possible meanings and interpretations to a single one. An ideal, 'utopian' illustration would have had to illustrate the slightest shade of meaning of each word, which is impossible. The words in which Vigenère expresses this opinion in his preface coincide literally (!) with those written more than three centuries later by Iurii Tynianov in his famous essay 'Illustrations' (Iurii Tynianov, *Poetika. Istoriia Literatury. Kino*, Nauka, Moscow, 1977, pp. 310-20).

13. Although not directly related to the process in question, one parallel from the history of theatre should be included: it was in the seventeenth century that actors and spectators were definitively separated, that is, reality was no longer mixed with its conventional representation in the space of the performance.

14. Vladimir Bychkov, 'Das Problem des Bildes, in der byzantinischen Ästhetik', *Wissenschaftliche Zeitschrift*, Martin-Luther-Universität, Halle, 1975, XXIV, 2, pp. 75-84; Henry Maguire, *Art and Eloquence in Byzantium*, Dumbarton Oak Papers, Princeton, 1981.

15. Ekaterina Dan'ko, 'Izobrazitel'noe iskusstvo v poezii Derzhavina', *XVIII vek*, 2, Nauka, Moscow-Leningrad, 1940, pp. 166-247.

16. L. Pumpianskii, *Klassicheskaia traditsiia: Sobranie trudov po istorii russkoi literatury*, Iaziki russkoi kul'tury, Moscow, 2000, p. 247.

17. See Aline Magnien, 'Callistrate et le discours sur la sculpture à l'âge moderne' in Philippe Hoffman et al., eds, *Antiquités Imaginaires*, Presses de L'Ecole Normale Supérieure, Paris, 1996, pp. 21-43.

18. Jean Seznec, *La survivance des dieux antiques*, Flammarion, Paris, 1993, p. 328.

19. The difference between the titles of Philostratus' and Callistratus' creations is quite significant: by entitling his work 'Images' Philostratus was trying to attract the spectator's attention to the described object itself, whereas Callistratus emphasized the very process of description.

20. *Diderot et l'art, de Boucher à David*, Ministère de la culture, Editions de la Réunion des musées nationaux, Paris, 1984, p. 451.

21. The literature on this subject being quite extensive, I mention only those studies which seem indispensable for the present topic: Yves Benot, *Diderot and Falconet*, Paris, 1958; A. Wilson, 'Correspondance de Diderot et Falconet', *The Romanic Review*, LI, 1960; A.B. Weinshenker, *Falconet, his Writing and his Friend Diderot*, Genève, 1966; H. Dieckmann, 'Diderot's letters to Falconet', *French Studies*, V, October, 1951, pp. 307 ff.

22. Count de Caylus was a predecessor of Diderot as an art critic: his first art reviews appeared in *Mercure de France* at the beginning of the 1750s, while Diderot came to art criticism no earlier than 1759.

23. The most thorough analysis of Falconet's theoretical texts one will find in: Michèle Beaulieu, 'Les "écrits" de Falconet sur la sculpture', *Bulletin de la société de l'Histoire de l'art français*, 1992, pp. 173-85; see also: J. von Schloesser, *Die Kunstliteratur*, Vienne, 1924, pp. 642-58. As for more general studies on the same subject, see P. Ratouis de Limay, *Les artistes écrivains*, Paris, 1921.

24. There exists another edition: *Œuvres complètes d'Etienne Falconet contenant la traduction des livres de Pline concernant la peinture et la sculpture avec des notes ... Précédées de la Vie de Falconet par P.C. Levesque*, 3 volumes, Paris, 1808.

25. *Pieces on Sculpture, and on the Statue of Peter the Great by M. Falconet & M. Diderot, translated by the Rev. Mr. Tooke, the Chapelain to the Factory at St. Petersbourg*, London, 1777.

26. Ibid., p. 6.

27. Ph. Fehl, 'The Placement of the Equestrian Statue of Marcus Aurelius in the Middle Ages', *Journal of the Warbourg and Courtauld Institutes*, 1974, pp. 362-7; M. Humbert, 'Marc-Aurèle place du Capitole', *Monuments historiques*, mai, 1985, pp. 100-2.

28. It is worth mentioning that Falconet's attitude towards Marcus Aurelius became one of the counts of an indictment in a speech delivered by David in the Convention. David exclaimed: 'This Falconet, who has prepared six thick volumes just to prove that the horse of Marcus Aurelius in Rome, the famous masterpiece of Antiquity, is not as good as his own, erected in St Petersburg, which will be hidden in the snows of the Neva so deeply that nobody will speak or even recall it any longer ...' (See L. Réau, *Falconet*, II, Paris, p. 490). Thus Falconet's lack of patriotism and loyalty towards the government was proved by his lack of respect towards the masterpieces of antiquity.

29. For a detailed and serious analysis of Falconet's observations on the statue of Marcus Aurelius and those of Diderot see H. Dieckmann and J. Seznec, 'The Horse of Marcus Aurelius. A Controversy between Diderot and Falconet', *Journal of the Warbourg and Courtauld Institutes*, 1952, pp. 198-228.

30. The main opponent of Falconet's theories was Winkelmann, who admired and supported archaic values, and who, by the way, detested Callistratus (Winkelmann wrote about him as

vehemently as if he were his contemporary). Thus the debate of Falconet and Winkelmann transformed the quarrel between ancients and moderns into one between *archaists* and *hellenists*.

31. Falconet and Diderot, *Pieces on Sculpture*, op. cit., p. 12.

32. Ibid., p. 11.

33. The 1760s in European art were marked by a particular interest in the representation of the physique of (especially galloping) horses: in France and Germany numerous anatomical atlases were published during this period; 1766 was notable for the huge carousel organized by Catherine the Great, in honour of which special medals were produced representing a horse racing at the hippodrome. Some scholars attribute this interest in the equestrian to the increasing oriental influence over occidental art in the eighteenth century (see Solomon Reinach, *La Representation du galop dans l'art ancien et moderne,* Paris, 1925).

34. Falconet, *Œuvres d'Etienne Falconet, statuaire*, op. cit., p. 292.

35. In this letter of December 6, 1773 Diderot tries to calm his friend and asks him, with a certain lassitude, to leave the matter aside, since the statue of Peter the Great is more important: 'Well, well, my friend, let us leave this horse of Marcus Aurelius. Whether it be beautiful, or whether it be ugly, what is it to me? I am not acquainted with the sculptor, and am totally uninterested in his work: let us speak however of yours' (*Pieces on Sculpture*, op. cit., p. 50).

36. N. Waxandall, Junior, *Cursory Remarks Made in a Tour through Some of the Northern Parts of Europe*, London, 1775, pp. 229-31.

37. Alexander Pushkin, *Selected Writings*, Moscow, Progress publishers, in 2 volumes, 1974, I, p. 95 (translated by I. Zheleznova).

38. Roman Jakobson, op.cit., p. 353.

39. Alexander Pushkin, op. cit., p. 96.

40. Boris Modzalevskii, *Biblioteka Pushkina* (*Bibliographicheskoe opisanie*), Imperatorskaia akedemiia nauk, St Petersburg, 1910, pp. 225-6.

41. Ibid., p. 198.

42. *The Works of John Keats*, The Wordsworth Poetry Library, 1994, p. 233.

43. The first and the most prominent article written on the subject, and to some extent the origin of all the rest, was that by Leo Spitzer: 'The "Ode on a Grecian Urn", or Content vs. Metagrammar' in Anna Hatcher, ed., *Essays on English and American Literature*, Princeton University Press, Princeton, 1962.

Pushkin's Imperial Image of St Petersburg Revisited

by

ALEXANDRA SMITH

Pushkin's portrayal of St Petersburg has attracted considerable attention among Pushkin scholars. It is possible to identify trends in their treatment of this topic. The trends include attempts to examine Pushkin's images of St Petersburg as part of the body of texts defined in Russian literary scholarship in these contexts: 'the Petersburg text' (Lotman and the Tartu school[1]); the descriptive approach (Tomashevskii[2]); the topographical approach (Mederskii[3]); the intertextual approach (Schwarzband, Kodjak[4]); and the mythological and mythopoetical approach (Jakobson[5], Bayley[6]).

These studies tend to focus on various aspects of Pushkin's Petersburg imagery. Yet they do not form a complete or coherent picture, and it remains unclear whether the topic 'Pushkin's Petersburg' has real credibility and whether Pushkin's texts with St Petersburg-bearing images actually have unity or display consistency.

To answer this it is necessary to have a closer look at Pushkin's poetics rather than ideological or socio-political issues which many scholars prefer to highlight. There has been some re-assessment recently in Russian scholarship of Peter the Great, and it is becoming clearer why St Petersburg was depicted in nineteenth-century literature in an ambivalent and contradictory way, as will be discussed below. Nevertheless, Pushkin's portrayal of St Petersburg brings some coherence into the topic of literature's depiction of St Petersburg, if Pushkin's texts are discussed in their cultural rather than their socio-political context. Such a perspective allows us to re-discover some of the intertextual links between Pushkin's Petersburg texts and (on the one hand) the Petrine Baroque, and (on the other) the visual as well as literary representations of other European cities, chiefly London - with which comparisons of St Petersburg were sometimes made in the first half of the nineteenth century.

It is also argued that Pushkin's 'kinetic' poetic model of a young European city anticipates Bergson's metaphysical concept of 'duration' (*durée*). Such an interpretation could develop the cohesion of St Petersburg in Pushkin's imagery, imagery that exemplifies changing reality in a Bergsonian sense. Thus it may be possible to explain the irrational aspects of Pushkin's portrayal of St Petersburg as part of the inner consciousness, or 'intuition', to use Bergson's terminology. Such an approach helps bring together various aspects of Pushkin's imagery, which before were interpreted as conflicting and contradictory. As a result, Pushkin's art discloses more unity than disparity, and makes Pushkin's treatment of St Petersburg more consistent with his reputation for having a harmonizing influence, a reputation that has been firmly held among Russian poets of the twentieth century. In Aleksander Blok's famous speech 'The Poet's

Role' he stresses Pushkin's preoccupation with inner concerns rather than with ideological or state affairs, one that underlines the child-like innocence embedded in Pushkin's writings. In the words of Blok, all Russians preserve in their memories from early childhood 'a happy name - Pushkin'.[7]

Blok's assessment of Pushkin's legacy in Russian culture defines Pushkin's work as part of national cultural memory. More importantly, Blok touches upon the universality of cultural memory, which he perceives as everlasting and dynamic. According to Blok, 'the poet is a child of harmony, and this gives him a role in the culture of the world. Three concerns are incumbent upon him: first, to liberate sounds from the native anarchic element in which they reside; second, to bring these sounds into harmony, or to give them form; and third, to transmit this harmony to the external world'.[8] This view of Pushkin as liberator of harmony enables Blok to highlight the dynamic mechanism of Pushkin's poetry, inviting a comparison of the poet with a composer who orchestrates the final transmission of harmony into the world. In other words the process, the dialogic nature of any poetic work results, in Blok's view, in participation in world culture.

Such a standpoint is very close to Bergson's view of memory and duration, and gives us an opportunity to assess Pushkin's work as part of the universal process of creativity. Bergson's concepts enable us to see the dynamic nature of Pushkin's work, leading us to the discovery of intertextual dialogism and reproduction of other cultural artefacts in his writings. Renata Lachmann has tested this approach in her analysis of Pushkin's poem *Monument*, linking intertextuality to cultural memory in general.[9] According to Lachmann, Acmeist poetics exemplifies Bergson's theory at its best, stressing the coexistence of all cultures (that is, producing a synchronic paradigm). In such a world-view, 'the past is grasped as becoming, as meaning that neither was nor is but that is, rather, always being projected into the future as deferred meaning. ... Deferral prevents the death of culture, and mnemonic writing guarantees deferral'.[10] The concept of intertextuality as cultural memory can be easily extended to the discussion of Pushkin's St Petersburg including non-verbal images, as well as beliefs and imagery of contemporary popular urban culture. What appears to be paramount to the discussion of Pushkin's Petersburg is Bergson's idea of the inner unity of matter and spirit, achieved through the spatialization of time.

To a great extent, Pushkin was a creator of St Petersburg in the same manner as Peter the Great. The observation William Mills Todd III makes about Pushkin's *Evgenii Onegin* can be easily extended to all Pushkin's texts on St Petersburg, since they fit the paradigm usually defined as 'the text within the text'. Thus, Mills Todd concludes that life and novel form a unity in Pushkin's *Evgenii Onegin* because they both manifest the same creative process.[11] The semiotic terminology allows us to introduce here the term 'text' in a broader meaning, applying it to St Petersburg as a cultural space, a text in its own right. Inversely, it can be said that Pushkin's Petersburg creates its own cultural space.

The relationship between Pushkin, the author of his Petersburg, and Peter the Great, the author of the city, can be best described as the anxiety of influence. To put it differently, Pushkin 'reads' St Petersburg as a book, as an evolving and open-ended text which can be used both for inscribing the poet's self and as a source of inspiration, as a context that helps Pushkin, the poet, to develop his own creative potential. This is especially true if we bear in mind that the St Petersburg of Pushkin's times was developing rapidly, changing its appearance in order to conform to the new Imperial image, with many features of the Petrine baroque being replaced with classical elements. Pushkin's vision of St Petersburg as expressed in *The Bronze Horseman* and in *The Queen of Spades* reflects the dynamic image of the city's cultural space in which different memories and cultural imprints co-existed, and with the classical 'solemn' image still very much evolving.

      This chapter proposes to view Pushkin's writings on St Petersburg as mnemonic writing, preserving the city traditionally perceived as 'Westernized' cultural space with a strongly marked 'young' identity, in the face of the Old Believers' belief that the city was doomed to vanish. It can be argued that Blok's representation of Pushkin, as a poet of child-like qualities, owes a good deal to Pushkin's self-identification with the young and vibrant city, the child of Peter the Great. Pushkin's representation of St Petersburg is far from static and it also bears the stamp of Pushkin's self on the city landscape. Arguably, Pushkin's Petersburg text 'transgresses its own boundaries and opens up into the greater text of culture, macrotext' articulating the 'flowing movement that runs through texts and that constitutes them'.[12]

      Two distinct periods in Pushkin's representation of St Petersburg in his texts are usually given special attention in Pushkin scholarship. One period comprises Pushkin's early years in Petersburg (1817-20) which may be characterized as the period of active intellectual and cultural life, when the young poet became increasingly involved in the social and cultural activities of the Russian capital. The second period runs from 1827 to 1837, marked by Pushkin's growing pessimism and somewhat split poetic persona. The latter arose from the failure of the Decembrist revolt and from Pushkin's social position as junior civil servant, humiliating in the eyes of the court and high society, as it did not match Pushkin's self-image of the first poet of Russia. It is important to bear in mind that most of Pushkin's poems on St Petersburg and Moscow before 1827 have not received much attention in Pushkin scholarship, and it is the second period which is known for the inscription of Petersburg urban life into Pushkin's texts. Such texts include *Evgenii Onegin*, *The Bronze Horseman* and *The Queen of Spades*.

      In spite of the large body of work devoted to Pushkin's 'Petersburg texts', it remains unclear why the poet expressed such strong anxieties about the urban life in the capital when, after the end of the war with Napoleon (1812-15), St Petersburg was developing so rapidly. Pushkin captured the new appearance of the city in a number of poems, especially in the opening sections of *The Bronze Horseman,* in which he inscribes into the text the glorious appearance of the renovated Admiralty building. It was the most striking innovation of the St Petersburg urban landscape in the period 1806-1827. The image of the renovated and improved city must have had enormous appeal to Pushkin on his return to St Petersburg in 1827 after several years of exile, although some of the grand projects were still in progress. St Isaac's cathedral, for example, was completed only after Pushkin's death. Yet in the early 1830s the forty-eight supporting columns of the cathedral portico attracted many admirers. One newspaper wrote:

> This work is the highest example of human stamina, might and knowledge. The most courageous projects of the Middle Ages cannot be compared with it, and are much inferior. As a good comparison, one might refer to Ancient Egypt, which represents the youthful stage of our Universe.[13]

Curiously, there are no references in Pushkin's poetry to this or to several other city developments. Clearly, Pushkin's vision has its own mythopoetic aspects. It can be argued that after 1827 they are aspects developing into a coherent mythopoetic model.

A view prevalent in Pushkin studies (for example the Tartu school) states that Pushkin opposes Petersburg to Moscow, in the manner of the Biblical distinction between Jerusalem as the city of God and Babylon as scarlet woman and city of exile. In my view, this approach to Pushkin's Petersburg requires modification since some texts are exempt from this paradigm. In the words of one scholar, the binary opposition 'Jerusalem - Babylon' can be presented as follows:

> Jerusalem is the true home of the chosen, God's site for the Temple and the throne. Yet it is subject to corruption and wavering allegiance and thus condemned by the prophets, particularly Hosea and Jeremiah. Babylon in contrast is the fallen city of sensuality, greed, and disobedience to God's will; there men worship idols and false values.[14]

This attitude can be sensed in Pushkin's own reference to St Petersburg as a cursed city. It is known that upon receiving news of the flood in November 1824 Pushkin wrote to his brother: 'The very thing for cursed Petersburg'.[15] Indeed, Pushkin's image of the old Moscow and the new capital invites such an opposition, but their representation is ambivalent both in *The Bronze Horseman* and in *The Queen of Spades.* This might be explained by the Romantic fashion of the 1830s with its promotion of male genius as Romantic hero. Young Petersburg fitted their image. This view was reflected in Pushkin's differentiation of the two cities on the basis of gender principles. Thus in *Evgenii*

Onegin Pushkin labels Moscow as grandmother. Furthermore, Pushkin does not see the two cities as equal any more, comparing the two capitals with two hearts that cannot co-exist in the same body.

In his essay 'The Journey from Moscow to St Petersburg' (1833-4) Pushkin summarizes his view thus: 'Peter the Great did not like Moscow ... The decline of Moscow is the inevitable consequence of the rise of St Petersburg. Two capitals cannot flourish at the same time in the same state - just as two hearts cannot co-exist in one human body'.[16] Yet some of Pushkin's poems do not distinguish strongly between the two cities. This is especially evident in the poem 'What a night! The hard frost ...' ('Какая ночь! Мороз трескучий ...') (1827) alluding to the execution of the rebellious *streltsy* by Peter the Great in Moscow's Red Square. The horse rider in this poem foreshadows the bronze horseman chasing Evgenii along the night streets of St Petersburg, yet the whole scene belongs to Moscow, the early capital of Russia, not St Petersburg. The Red Square that Pushkin depicts still bears all the marks of the bloody execution:

> ... And the whole of Moscow sleeps quietly,
> Disturbing fear forgotten.
> And the square stands in the darkness of the night,
> Still full of the painful memories of execution.[17]

Yet the violent scene which Pushkin graphically depicts with dead bodies, blood, and the burning ashes of human bones is merged with the portrayal of a young executioner riding through the square to a meeting with his beloved. If anything it is the horse, not the rider, which conveys some disgust with the scene, as well as hesitation and anxiety. The rider persuades the horse to ride forward, forgetting the horror they both witnessed:

> '... What are you afraid of? What is it?
> Didn't we ride here yesterday,
> Stamping viciously on the traitors of the Tsar?
> ... My swift horse, my fearless horse,
> Ride forward, fly! ...' And the tired horse
> Ran through the pillars, underneath the hanging body ...[18]

In this poem Pushkin's vision of Moscow is virtually indistinguishable from a similar scene of the chaos and violence in post-flood St Petersburg as presented in *The Bronze Horseman*. Therefore it is questionable whether *The Bronze Horseman* depends much on the imagery of Adam Mickiewicz who recorded his impressions of the flood in such poems as *The Monument of Peter the Great* (*Pomnik Piotra Wielkiego*) and *Oleszkiewiecz*. In the latter poem the Polish painter and freemason Oleszkiewiecz acts as a prophet, comparing St Petersburg with a new Babylon and predicting its demise. In the words of M.N. Virolainen,

Pushkin's *The Bronze Horseman* contains polemical allusions to Mickiewicz's poems of which Pushkin was aware.[19] However, when juxtaposing these poems with Pushkin's poem about Moscow 'What a night! The hard frost …', it is difficult to agree with Schwarzband who insists on Pushkin's appropriation of these images from Mickiewicz's work. Schwarzband states that 'perhaps … Mickiewicz's poem *The Monument of Peter the Great* … inspired Pushkin to use the horse as an allegory of Russia, and the rider as an allegory of the autocracy'.[20] Clearly in 'What a night! The hard frost …' written about Moscow and preceding *The Bronze Horseman*, Pushkin had already created such an allegorical vision. This observation supports the view of John Bayley, who emphasizes that Pushkin knew Mickiewicz's poem *Forefathers' Eve* (*Dziady*) which describes St Petersburg; however everything about the poem must have outraged his æsthetic sense, but like the grit in the oyster it worked in him until the final casting of the pearl at Boldino in 1833. *The Bronze Horseman* is not a reply to Mickiewicz's poem, but it might not have been written without it.[21] Surprisingly, the possibility of self-reference in Pushkin's work has escaped scholars' attention. Yet 'What a night! The hard frost …' simply continues Pushkin's comparison of the Decembrist conspiracy in *Stanzas* (1826) with the mutiny of the Moscow *streltsy* at the beginning of Peter's reign. In this respect, Pushkin presents both cities as civilized urban places which had lost their innocence and appeal to the less privileged.

In many ways both Moscow and St Petersburg look equally appealing in Pushkin's verse novel *Evgenii Onegin*, boasting a huge range of social gatherings and cultural life, with a dynamic and diverse urban life. There are several scenes presented in a kinetic manner: as if the busy city life is seen through the eyes of a person taking a ride through the streets of Moscow and St Petersburg. The description in *Evgenii Onegin* of Moscow's busy Tverskaia Street as perceived by Tatiana (7: XXXVIII) strongly resembles, in its lively kaleidoscopic representation, St Petersburg's busy streets as seen by Onegin in the early hours of the morning (1: XXXV). Commenting on the liveliness and dynamism Pushkin employs in *Evgenii Onegin*, one of the most important Russian critics of the first half of the nineteenth century, N.I. Nadezhdin, compared Pushkin's portrayal of urban life with the paintings and engravings of the English artist William Hogarth (1697-1764). Hogarth's satirical realism and lively representation of life captured the imagination of Pushkin and his contemporaries. In his review of *Evgenii Onegin* Nadezhdin writes with great enthusiasm that Pushkin's 'portrayal of Moscow is truly Hogarthian! Pushkin's talent here is at its best'.[22] Hogarth's prints and engravings were well known in Russia in the first half of the nineteenth century. Petr Viazemskii mentions his name as being among the most influential artists in Russian cultural development of this period.[23] It is as if Nadezhdin was anxious to follow the example of the eighteenth-century English writers whose verbal portraits and interiors were imitative of Hogarth's art.

Nadezhdin's comments on the 'Englishness' and 'Hogarthian qualities' of Pushkin's artistic world extend to observations on a more general use of irony and parody in Pushkin's work. The critic defines Pushkin's poetics as 'simply a parody', claiming that

> Pushkin's muse is a mischievous young girl, who does not care tuppence for the world. Her element is to mock at everything, good and bad ... not out of spite or scorn, but simply out of desire to poke fun. It is this which shapes in a particular way Pushkin's poetic process and clearly distinguishes it from *Byronic* misanthropy or the humour of Jean-Paul Richter ... There is nothing that can be done about it ... what is true, is true ... A master can mock and ridicule ... provided, of course, he has a sense of honour and proportion. And if one can be great in small matters, then it is perfectly possible to call Pushkin a genius - *at caricature!*[24]

Nadezhdin's view of Pushkin has become increasingly credible in recent Russian studies on Pushkin,[25] despite being vigorously dismissed or marginalized in Soviet scholarship.[26] One scholar suggests the presence of carnivalesque qualities (in the Bakhtinian sense) in Pushkin's texts. It would not be overdoing it to take this point further and map out the co-presence of at least two pre-texts, two stylistic influences in Pushkin's work that relate to the images of St Petersburg.

As Nadezhdin points out, Pushkin appropriates playfulness and dynamic impressionism in his poetry with great success. Both Pushkin and Hogarth share a great love for theatre and they both mock the theatrical in the everyday life of the middle class and the aristocracy. Hogarth's innovative techniques lie in reviving the baroque, introducing new themes and a vast new world of descriptive realism that occasionally blend irrational elements of fantasy which one critic said 'derived from popular art and from mannerism', and were 'in seeming contradiction with his inherent and increasing realism'.[27] To a great extent the same words can be applied to Pushkin. Pushkin's poem *Peter the Great's Feast* verbally reproduces some popular images of St Petersburg which appeared on many engravings of the two Russian eighteenth-century artists Ivan and Aleksei Zubov. Their engravings were imitative of the popular art of *lubok* and were promoting ideologically charged imperial images of the new Russian capital St Petersburg anxious to boost its trade with Europe.

The most famous engraving produced by Aleksei Zubov is the 1716 panorama of St Petersburg showing several important unfinished projects as being completed. In effect Zubov presented the future look of the city as its present one. In the same manner Pushkin wrote his utopian-like prophecy of St Petersburg's future diverse cultural space into *The Bronze Horseman*. The

imagery of Zubov's engraving is politically charged and is a prototype image
for Pushkin's *Peter the Great's Feast*. Lindsey Hughes describes the engraving:

> Like many views of the city, it focuses not on the buildings, which are
> confined to a narrow strip in the middle ground, but on the ships -
> warships, yachts, barges, and a sloop bearing Peter and Catherine - in
> the foreground. The sky takes up more than half the sheet, with hosts
> of heaven bearing a ribbon with the city's name. It shows St
> Petersburg from an 'impossible' angle, ignoring the rules of aerial
> perspective, while at the same time showing buildings in their correct
> order as a strip of façades. Unfinished projects (for example, the spire
> of Peter-Paul Cathedral) are shown completed ... Aleksei Zubov was
> able to capture the 'spirit of the age' as well as its concrete image.[28]

Peter the Great's Feast focuses primarily on the boats, yachts, Russian flags,
military victories of Peter the Great and cargo ships, reproducing the festive
atmosphere of the Petrine period:

> The multi-coloured flags of the ships
> Flutter joyfully above the Neva river,
> The loud harmonious songs of the rowers
> Reach the shores from the boats ...
> What does the Russian tsar celebrate
> In the little city Petersburg?
> Why the shouts and loud shots,
> And the squadron is on the river? ...
> Perhaps, our young fleet is greeting its father
> Brandt's old boat? ...[29]

It is a commonplace to suggest that Pushkin's poem illustrates Peter the Great's
ability to forgive his enemies, hinting that Nicholas I should pardon the
Decembrist conspirators who were living in exile in Siberia. (The poem was
written in 1835 and was intended to mark the anniversary of the Decembrist
revolt.) While this is true, it is just as important to note that to achieve this
Pushkin reproduces a very popular image of St Petersburg celebrating the young
Russian Empire. Echoing Zubov's engraving, Pushkin refers to Catherine, Peter
the Great's wife:

> Did Catherine give birth?
> Does she celebrate her Saint's day,
> This dark-browed wife
> Of the miracle-maker giant? ...[30]

In this stanza Pushkin veils his allusion to the ever-increasing prosperity and fertility of the re-invented empire in overtones and imagery readily present in Russian popular culture (for example, 'dark-browed wife'; 'miracle-maker giant').

This is a twofold device. Pushkin's image of Empress Catherine I reflects the background of Peter the Great's wife that, together with his inclination towards democracy (including popular Yuletide festivities, fireworks, Russian court carnivals, the 'Drunken Assembly', parties, etc.), contributed to his image in popular literature as a tsar-craftsman, a people's tsar. Catherine progressed 'through the roles of camp-follower, mistress, official companion, wife, empress-consort, and, from 1725 to 1727, empress in her own right'.[31] Pushkin's image of Catherine as mother of the nation, a typical popular peasant goddess of fertility, so to speak, might be attributed to the fact that one of her pet names in Peter the Great's household was 'matka', meaning an old girl, mother and uterus - all at the same time. On the other hand, Pushkin as author of the poem inscribes his own voice into the festivities of Peter the Great, the Russian Bacchus. This point brings closer an understanding of the mechanism Pushkin employs, using the Petersburg setting, to promote his own hedonistic image (partially reflected in *Evgenii Onegin* and in some poems dedicated to various Petersburg friends, for example *To Galich*). This image produced a great effect on twentieth-century readers of Pushkin. As mentioned above, Blok associated Pushkin's name with the celebration of life and joyful carnival. In her essay 'My Pushkin' Tsvetaeva reflects on the excitement she felt as a child when reading Pushkin's *Peter the Great's Feast*. She found particularly striking and amusing the reference to the popular image of the Empress together with references to the noises produced by party-goers and cannons.[32] In spite of the fact that Pushkin declared England the 'fatherland of caricature and parody',[33] the Petrine culture was full of carnivalesque qualities that inspired parody and mockery. Furthermore, Pushkin draws attention to activities of Peter the Great that have highly questionable relevance to the state. It appears that Pushkin depicts with warmth and sympathy Peter the Great's whimsical and anarchistic qualities that would attract criticism from the more conservative representatives of Russian culture and from Western observers. Yet the image of the 'shaken' Neva at the end of the poem functions as a mark of the irony in this poem, alluding to the assault on the cultural memory of the nation and playing on the metaphor that, in popular cultural memory, associated Peter the Great with the pagan god of thunder who could strike again.

Here it may also be mentioned that Pushkin's *Peter the Great's Feast* conceals autobiographical overtones. Thus, Fedor Musin-Pushkin, one of Pushkin's ancestors, was executed by Peter the Great for participating in the 1697 conspiracy against the Tsar. Pushkin mentions Fedor in the poem *My Genealogy* (1830): 'My ancestor had a quarrel with Peter the Great'. Yet Ivan Musin-Pushkin, another Pushkin ancestor, took part in the greatest Peter the

Great-organized spectacle - Zotov's 1715 wedding, a real landmark in the history of the orgies of the Drunken Assembly. Ivan Musin-Pushkin was dressed in Venetian costume.[34] Noting the carnivalesque overtones in Pushkin's texts that touch upon the theme of St Petersburg or of Peter the Great, it seems highly significant that Pushkin continues the Venetian motif in his representation of St Petersburg, introducing biographical allusions into his text.[35] As for the poem's setting, Pushkin refers to Peter the Great's celebrations of his 1714 victory at sea over Swedish war-ships, which led to the annexation of Finland. In his historical work *A History of Peter the Great* Pushkin details the victory celebrations of Peter the Great's 'naval' Poltava, with abundant gunfire across St Petersburg and Empress Catherine's giving birth to a daughter Margarita (wrongly mentioned by Pushkin as Natalia in his *History*).[36] A few months later, at the beginning of 1715, Peter the Great pardoned some officials involved in a financial scandal (members of Peter the Great's Treasury were sent to Siberia), celebrating it with gunfire and other festive activities. Just at this time Musin-Pushkin came to be dressed in Venetian costume for a carnival at the 'mock wedding' of a 'young groom', Zotov (who was over eighty years old), organized by Peter the Great in Moscow in January 1715. In the words of one of the witnesses, it was 'a world turned upside down', when the mock Tsar was carried in a sledge pulled by bears.[37]

Taking into account Pushkin's work in the archives as a historian, it is difficult to imagine that *Peter the Great's Feast* contains any of Pushkin's sincere admiration or sympathy. Pushkin's veiling of his didactic message to Nicholas I about the Decembrists sent to Siberia appears to be highly ambivalent. Could Pushkin really be celebrating such a carnival? Lindsey Hughes points out that there were many critical accounts of the forced and unspontaneous nature of the festivities: 'These and similar incidents confirm the suspicion that Peter's masquerades were not true carnival at all, in the sense that "people are liberated from authority, behaviour is unfettered and hierarchy is suspended". On the contrary, Peter's "courtly carnival" celebrated authority as sacred'.[38]

Contrary to the established view that Pushkin's *Peter the Great's Feast* contains a sympathetic account of the Russian Tsar, I argue that Pushkin's references to the popular image of Peter the Great suggest an imitation of the popular imagination to parodic effect. The great importance of the occasion for the Russian Empire is overshadowed in Pushkin's narration by actions of personal glorification. Thus, Pushkin's Peter, the autocratic leader, celebrates himself. Arguably Pushkin, the author in his own right, produces his own version of events to undermine the historical figure of Peter the Great, subverting Peter's pseudo-carnival. Pushkin ridicules as well as praises Peter the Great in a carnivalistic manner, developing Peter's masquerade into a true carnival.

This poem exemplifies, in my view, one of the most typical uses of irony, definable as *blame by praise*. It should be borne in mind, too, that

Pushkin's *Peter the Great's Feast* mocks the naivety of popular belief in a benevolent autocrat. If anything, abundant references to cannons and guns produce a negative effect on readers. At the same time as playing on the popular motif of the benevolent Tsar, Pushkin conceals his doubts about the noble nature of Nicholas I, or for that matter any other Russian autocrat.

To support this observation, we can examine Pushkin's treatment of the theme of carnival and autocracy in an early Pushkin poem hitherto undiscussed in the context of the Petersburg theme. Pushkin conveys his doubts of the true nature of Nicholas I's 'carnival' in the poem 'When the Tsar was frowning ...' ('Брови царь нахмуря ...') (1825). In this poem Pushkin's Nicholas I plays a practical joke on his audience, suggesting that Falconet's monument of Peter the Great has miraculously disappeared from its usual place:

> When the Tsar was frowning,
> He told his companion that, 'Yesterday
> The storm pushed down
> The monument to Peter'.
>
> The companion was frightened to death,
> Asking 'Is that so? I didn't know! ...'
> The Tsar burst into laughter,
> Saying, 'It's an April Fool, my dear!'[39]

This poem implicitly links Nicholas I to Peter the Great in mentioning execution by hanging (a concealed homage to the hanged Decembrists), suggesting that the beginning of Nicholas' reign was marked with blood and victimization of some of his subjects, and repeating Pushkin's view of the tragedy of Peter the Great. The poem 'When the Tsar was frowning ...' can be compared with observations Pushkin makes in his essay 'A Journey from Moscow to St Petersburg'. In this essay Pushkin states that 'Peter I did not like Moscow where everywhere he went he faced painful memories of revolts and executions, an extremely traditional way of life and the obstinate resistance of bigotry and prejudices'.[40] In 'When the Tsar was frowning ...' Pushkin satirically conveys the Russian Tsar haunted by the legacy of his predecessor Peter, with whom he wanted to be compared. (The column marking the reign of Alexander I was built on the orders of Nicholas I, whose intention was to produce a grand monument that could overshadow Peter's fortress and its tall bell-tower.) Nicholas I was criticized by Pushkin and his contemporaries not only for his treatment of the Decembrists but also for his growing interference in censorship and failure to organize evacuation and help for victims of the famous St Petersburg flood of November 1824. Pushkin detects in Nicholas I signs of the anxiety of influence, as well as a tendency towards organizing ever more masquerades that act to confer sanctity on autocracy rather than to liberate the suppressed.

It is not coincidental that Pushkin employs irony in his depiction of Peter and Nicholas. In 'What a night! The hard frost ...' Pushkin uses the first phrase as a mark of irony, suggesting that the poem contains a discourse on love (in the manner of many nineteenth-century love poems) but in the context of the poem its meaning unravels itself as pure mockery. Similarly in 'When the Tsar was frowning ...' Pushkin makes a jester of the Tsar who pretends to be horrified rather than amused. This time St Petersburg with its famous monument to Peter the Great appears a perfect setting for such jokes.

The joke about the moving statue of Peter the Great appears in *The Bronze Horseman*. It has received extensive treatment in Pushkin scholarship. Virolainen, however, argues that there were many legends about the moving statue, including Count A.N. Golitsyn's dream, but all of them were likely to have been inspired by Pushkin's imagination as expressed in *The Bronze Horseman*.[41] The outline of this legend is important because Pushkin's 'When the Tsar was frowning ...' supports an opposite view to Virolainen, that Pushkin was aware of the legend long before writing *The Bronze Horseman* (1833). According to the legend, in 1812 Alexander I intended to move the monument, but Count Golitsyn saw a 'good omen' in his dream and warned him not to do it. In Golitsyn's words, he saw himself walk towards Elagin Island to deliver a report to the Tsar. The Bronze Horseman chased Golitsyn on his way to the palace, and in front of the palace warned the Tsar and Golitsyn that it was not to be moved, because it served as the protector of the city. It is known Golitsyn recounted the dream to Alexander I who changed his mind about moving the monument.[42] Pushkin's version differs in that Alexander I spreads this legend himself, with the purpose of terrorizing his subordinates. Pushkin adds a humorous twist to the story, too.

There may have been many other legends of Peter the Great's statue circulating in St Petersburg, contributing to the growing body of urban tales that accompany the growth of any important trade centre or port city. Falconet himself was partly responsible for the impression his sculpture produced on its observers. First of all, the statue itself was to some extent a parody of Italian equestrian statues, bringing carnivalesque overtones to the city's landscape. According to the critic George Levitine, Falconet chose a simple concept, avoiding any overt symbolic detail:

> In this conception, Falconet departed from the main tradition of equestrian monuments, which took its source in the Roman statue of Marcus Aurelius, in the Capitoline square. This tradition was based on the image of a triumphant horseman mounted on a powerful steed, majestically advancing at a walking pace on the flat surface of a geometrically shaped pedestal. Exemplified during the Italian Renaissance by Donatello's 'Gattamelata' (Padua) and Verocchio's 'Colleoni' (Venice), this type of equestrian representation culminated

in France in Girardon's famous statue of Louis XIV, which stood in the Place Vendôme, in Paris.[43]

There is an inner symbolic meaning in Falconet's equestrian statue, detectable to spectators, arising from Falconet's unusual placing of the monument on the edge of a rocky elevation. This added a certain twist to the old theme, producing an unprecedented dramatic context. However, Falconet explains in some of his letters that he portrayed 'Peter the Great not as a conqueror, but as a benevolent reformer and legislator; the monarch of the "philosophers" and the benefactor of the new Russia'.[44] As Levitine points out:

> In his writings, Falconet repeatedly explained the meaning of various aspects of his statue. Instead of the traditional pseudo-Roman martial attire, the tsar is given a 'heroic' but nondescript garb which, according to the sculptor, belongs to 'men of all times'. The sculptor acknowledges the fact that this garb recalls the shirt worn by Volga boatmen, and one can note an additional, distinctly Russian, touch in the wolf skin used in the monarch's saddle ... He has reached the summit of the rocky elevation that symbolizes the difficulties he has overcome.[45]

Surprisingly, the irony embedded in Falconet's monument has not been adequately discussed. Some distinctly 'barbaric' features of Falconet's horseman reflect the fact that Peter the Great was a jester, disguising himself as a 'people's Tsar'.

It should be noted that from the very beginning of the project there were several factors to inspire the creation of local legends. The monument itself was a living memory of the saga associated with the history of its creation. One of the most striking examples is the stone forming the statue's base. This was made from part of what was known in Russia as the 'Thunderstone' weighing over three million pounds. This gigantic monolith was brought from the Karelian swamp where according to Karelian legend Peter the Great had used it many times as an observation point. The monument itself became part of urban folklore. There were numerous accounts of people witnessing some movement of the statue. The vast space surrounding the monument chiefly contributed to this 'kinetic' effect, as did some important features of the monument itself. In Levitine's view:

> It is not a mere question of size. The arresting effect of this silhouette is also the result of the powerful ascending diagonal movement that abruptly releases its energy after having reached its apogee. Animated by a different rhythm, the theme of upward élan, culmination and break is repeated twice: in the bronze horseman, with the horse rearing over

emptiness, and its mountain-like base, with the jutting shape of the cliff. Naturally this theme is the energizing force of the great triangle that gives the group its monumental character.[46]

The main achievement of the sculptor lies in the theatrically conceived staging. Some contemporaries, including Diderot, referred to Falconet's monument to Peter the Great as 'epic drama', or even 'Falconet's epic poem'.[47]

Theatricality formed an essential part of the Petrine period, and can be seen as part of the living legacy of Peter the Great in St Petersburg. It is not surprising that theatricality was on Pushkin's mind when he wrote such Petersburg tales as *The Queen of Spades*, *The Little House in Kolomna*, *The Bronze Horseman* and *The Lonely Little House on Vassilevskii Island*. It is interesting that the famous flood in St Petersburg significantly undermined popular belief in Peter the Great's God-like and miracle-making qualities. Falconet's monument became the embodiment of Peter the Great's qualities as a protector of the city (perhaps, in the same way as St George served as a protector of Moscow in popular culture).

As Levitine puts it, 'Benevolent or ominous, Peter the Great came to be popular as the jealous guardian of the destiny of the city, a kind of awesome palladium'.[46] As mentioned above, Pushkin's 'When the Tsar was frowning ...' refers to an act of mockery concerning Falconet's statue. Alexander I's attitude was not unique. It is known that Countess Anna Tolstaia, a friend of Pushkin, visited Falconet's monument after the flood of St Petersburg on 7 November 1824, and expressed her disgust at the monument's failure to protect the city by sticking out her tongue at the statue.[48]

The flood produced mixed responses. Some reflected on this event with humour (see the satirical poem in the style of Béranger, written on the day after the event by Aleksandr Izmailov - 'God decided to punish all the sinful here ...'). Others described it in an apocalyptic vein. The number of the texts (especially prose tales) bearing the marks of the unravelling Apocalypse outweighs the number of more humorous or satirical texts. Such works include the historical tale *The Black Box* (1833) (*Черный ящик*) by K.P. Massalskii, a novella *A Dead Man's Joke* (*Живой мертвец*) by V. F. Odoevskii (published in 1833 in the almanac *Dennitsa*), a Petersburg tale *The Feast of Death* (*Торжество смерти*) by V.S. Pecherin (1833), to name just a few. It seems that Pushkin incorporated both tendencies in his Petersburg tales, embedding some parodies on existing texts, too. Among the sources Pushkin uses in *The Bronze Horseman*, Virolainen lists a great number of anecdotes and historical accounts of responses to the flood.[50]

In several ways Virolainen interprets *The Bronze Horseman* as an example of polyphony in the Bakhtinian sense. In Virolainen's view, the historical truth emerges as a collection of voices.[51] Virolainen's opinion appears far-fetched, stretching to some analogies with Dostoevskii's novels which

Bakhtin examined in great detail. To support such a view one needs to rely on the evidence of the dialogical nature of the text. It is difficult, however, to find consistent evidence of dialogue in the narrative nature of *The Bronze Horseman*. The characteristics of Pushkin's narrative are still blurred. There is no agreement between scholars, for example, on which points of view are represented in *The Bronze Horseman*. In contrast to Pushkin's texts, Dostoevskii's novels contain various ideological trends and points of view with clear marks, that is, every voice is definable and distinctive. This is not the case with Pushkin. Evgenii's madness in *The Bronze Horseman* is not readily recognizable. Some scholars see this as the embodiment of realism, while others link it to Romantic tradition, to Shakespeare's drama, or to the representation of the holy fool in Russian popular culture.[52] Perhaps it is more appropriate to characterize *The Bronze Horseman* and other Petersburg tales by Pushkin as representation of cultural memory, expressing anxieties about the city's future destiny.

Under close examination Pushkin's Petersburg texts reveal many links with the popular mythology of the city not primarily centred on Falconet's statue. Thus, Ospovat and Timenchik relate people's fear of the monument to Alexander I, the new landmark of the city unveiled by Nicholas I to the public on 30 August 1834. Pushkin avoided the ceremony, finding it humiliating to appear there as a junior civil servant. Commenting on the enormous weight and height of the column, Countess Anna Tolstaia predicted that it would fall down, and avoided riding near it in her carriage. Alexander I's column became a target of many jokes.[53] Given both popular fears and jokes it is surprising that in the poem *The Monument* (1836) Pushkin chose Alexander's column in front of the Winter Palace for comparison with his own art, the non-verbal monument. Pushkin in referring to the column is suggesting that his own immortalized self be located in the space of St Petersburg. By placing himself in the cultural space of St Petersburg, Pushkin explored the opportunity of reaching a vast audience, making his image as popular and ambivalent as the image of the city itself. Thereby the poet secured his immortality: linking himself to the cultural memory of the city, advancing his ability to mimic different texts as the main virtue of his writing. Furthermore, Pushkin's characterization of himself in *The Monument* as a person who 'told the truth to the Tsars with a smile on his face' compares the poet with Evgenii, his protagonist in *The Bronze Horseman*. Both the prophetic and the humorous traits in Pushkin's art come together when his Petersburg tales are viewed as portraying the city as 'comic apocalypse' (to borrow the definition Mark Seiden applied to Dickens' London[54]).

Pushkin reflected the mood of his St Petersburg and European contemporaries when he expressed disillusion with the noise and growing commercialization of modern, European St Petersburg, the youngest of European capitals. Pushkin's contrasting view of Moscow and St Petersburg in *Evgenii Onegin*, manifesting the archetypal 'Jerusalem-Babylon' model, is comparable to the view of London found in late eighteenth-century British literary tradition.

(The 'Babylonian' view of St Petersburg is strongly pronounced in Pushkin's tale *The Lonely Little House on Vassilevskii Island*, in which the protagonist is a victim of corrupting St Petersburg and withdraws from urban life as a result of his misfortunes.) As one critic concludes:

> Hence the ambivalence that marks the eighteenth-century's confrontation with the city and the deep nostalgia felt by many writers toward the past represented by the classical tradition. They would have liked to live in an idealized classical city, an Athens or Augustan Rome of their imagination - a city of culture in the truest sense. Yet the noise and perpetual whirl of commercial and criminal London kept closing in on them. They couldn't really reconcile the two images, although one has a sense of their having tried desperately to do so. It remained for the Romantics utterly to reject the city as a meaningless and trivial experience.[55]

These words are also applicable, with some modification, to Pushkin's world view. Anna Akhmatova noted the decaying atmosphere of Pushkin's St Petersburg and compared the image of the city in the first chapter of *Evgenii Onegin* with that presented in *The Bronze Horseman*:

> In the first example we see a charming native land through the eyes of Evgenii Onegin, the young exile; in the second example we see Petersburg as a pigsty as presented in Pushkin's letters; it is merciless and gloomy ... The diversity and colourfulness of the scenes in *Eugene Onegin* had vanished in *The Bronze Horseman* ... what is left is the impenetrable darkness and whores. It expresses Pushkin's cry over human life. What is felt is the displacement of the author of *The Bronze Horseman*.[56]

To Akhmatova's observations can be added Pushkin's thoughts about decaying St Petersburg in *Evgenii Onegin*, which she does not refer to. In the first chapter (stanza XXXV) Pushkin depicts the noisy scene of a St Petersburg morning in an ironic way. Pushkin refers to 'the pleasant noises of the morning' in the context of an unappealing St Petersburg setting: all images refer either to military training (allusions to the noises of drums - 'St Petersburg, as busy as ever, had been woken up by drums') or to trade and business activities. We see these morning activities through the eyes of young Onegin returning home exhausted from the ball in the early hours of the morning, so it is difficult not to interpret Pushkin's remark about the pleasant noises of the morning as ironic. Pushkin's ironic viewpoint is also felt in the same chapter's allusion to the blue smoke of chimneys spiralling high into the sky. In this chapter the winter morning landscape is associated with pollution and a busy pace of life, not as enjoyable as the atmosphere Pushkin portrays in his other scenes that romantically idealize winter experiences in the country.

Scholars have overlooked one important aspect of Pushkin's Petersburg. As mentioned earlier, English writers developed the image of the classical city as a product of their imagination, ascribing to it the qualities of truly cultural space. In the context of this comparison, it is important to address the question of Pushkin's ideal city. Did he develop such a view of the classical city? In my view Pushkin expresses his longing for Venice, imagining it as a truly classical and peaceful cultural space. In the opening chapter of *Eugene Onegin* (1: XLIX) Pushkin vividly depicts Venice as a desirable location where he will be free and in love with a Venetian girl, enjoying a ride in a 'mysterious gondola'.[57] In the poem 'Near the places, where a golden Venice rules ...'(1827) Pushkin reproduces the same dream of a peaceful and idyllic ride in a gondola through the canals of Venice. Pushkin compares himself to a young Venetian singing love songs and thinking of sacred poems. In the context of the European tradition of the representation of city life in the pre-Romantic and Romantic period, one may suggest that Pushkin's juxtaposition of Venice and St Petersburg is not coincidental and that it alludes to the image of the still evolving city. This view can be supported by reference to the concealed homage to Venice in *The Bronze Horseman*. Thus at the beginning of *The Bronze Horseman* Pushkin incorporates the words of Venetian citizen Francesco Algarotti, who in a letter in 1739 compared St Petersburg with 'the great window recently opened in the north through which Russia looks on Europe'.[58] In the Notes to *The Bronze Horseman* Pushkin identifies this quotation as a source of his metaphor attributed in the poem to Peter the Great: 'It is determined by Nature for us to cut a window here into Europe'. It is interesting that Pushkin depicts Peter as a mystic and a seer, as if the vision of the city came to him as an inspiration from Venice.

This point should not be overstated however, in the light of the fact that Peter the Great's acquaintance with Venice remains problematic. It is known, for example, that the mutiny of *streltsy* (reflected upon in 'What a night! The hard frost ...') prevented Peter from visiting Venice (he was on his way to Venice but the news of mutiny made him cancel the trip). Pushkin's allusions to Venice are rare, but they do convey mystical overtones suggesting a Romantically idealized cultural space where poetry flourishes and enjoys freedom of expression, allowing spontaneity and exciting ground for mimicry. In this respect, Pushkin's ideal poet is Charskii, protagonist in the tale *Egyptian Nights* (1835). He is a somewhat mystical messenger, reminding Pushkin and his friends of Naples and other Italian locations, where free improvising is a commonplace. Perhaps, Pushkin uses the image of Venice as a political allusion too, fulfilling Mickiewicz's prophecy of the downfall of autocracy in Russia?[59] In the context of Pushkin's poetics, windows are associated with dreaming and seeing into the future. This is particularly evident in Pushkin's portrayal of Tatiana Larina in

Evgenii Onegin and in the poem *To My Nanny*, where both women look through the window and into the future, anticipating events and visitors. By the same token, Pushkin's appropriation of Algarotti's metaphor of St Petersburg as a window looking upon Europe in *The Bronze Horseman* can be treated in the same context, as if Pushkin adds to his list of visionaries not only Tatiana Larina, but Peter the Great, too, and even himself, since the city-window allows the poet to see horizons remote both in place and time (the ideal city of Venice, for example, with liberal atmosphere and free artistic expression).

The image of Venice in Pushkin's poetry can be best described in Bergsonian terms, as an intuitive vision of the future experienced by the poet as a mystical present (see for example, the usage discussed above of the word 'mystical' in Pushkin's references to Venice). It is also important to bear in mind that in Pushkin's dreaming of Venice in 'Near the places where a golden Venice rules …' the poet experiences a prophetic vision in the night, as if this state already foresees Bergson's concept of duration. In Bergson's words, it is a miraculous combination of 'a multiplicity of successive states of consciousness' and of 'a unity that binds them together': 'Duration will be the "synthesis" of this unity and this multiplicity, a mysterious operation which takes place in the darkness'.[60] Bergson brings together temporal and spatial concepts, talking of the flow of duration and comparing it with the flow of a river. In the light of this concept, Pushkin's presentation of himself in the poem 'Near the places where a golden Venice rules …' as a singer in a gondola/boat appears to be profound and far-reaching: he is a seer and a mystic who notices the unfolding images of future Time.

The juxtaposition of St Petersburg and Venice is fully developed in the Russian modernist and post-modernist poetic vision. Such a view contributes to a broader understanding of Pushkin's St Petersburg, the space where Pushkin located many themes and images which were to dominate Russian literature in the next hundred years. As Seiden comments:

> In *The Bronze Horseman* Pushkin shifted the focus of Russian literature from the planned, rational aspects of eighteenth-century Petersburg to the issue which was to dominate so much of nineteenth-century literature: the plight of the insulted and injured in the city.[61]

To modify the socio-political implications of Seiden's view, it should be added that Pushkin reflected on the ambivalent nature of the perception of the city in the nineteenth century, especially after 1825. Pushkin gave greater prominence than did his predecessors to the irrational fears and intuitive tendencies expressed in the urban popular culture of his time.

An extensive intertextual analysis of *The Bronze Horseman*, underlying many of the subtexts found in anecdotes and tales, has been undertaken by Timenchik and Ospovat.[62] Their study opens the possibility of examining further the role of metatextuality in Pushkin's works as regards the representation of St Petersburg. This chapter has attempted to combine the intertextual approach with the psychoanalytical and philosophical, focusing on Pushkin's poetics. It suggests that Pushkin inscribes himself into the broader Petersburg text, making his text part of the cultural memory of the city, participating in both national and world cultures. Such an interpretation of Pushkin's Petersburg texts is possible if we compare Pushkin's inscription of visionary messages with, for example, that of William Blake, who predicted the downfall of London. John Bayley points to a significant difference between the two poets, stressing that in Blake's case:

> Like most poems of the great English romantics they are part of the complex and yet continuous life of the poet's consciousness, and must be understood in its total dimension. The reverse is true of Pushkin's poems. Inherently dramatic, each poem is complete in itself: to read it in the life of others will not extend or modify its meaning. In 'The Prophet' Pushkin incarnates himself as 'prophecy', not as the message a prophet brings.[63]

In the light of Bayley's observations, it would be appropriate to suggest that in his poem *The Monument* (1836) Pushkin reflects on precisely the fact that he incarnated himself as a prophecy in the cultural space of St Petersburg as conveyed in his Petersburg texts.

In *The Monument* the future image of the city unfolds: it is the city where the non-verbal, non-materialistic monument of the poet himself (represented, perhaps, as pure thought, or a part of the oral tradition and cultural memory) will produce a more overpowering effect upon the audience than the monuments of Pushkin's autocratic predecessors and other creators of the Petersburg text. It is as if Pushkin portrays himself in *The Monument* as witnessing how the false idols and inferior cultural landmarks are collapsing, thereby giving prominence to the immortal voice of the Pushkin, the Russian Orpheus, who so aptly compared himself with a Venetian singer-boatman.

NOTES

1. See, for example, Iu. M. Lotman, 'Simvolika Peterburga i problemy semiotiki goroda', in Iu. M. Lotman, ed., Semiotika: Trudy po znakovym sistemam, *XVIII, Uchenye zapiski Tartuskogo gosudarstvennogo universiteta*, 664, Tartu, 1984, pp. 30-45; Z.G Mintz et al., 'Peterburgskii tekst i russkii simvolism' in ibid., pp. 78-92.

2. B. Tomashevskii, 'Peterburg v tvorchestve Pushkina', in B.V. Tomashevskii, *Pushkinskii Peterburg*, Leningradskoe Gazetno-zhurnal'noe knizhnoe izdatel'stvo, Leningrad, 1949, pp. 3-40.

3. L. Mederskii,'Arkhitekturnyi oblik pushkinskogo Peterburga', in ibid., pp. 285-352.

4. S. Schwarzband, *The Logic of Pushkin's Artistic Quest: From 'Yezersky' to 'The Queen of Spades'*, The Magnes Press, The Hebrew University, Jerusalem, 1988; Andrej Kodjak, '"The Queen of Spades" in the Context of the Faust Legend', in Andrej Kodjak et al., eds, *Alexander Pushkin: A Symposium on the 175th Anniversary of His Birth*, New York University Press, New York, 1976, pp. 87-118.

5. R. Jakobson, *Pushkin and His Sculptural Myth*, The Hague, Paris, 1975.

6. John Bayley, *Pushkin: A Comparative Commentary*, Cambridge University Press, Cambridge, 1971.

7. Aleksandr Blok, 'The Poet's Role', quoted from D.J. Richards and C.R.S. Cockrell, editors and translators, *Russian Views of Pushkin*, Willem A. Meeuws, Publisher, Oxford, 1976, pp. 127-134 (127).

8. Ibid., p. 129.

9. Renate Lachmann (translated by Roy Sellars and Antony Wall) 'Intertextuality as an Act of Memory: Pushkin's Transposition of Horace', in id., *Memory and Literature: Intertextuality in Russian Modernism*, University of Minnesota Press, 1997, pp. 194-221.

10. Ibid., p. 234.

11. William Mills Todd III, '"Evgenii Onegin": roman zhizni' in id., ed., *Sovremennoe amerikanskoe pushkinovedenie: sbornik statei*, 'Akademicheskii proekt', St Petersburg, 1999, p.180.

12. Lachman, op. cit., p. 234.

13. Quoted from L. Mederskii, 'Arkhitekturnyi oblik pushkinskogo Peterburga', in B.V. Tomashevskii, ed., *Pushkinskii Peterburg*, Leningradskoe gazetno-zhurnal'noe knizhnoe izdatel'stvo, Leningrad, 1949, p. 304. (Translation is mine. Further quotations from Russian texts are given here in my translation, too.)

14. Arthur J. Witzman, 'Eighteenth-Century London: Urban Paradise or Fallen City?', *Journal of the History of Ideas*, XXXVI, 3, July-September 1975, p. 471.

15. Quoted from A.S. Pushkin, *The Bronze Horseman*, edited with introduction by T.E. Little, Bristol Classical Press, Bristol, 1991, p. xii.

16. A. S. Pushkin, 'Puteshestvie iz Moskvy v Peterburg' in *Sobranie sochinenii v desiati tomakh*, ed. D.D. Blagoi et al., VI, Gosudarstvennoe izdatel'stvo khudozhestvennoi literatury, Moscow, 1962, p. 383.

17. A.S. Pushkin, *Polnoe sobranie sochinenii v desiati tomakh*, second edition, ed. B.V. Tomashevskii, III (Stikhotvoreniia 1827-1836 gg.), Izdatel'stvo Akademii Nauk SSSR, Moscow, 1957, p. 484.

18. Loc. cit.

19. M.N. Virolainen, 'Mednyi vsadnik: peterburgskaia povest'', *Zvezda*, 6, 1999, pp. 208-19 (208).

20. Schwarzband, op. cit., p. 76.

21. John Bayley, op. cit., p.131.

22. N. Nadezhdin, *Vestnik Evropy*, CLXX, 7, 1830, pp. 195-223; quoted from S. Mashinskii, ed., *V mire Pushkina*, Sovetskii pisatel', Moscow, 1974, p. 350.

23. Thus, for example, Viazemskii comments on Smirnova-Rosset, as follows: 'Our beautiful lady could comprehend the art of Raphael, neither did she ignore the art of Turner and Hogarth'. Quoted from A. O. Smirnova-Rosset, *Dnevnik: Vospominaniia*, Nauka, Moscow, 1989, p. 589.

24. Quoted from Richards and Cockrell, op.cit., p. 246.

25. See, for example M.G. Sokolianskii, 'Ironiia v romane "Evgenii Onegin"', *Izvestiia Akademii nauk: seriia literatury i iazyka*, LVIII, 2, 1999, pp. 34-43; V.S. Baevskii, 'Dominanty khudozhestvennoi evoliutsii Pushkina', ibid., pp. 23-33.

26. See, for example, Blagoi's prescriptive recommendation to ignore such as view: 'To see in Pushkin's poetry merely the "elegance of a caricaturist", "amusing prattle", the masterly ability to "turn nature inside-out", and, as a result, to view him simply as a "genius of caricature", a "master of parody" is to misunderstand it completely. (Most of Nadezhdin's articles on Pushkin are an example of such a crude misinterpretation).' Quoted from Richards and Cockrell, op. cit., p. 246.

27. Frederick Antal, *Hogarth and His Place in European Art*, Routledge and Kegan Paul, London, 1962, p. 25.

28. Lindsey Hughes, *Russia In the Age of Peter the Great*, Yale University Press, New Haven and London, 1998, p. 233.

29. Pushkin, op. cit. (note 17), p. 350.

30. Ibid., p. 351.

31. Hughes, op. cit., p. 394.

32. Marina Tsvetaeva, *Moi Pushkin*, Sovetskii pisatel', Moscow, 1967, pp. 73-4.

33. A.S. Pushkin, *Sobranie sochinenie v desiati tomakh*, VII, 'Kritika i publitsistika', Nauka, Leningrad, 1978, p. 101.

34. Hughes, op. cit., p. 253.

35. Pushkin knew the history of the Petrine period very well, especially through his work on Peter the Great in the state archives. Pushkin contemplated writing a book on the history of Peter the Great's reign since 1827 but he started working officially in the archives in 1831. Ivan Musin-Pushkin was the last 'boyar' to be awarded this title by Peter the Great. Following heroic deeds during the battle in Poltava, Musin-Pushkin, a close ally of the Tsar, was promoted rapidly by Peter the Great, becoming one of the Senators of the newly created Senate. Pushkin refers to him extensively in his unfinished historical work *A History of Peter the Great* which was not approved for publication by Nicholas I because of its portrayal of crude and unflattering scenes from Peter the Great's life.

36. A.S. Pushkin, 'Istoriia Petra: podgotovitel'nye teksty', *Sobranie sochinenii v desiati tomakh*, IX, ed. B.V. Tomashevskii, Izdatel'stvo Akademii Nauk SSSR, Moscow, 1958, pp. 5-464 (337).

37. Hughes, op. cit., p. 253.

38. Ibid., p. 266.

39. Pushkin, op. cit. (note 17), II, p. 316.

40. Pushkin, 'Puteshestvie iz Peterburga v Moskvu', op. cit., p. 189.

41. Virolainen, op. cit., p. 213.

42. Loc. cit.

43. George Levitine, *The Sculpture of Falconet*, New York Graphic Society Ltd., Greenwich, Connecticut, 1972, p. 54. On Falconet more generally see chapter 6 of the present volume.

44. Ibid., p. 55.

45. Ibid., pp. 55-6.

46. Ibid., pp. 59-60.

47. Ibid., p. 60.

48. Ibid., p. 59.

49. See, for example, the discussion of this episode in A.L. Ospovat and R.D. Timenchik, *Pechal'nu povest' sokhranit'*, Kniga, Moscow, 1987, p. 24.

50. Virolainen, op. cit., p. 217.

51. Ibid., p. 219.

52. See the discussion of this point in Virolainen's article: ibid., p. 211.

53. Ospovat, op. cit., p. 47.

54. Mark Alexander Seiden, *Dickens' London: The City as Comic Apocalypsis*, unpublished PhD thesis, Cornell University, 1967.

55. Weitzman, op. cit., p. 479.

56. Quoted from Schwarzband, op. cit., p. 222.

57. Pushkin, op. cit. (Note 17), V, Moscow, 1957, p. 30.

58. Quoted from Hughes, op. cit., p. 210.

59. See the discussion of Mickiewicz's poem *Oleszkiewicz* in Little, ed., op. cit., p. 33.

60. Henri Bergson, *An Introduction to Metaphysics*, translated by T.E. Hulme, Macmillan and Co., Ltd, London, 1913, p. 49.

61. Seiden, op. cit., p. 2.

62. Ospovat, op. cit.

63. Bayley, op. cit. p. 145.

Notes of Confusion: On the Footnotes to
The Bronze Horseman

by

MICHAEL BASKER

The following analysis of the footnotes to *The Bronze Horseman* stems from the practical experience of producing detailed annotations to a student edition of Pushkin's poem. At the outset of that project, the obvious editorial question with regard to the author's five short notes had simply been whether to annotate or not: in other words, whether to burden the student reader with footnotes to Pushkin's footnotes. The unexpected complication lay in the sheer volume of commentary that the seemingly flippant, almost inconsequential notes proved to engender. Far from performing a conventional, merely subordinate function of textual elucidation, they appeared, paradoxically, to invite more elaborate explanation than anything in the poem it was their ostensible purpose to illumine. This clearly indicated that the notes should be treated as a fully constituent part of the author's text, and annotated accordingly. But such a task first necessitated a more precise understanding of the functions of the notes.

By virtue of their position at the margin of the text - placed, as it were, between author and poem, and even between author and reader, partially by-passing the poem itself - Pushkin's footnotes might be assumed to have particular bearing on two issues of considerable importance to an interpretation of *The Bronze Horseman*: authorial attitude, and the relevance of extra-textual material. To state the obvious: much of the variety of critical opinion concerning the poem patently derives from the elusiveness of the author's position. So, for example, there is critical disagreement even at the most fundamental level of whether the voice which declares love for 'Peter's creation' should be considered equally, or more, or less authoritative than the voice which declares a conflicting sympathy for the suffering of 'poor Evgenii' - especially in that the closing description of Evgenii's demise and burial echoes and arguably returns the reader to the nearly forgotten terms - and mood, and voice - of the opening eulogy. At the very least, then, the footnotes merit examination as a separate aspect of authorial participation, from which, however naive the expectation in the case of Pushkin, a particularly unmediated formulation of attitude (or manipulation of response) might conceivably be sought.

In practice, of course, the poem's richness of meaning arises as much from lack of homogeneity within each single paragraph, where persistent shifts of linguistic register and generic convention mirror semantic ambiguities, as from broader contrasts in narrative voice between one section and another. This intratextual complexity is potentially much compounded by the the possibility of extra-textual reference. Andrei Belyi, for instance, long ago demonstrated that it is not difficult to compile a series of extracts from Pushkin's correspondence which seems intriguingly subversive of the poet's repeated protestations of 'love' for St Petersburg, or indeed for such specific characteristics as the 'блеск и шум и говор балов' ('sparkle, and sound, and talk of balls') celebrated in the 'Introduction'.[1] It is usual, even *de rigueur*, to discount such extraneous evidence of authorial attitude as irrelevant or at best peripheral to the task of textual interpretation; but it seems not implausible that Pushkin's unusual footnotes, with their orientation beyond as well as towards the poetic text, might also sanction (or necessitate) a broadening of conventional approaches.

To some extent, my analysis is also conceived in response to the detailed recent discussion of the poem's footnotes in Samuil Shvartsband's meticulously researched and challengingly provocative analysis of Pushkin's 'artistic quest' during the mid-1830s. Shvartsband contends that by including the footnotes in the fair copy submitted to the personal scrutiny of Nicholas I:

> Pushkin hoped that his allusions (mention of the Italian historian Algarotti, the Russian poets Viazeskii and Ruban, the Serb Miloradovich and the German Benkendorf) would allow him to 'smuggle through' the only thing necessary to an understanding of the poem - the name of A. Mickiewicz, the Polish poet forbidden in Russia.[2]

For Shvartsband, only two notes (three and five) have genuine significance, while the remainder are essentially a smokescreen to mislead the censor. The view is intriguing not least for the implication that the notes share no single, intrinsic function, and that the role of notes one, two, and four renders futile the search for any such function. This is predicated, however, on a rigorous definition of Pushkin's artistic purpose which is perhaps more compelling than the 'Decembrist' readings of *The Bronze Horseman* and its notes offered by a number of Soviet critics, but troubling in its neglect of anything which falls outside that critical defintion. My own observation is that what the footnotes have primarily in common, and contribute to a reading of the whole, is an unremitting concern with multiplicity as opposed to purposeful singularity of meaning: a mentally subversive openness, which, as we shall see, nevertheless revolves in part around the politically subversive closedness perceived by the émigré critic. In pursuing this argument below, I attempt what amounts to a close contextual reading of each note. I begin with notes three and five, which are treated at length by Shvartsband, but where I would nevertheless claim to add something of my own. Continuing in roughly increasing order of laconicism of annotation, I then proceed through notes one, four and two.

NOTE THREE

> Мицкевич прекрасными стихами описал день, предшествовавший Петербургскому наводнению, в одном из лучших своих стихотворений *Oleszkiewicz*. Жаль только, что описание его не точно. Снегу не было Ё Нева не была покрыта льдом. Наше описание вернее, хотя в нем и нет ярких красок польского поэта.

> (Mickiewicz has described the day preceding the Petersburg flood in beautiful lines from one of his best poems, *Oleskieiwicz*. It is just a pity that his description is not accurate. There was no snow; the Neva was not covered in ice. Our description is truer, though it lacks the bright colours of the Polish poet.)[3]

This third of Pushkin's authorial notes is inserted into the text of part one after the line 'И бледный день уж настает ...' ('And the pale day already dawns'; line 166). It is at once followed by the emotive exclamation 'Ужасный день!' ('Dreadful day!'; line 167). The 'pale' and 'dreadful' day is of course that of the flood of 7 November 1824 (the Neva did not burst its banks until well after dawn, at some time between 10 and 11 a.m.);[4] the passage in question occurs immediately after Evgenii's nocturnal musings on the weather and the rising waters, his job, prospects of marriage, and future life and death with Parasha. All seems straightforward - except that the footnote involves a symptomatic obfuscation. The subtitle of Mickiewicz's poem *Oleszkiewicz* - which Pushkin can be assumed to have known well, for he had taken the trouble to copy it in full into a working notebook, and had its proscribed Parisian publication with him at Boldino as he wrote *The Bronze Horseman*[5] - was *The Day **Preceding** the Inundation of St Petersburg in 1824* (*Dzien **przed** powodzią Peterzburską, 1824* [my emphasis]). The day to which Pushkin's footnote alludes is in other words not the day to which the text of his poem refers. But nor, despite his subtitle, does Mickiewicz properly describe the *day* before the flood. Just as it is 'already late and dark' (line 103) when Pushkin's Evgenii is first introduced, returning home on the eve of the disaster, so Mickiewicz's dark, lantern-lit narrative begins with the gathering dusk, and comes to a close at the dead of night, when all are in their beds.

The subject-matter of *Oleszkiewicz* is less problematic. Oleskiewicz, a venerable Polish artist, Mason and occultist, 'well known in St Petersburg', according to the footnote supplied by Mickiewicz, 'for his virtues, his deep learning and his mystic prophecies',[6] is observed by a group of his compatriots as he mysteriously measures the depths of a tributary of the Neva. His calculations move him to pronounce aloud on the impending flood, which he describes as the second 'but not the last' of three Biblical trials miraculously sent by the Lord to shake the 'Assyrian throne', the 'foundations of Babylon'.[7] The third will be more terrible still. Oleszkiewicz moves on through the night, and halts to speak again in view of the Winter Palace, where the 'aging soul' of Alexander has sunk 'ever deeper under Satan's guile'. It is because Alexander has flouted the will of the Lord that Divine wrath will be visited on his people, and the poem closes with the 'unchained oceans' poised to break upon the city. This stark prophecy, of disaster preceding cataclysmic disaster, is all the more powerfully emphatic in that *Oleszkiewicz* is the sixth and final poem of the *Digression* (*Ustęp*), which itself brings to a close part three of Mickiewicz's *Forefathers' Eve* (*Dziady*). It is followed only by the vitriolic epilogue-dedication *To Russian Friends* (*Do przyjaciół Moskali*).

The poem's references to (melting) snow and ice, to which Pushkin takes exception in his note, are a fleeting and seemingly peripheral preliminary. One recent critic has therefore taken Pushkin's pedantry in this matter as a covert allusion to the Decembrist Revolt, when ice and snow were indeed abundantly present.[8] Over the *Digression* as a whole, however, the freezing, hostile Russian climate forms a persistent leitmotif, which stands as an unmistakable symbol of lifeless, autocratic oppression. It is generally agreed, moreover, that Pushkin's famous affirmation of love for the Petersburg winter in the 'Introduction' to *The Bronze Horseman* ('Люблю зимы твоей жестокой / Недвижный воздух и мороз, / Бег санок вдоль Невы широкой, / Девичьи лица ярче роз ...' [lines 59-62] ['I love your cruel winter's / Immobile air and frost, / The rush of sleighs along the wide Neva, / Maidens' faces brighter than roses ...']) involves a polemical rebuttal of precisely this aspect of Mickiewicz's satire (with a more specific rejoinder to Mickiewicz's unflattering description in poem three of the *Digression* of a frost-afflicted lady of the capital, her face 'crab-red and snowy white of hue').[9] There is therefore little reason not to read in similar vein Pushkin's footnoted reference to metereological misrepresentation in *Oleszkiewicz*: as a rejection both of Mickiewicz's uncompromising denunciation of Alexander I's rule, and of his prediction of the imminent, inevitable, justly deserved fall of autocracy. As Shvartsband argues, if Mickiewicz cannot be relied upon even to get the weather right, his poem can easily be dimsissed as nothing more than what Pushkin terms 'beautiful lines' and 'bright colours'.[10] Mickiewicz's prophetic-apocalyptic interpretation of the flood is not well-grounded in truth.

The concern with 'accuracy' and 'fidelity' which Pushkin's footnote accordingly emphasizes is consistent with a similar insistence in his 'Foreword' to the poem: 'The event described in this tale is based on the truth. The details of the flood are taken from journals of the time. The curious may consult the account compiled by V.N. Berkh'. (It might be observed that this invocation of extra-textual reality, and Pushkin's quite specific reference to documentary sources including Berkh's 1826 compilation *A Detailed Historical Account of All the Floods that Have Occurred in Saint Petersburg* [*Подробное историческое   известие о всех наводнениях, бывших в Санктпетербурге*], lend his brief 'Foreword' the characteristics of another, preliminary footnote.) The claim to authenticity is perhaps not substantially altered either by the unspoken implication that Pushkin - who had been confined in exile at Mikhailovskoe in 1824, at the time of the 'event' the poem describes - was obliged to use secondary sources rather than first-hand observation; or by the consideration that the section of Berkh's pamphlet devoted to the flood of 1824 was written by Faddei Bulgarin (whom Pushkin not surprisingly refrains from naming).[11] We shall nevertheless have occasion to return below to Pushkin's assessment of the accounts of Berkh and others as an official half-truth, open to dispute. As for his claim to greater veracity than Mickiewicz, the polemical assertion of factual authority in the footnote is tacitly replicated by the poetics of the text. In place of Mickiewicz's high Romanticism, Pushkin provides in the passage which leads up to note three a sustained example of the unflamboyant realism perhaps appropriate to a 'Petersburg tale' (*Петербургская повесть*).[12] At roughly the same time of the same night during which Mickiewicz presents Oleszkiewicz and his sombre prophecies, Pushkin depicts Evgenii and his unsublime thoughts. Oleszkiewicz seems tireless; Evgenii does eventually close his sleepy eyes. Instead of the disputed snow which in Mickiewicz melts into a 'Stygian' flood, Pushkin describes (cf. 'our description is truer') rain and November wind; and it might be argued that in marked contrast to the 'beautiful lines' he attributes to Mickiewicz, Pushkin affects an unglamorous prosaicism. As so often in *The Bronze Horseman*, he obscures the metrical contour and disrupts the rhythm of his verse by a combination of frequent enjambement and mid-line syntactic breaks; and he underscores his departure from the conventionally poetic with a liberal dose of colloquial particles and conjunctions (Так; не так; чтобы; наконец; И вот; уж). And if Pushkin finds 'bright colours' in Mickiewicz, his own work offers a 'pale' dawn:

> Так он мечтал. И грустно было
> Ему в ту ночь, и он желал,
> Чтоб ветер дул не так уныло
> И чтобы дождь в окно стучал
> Не так сердито ...
> Сонны очи
> Он наконец закрыл. И вот
> Редеет мгла ненастной ночи
> И бледный день уж настает ... [3]
> Ужасный день!

(ll. 159-67)

(Those were his dreams. And he felt sad
On that night, and he wished
That the wind did not blow so dismally
And that the rain did not beat against the window
So angrily ...
His somnolent eyes
He closed at last. And now
The gloom of the inclement night thins,
And the pale day already dawns...
Dreadful day!)

While this series of juxtapositions appears entirely clear-cut, it is nevertheless compromised from within: the first five of the lines just quoted have an unmistakable source - quite astonishing in a Realist context - in the opening episodes of that quintessential exemplar of the Gothic 'tale of terror', Charles Maturin's *Melmoth the Wanderer*:

> John looked at his manuscript with some reluctance, opened it, passed over the first lines, and as the wind sighed round the desolate apartment, and the rain pattered with a mournful sound against the dismantled window, wished - what did he wish for? - he wished the sound of the wind less dismal, and the dash of the rain less montonous. - He may be forgiven, it was past midnight, and there was not a human being awake but himself within ten miles ...[13]

Not entirely perversely, Pushkin's borrowing from Maturin could in one respect be taken to confirm the Realist pattern. Pushkin, like Maturin (and of course Mickiewicz), is prepared to portray ужас (horror): but in demonstrative contrast to the nocturnal terror spawned by the Gothic-Romantic imagination, his text presents a horror which is objective and diurnal - the stark, waking *reality* of an 'ужасный день'. Yet if Pushkin is invoking the Romantic in order to distance himself from it, Maturin's Romanticism - surely a reflection of the author-narrator's bookishness, rather than Evgenii's - does nevertheless inform the presentation of Evgenii's 'reality'. And it is plain from what follows that Pushkin's divergence from the Romantic model is indeed less than complete.

Evgenii is lost to the narrative for a while, until he re-emerges astride the marble lion outside the Lobanov-Rostovskii mansion, and has a vision (or imagines a scene) of uncertain ontological status: 'Или во сне / Он это видит?' ('Or is it in a dream / That he sees this?'). The Romantic dream motif is familiar enough even from Pushkin's own earlier work,[14] and there may be a further specific parallel to Melmoth the younger, as he eventually lays aside the manuscript at the end of the third chapter of Maturin's novel: 'But (for Melmoth never could decide) was it in a dream or not that he saw the figure of his ancestor appear at the door? ... Melmoth started, sprung from his bed, it was broad daylight'.[15] Evgenii henceforth becomes a homeless 'wanderer', filled with 'dreadful' thoughts,[16] and has a second, more horrific, though scarcely more objectively 'real' vision, of Peter (his metaphorical progenitor?) or his statue in sinister, quasi-demonic, reanimated form.[17] (Melmoth's less metaphorical, unequivocally demonic, reanimated ancestor whispers 'I am alive - I am beside you'.)[18] For all its anti-Romanticism, Pushkin's text remains much beholden to Romantic stereotypes. In similar fashion, it is anti-apocalyptic-eschatological, at the point where note three engages in polemic with Mickiewicz, and yet elsewhere apocalyptic on its own account.[19] Small wonder, then, that it lays claim to accuracy and realistic truth in a footnote which itself contains a factual inaccuracy (the 'wrong' day!); and that the broad spirit of the footnote is contravened by the precise detail of the accompanying text.

NOTE FIVE

The other footnote to make reference to Mickiewicz conveys an initial impression of informative, academic brevity: 'Смотри описание памятника в Мицкевиче. Оно заимствовано из Рубана - как замечает сам Мицкевич'. ('See the description of the monument in Mickiewicz. It is taken from Ruban - as Mickiewicz himself observes'.) On closer consideration, however, significant contrarieties again emerge.

Unlike note three, which attaches to one of the poem's less prominent lines, the fifth footnote is related to one of its most striking and politically sensitive passages: 'О мощный властелин судьбы! / Не так ли ты над самой бездной, / На высоте, уздой железной / Россию поднял на дыбы?' (lines 420-3) ('O powerful master of fate! / Have you not thus, over the very abyss, / On high, with iron bridle, / Raised Russia on to its hind legs?')

The overt function of the note is to indicate that the terms in which Pushkin portrays the monument are not his own invention. They derive from Mickiewicz, who borrowed in turn from the poet and historian Vasilii Grigorevich Ruban (1742-95): specifically, as will be confirmed below, from Ruban's eight-line poem of 1770, *Inscription for the Stone Intended as a Pedestal for the Statue of the Emperor Peter the Great* (*Надпись к камню, назначенному для подножия статуи императора Петра Великого*). For Ruban, the so-called 'Thunder Stone' was superior to the pagan wonders of the ancient world - the Colossus of Rhodes or the pyramids of the Nile. It is truly miraculous, for it is 'not made by hands', and its arrival in St Petersburg, obedient to 'the voice of God from Catherine's lips', confirms both Catherine and Peter as the vessels of Divine will and favour.[20] Although any reference to Mickiewicz is potentially provocative, a footnote alluding also to Ruban - whose poem was widely known in Pushkin's day, and commonly regarded as his most (or only!) memorable piece[21] - could in other words be taken to indicate that Pushkin's description of the rearing statue is fundamentally sound. Pushkin may have enjoyed a subversive awareness that Nicholas found the elevation of Catherine to equality with Peter personally distasteful;[22] but its political origins are outwardly impeccable.

Clearly, however, it is at least equally possible to interpret quite differently a note which makes combined reference to both Mickiewicz and Ruban: the fierce critic of Russian autocracy, and its devoted apologist. If the incongruity of their juxtaposition is too striking to ignore, the obvious implication is that the text, too, is deeply equivocal in its attitude to state and statue: at once both 'for' and 'against' the statue and everything it might connote, in much the same way, perhaps, that it is simultaneously both Romantic and non-Romantic, apocalyptic and non-apocalyptic. The only difficulty in this - as the reaction of Pushkin's first reader, Nicholas I, seems to confirm - is that a footnote which is itself ambiguous seems scarcely necessary to emphasize the inherent ambiguity of the image of the rearing statue, poised on the edge of the abyss.[23] Unless the purpose of the note is somehow to (re-)assert the relevance of Mickiewicz to Pushkin's conceptions - and presumably to do so in a way different to note three - it is liable to appear ineffectually redundant. (Moreover, the impression of redundancy was perhaps reinforced by Pushkin's unhelpful obscurity. Mickiewicz's *Digression* was unpublished and forbidden in Russia in 1833. Though censorship undoubtedly prompted caution, Pushkin was more reticent - or off-hand? - even than in note three in identifying his sources, and offered no illustrative quotation to supplement his meagre references.)

The particularly well-informed reader - or an exceptionally determined 'curious' reader, such as the 'Foreword' enjoins to seek elucidatory information - will nevertheless recognize that the 'description in Mickiewicz' to which the note so cryptically alludes is from *The Digression's* fourth poem, *The Monument of Peter the Great* (*Pomnik Piotra Wielkiego*):

> Car Piotr wypuszczał rumakowi wodze,
> Widać, że leciał tratując po drodze;
> Od razu wskoczył aż na sam brzeg skały.
> Już koń szalony wzniósł w górę kopyta,
> Car go nie trzyma, koń wędzidłem zgrzyta,
> Zgadniesz, że spadnie i pryśnie w kawały.

> (His charger's reins Tsar Peter has released;
> It has been flying down the road, perchance,
> And here the precipice checks its advance.
> With hoofs aloft now stands the maddened beast,
> Champing its bit unchecked, with slackened rein:
> You guess that it will fall and be destroyed.)[24]

Though the wording of the footnote implies similarity, these lines provide obvious grounds for contrast rather than direct comparison with Pushkin's text. Mickiewicz's rider has loosened the reins and is unable to control his horse. Only the precipice checks its 'flight', and though it now rears aloft at the edge in (literally) frozen motion, the poem's remaining few lines make clear that a thaw will eventually come, and horse and rider must indeed topple. In this context, Pushkin's description seems a model of political loyalty. His 'powerful master of fate' controls his horse with an 'iron bridle'. The Tsar, not the precipice, holds its gallop in dramatic check, and he draws his mount upward with a deliberateness which must surely connote triumphant realization of destiny rather than heedless courting of imminent disaster.

While this indeed comes close to emphatically repetitive reinforcement of the refutation of Mickiewicz's political position in note three, one potentially significant difference is a greater degree of personal involvement. Mickiewicz's 'description' is presented not as that of the Polish author-narrator, but of 'a Russian bard / Famous for his songs through all the North'.[25] Pushkin was at once inclined to relate this figure to himself. The identity was regarded as 'obvious' by the two poets' mutual friend, Prince P.A. Viazemskii (of whom more presently);[26] and it has been widely accepted in studies of Pushkin's relationship to Mickiewicz.[27] Nor, however, could Pushkin have failed to see himself also in the unflattering portrait of the poet who 'betrays his free soul to the tsar for hire' and 'with venal tongue … lauds the tyrant' in *the Digression's* epilogue, *To Russian Friends*.[28] Shvartsband contends that Pushkin's footntote - or more precisely, the textual contrast to which it draws oblique attention - represents a considered attempt to deny his connection with Mickiewicz's first 'bard', and so to reject any imputation of political duplicity arising from conflicting portraits at two different points of *The Digression*.[29] But this is to postulate a puzzlingly obscure method of refuting an identity which others found self-evident; and as we shall see, the argument apparently ignores the second sentence of Pushkin's note.

If we suppose instead that Pushkin - in a literary epoch whose fondness for prototypes he indulged to the full - did not seek to reject outright his identity with Mickiewicz's bard, then his note and related text must be taken to imply either that Mickiewicz distorts the truth in attributing to Pushkin as 'Russian bard' sentiments which he did not share; or that the author of *The Bronze Horseman* had himself radically altered - to the point described in *To Russian Friends* - from a time when, in personal conversation with the Polish poet, he might have concurred that the Russian autocracy amounted to ill-directed rule by a 'wielder of the knout' ('Car knutowładny').[30] Viazemskii, some forty years later, lent authority to the former alternative, maintaining that Mickiewicz 'attributes to Pushkin words that he undoubtedly did not utter; but this is poetic and political licence'.[31] Nor is it surprising that veracity is once more an explicit textual issue. Mickiewicz, in a footnote of his own to *The Monument of Peter the*

Great, insisted that his poem was based on accurate observation: 'The colossal equestrian statue of Peter, designed by Falconet, and the statue of Marcus Aurelius that now stands in Rome on the Capitoline Hill are here faithfully described'.[32] There seems litle doubt that Pushkin mimicked this wording in his third footnote. The implication of the textual contrast encouraged by note five is of course that Mickiewicz's claim to faithful rendition is ill-founded. Mickiewicz distorts the image of the statue, which Pushkin corrects and reinterprets. It might therefore be inferred that Mickiewicz also distorts the image of Pushkin as Russian bard.

This relatively clear-cut piece of self-vindication is, however, substantially subverted by the curious second sentence of Pushkin's footnote: 'It is taken from Ruban - as Mickiewicz himself observes'. Mickiewicz's 'observation' comes in another footnote to a single line of his poem, describing how the statue's huge granite pedestal is transported 'from Finland's shore' on Catherine's order, 'And falls into its place at her command'. It states: 'This line is translated from a Russian poet whose name I do not remember'.[33] In supplying the missing name of Ruban, Pushkin could again claim greater accuracy than Mickiewicz. Yet his conscientious (and patriotic?) concern for precision might seem ironic in a series of footnotes beginning with a casual 'somewhere' in reference to Algarotti (note one); and such irony is greatly compounded by a grotesque imprecision in the note's imputation that not just a single line, but the entire 'description of the monument' which is the essential subject-matter of Mickiewicz's poem, was 'taken from Ruban'. At best, this reflects a wilful misreading of the heavy irony in Mickiewicz's description of the statue's autocratic origins and connotations. It also betrays a confusion of the Classical (Ruban) and the Romantic (Mickiewicz) so astonishing in Pushkin that it can scarcely be taken seriously. The charge of unoriginality is all the more preposterous in that the poem by Ruban to which 'Mickiewicz himself' alludes does not depict the *statue* of the imperial horseman at all: it merely commemorates the arrival in St Petersburg - a full twelve years before the statue's ceremonial unveiling - of the piece of granite intended for its pedestal. An obvious conclusion is that Pushkin, understandably resentful of his own distorted representation by Mickiewicz, somewhat petulantly out-distorts Mickiewicz in response.

But the 'alternative' interpretation is equally and perhaps simultaneously conceivable. If the first sentence of note five, taken alone, is clear - Pushkin is more loyal than Mickiewicz - the second introduces a startling incongruity: Mickiewicz himself is indebted to a sycophantically loyalist source. These profoundly incompatible statements are particularly inappropriate to the uncompromisingly single-minded Polish poet. By contrast, however, the ability to encompass mutually exclusive meanings (and to combine contrasting generic features - Classical-odic, Romantic, Realist) seems thoroughly characteristic of Pushkin, whose very footnote is near-impenetrably inconsistent.

It embodies a tension between deceptive semblance of surface simplicity and elusive underlying complexity; and engenders nothing if not further reflection on notions of exactitude/inexactitude, consistency/inconsistency. Perhaps, then, Pushkin's overt focus on Mickiewicz reveals something of greater relevance to himself, and the annotation which invites comparison between his description of the statue and that by Mickiewicz's 'bard' does after all involve an underlying admission of his own change of political heart. It is tempting to conjecture that the element of shame involved in this painfully oblique admission was partially transposed into the resentment against Mickiewicz noted in the previous paragraph.

The technique of self-revelation through attention to another writer is not unfamiliar in Pushkin (indeed, Belyi appears to detect a comparable procedure behind the flippant reference to Count Khvostov in part two of *The Bronze Horseman*).[34] Moreover, Ruban, too, was evidently of greater concern to Pushkin than to Mickiewicz; at any rate, Pushkin was again mindful of Ruban's *Inscription* when he composed his *Monument* in 1836.[35] And the oblique obscurity of Pushkin's footnote also becomes more comprehensible in view of the intensely personal and potentially troubling nature of the delicate ideological issue involved. Doubtless, however, the private unease in relation to Mickiewicz which Pushkin seems to signal at the very margin of his text was not limited to his awareness of an alteration over time in attitude to the autocracy. It presumably extended also to the continuing capacity for inner inconstancy or contrariety (including, as we saw in the polemic against Mickiewicz in note three, in ways subversive of his own position) which made him so different from his uncompromising Polish counterpart. This capacity is further manifest in the three remaining notes.

NOTES ONE AND FOUR

The almost parodically casual 'somewhere (or other)' which begins the first of the poem's footnotes has led to critical disagreement concerning Pushkin's exact source: 'Альгаротти где-то сказал: "Pétersbourg est la fenêtre par laquelle la Russie regarde en Europe"' ('Algarotti somewhere said: "Petersburg is the window through which Russia looks on to Europe"'). N.V. Izmailov, summarizing previous research, has indicated that the phrase could have been taken directly from the French translation of the Italian Enlightenment author's *Lettere sulla Russia* (1739), or borrowed second-hand from a compilation of 1802 (*Tableau général de la Russie moderne et situation politique de cet Empire au commencement du XIXe siècle*) which Pushkin is known to have had in his library. In either case, Pushkin took an interest in Algarotti's dictum as early as 1826-7, while he was working on chapters four and five of *Evgenii Onegin*.[36] More significant for interpretation of *The Bronze Horseman*, however, is the relationship of Pushkin's footnote to his poetic text, which is that of foreign original - or rather, foreign (French) translation of foreign (Italian) original - to Russian 'translation'. Coincidentally or not, the collocation of different linguistic (and stylistic) systems (Russian-foreign or Russian-Russian) is far more readily associated precisely with *Onegin*, where 'translation' is both explicitly thematized, and an important component of the novel's poetics.[37] In *The Bronze Horseman*, the habitual polarities of foreign/poetic: Russian/ prosaic have been superficially reversed.[38] The (cultural?) discrepancy between French prose annotation and associated lines of Russian verse ('Природой здесь нам суждено / В Европу прорубить окно' [lines 15-16] ['By nature we are fated here / To cut a window on to Europe]) is none the less fruitfully productive of meaning.

In the French quotation from Algarotti, the verb *regarder* characterizes a generalized and essentially static contemplation. This is transformed in Pushkin's Russian 'translation', which substitutes the person of Peter the Great for the impersonal *la Russie*, and presents Peter's mental confrontation with destiny as vigorous action. Moreover, Pushkin's choice of active verb - 'прорубить' - particularly suggests the use of an axe, and so (most charitably) evokes admiration for Peter in his practical guise of carpenter-builder. To the extent that the verb tends to convey rough force rather than sophisticated precision, there is also a potential irony: the 'window' which will open Russian darkness to Western light (the Enlightenment of Algarotti and others) will be fashioned by Peter not with refined western tools, but with the traditional implement of the Russian peasant. And of course the axe in the hands of Peter the Great might also suggest sinister menace: the cruelty of the executioner, who was reputed to have wielded the axe personally against many of the *Streltsy* in 1698 and 1699.[39] Thus the discrepancy between note and text serves both to commend Peter's energy and to indicate the dark underside of his wilful project of enlightenment.[40] The note complicates and subverts the surface meaning of the text (praise of Peter's vision), and perhaps anticipates thereby the type of complex reading admissible throughout the laudatory 'Introduction'.

Though we must return briefly to note one below, this is nevertheless straightforward enough by comparison to the 'Mickiewicz' notes; and note four seems more transparent still in underscoring an irony plainly inherent in the text. This note could scarcely be more perfunctory: 'Граф Милорадович и генерал-адъютант Бенкендорф' ('Count Miloradovich and Adjutant-General Benkendorf'). It appears to perform the simplest of footnote functions in its minimalist identification of textual referents, and is attached to the passage near the close of part one which describes the relief efforts made at Alexander's behest in immediate response to the flood:

Царь молвил - из конца в конец
По ближним улицам и дальным

В опасный путь средь бурных вод
Его пустились генералы[4]
Спасать и страхом обуялый
И дома тонущий народ.   (lines 214-9)

(The Tsar pronounced - from end to end
By near streets and far
On a dangerous path amid stormy waters
His generals set forth
To save the people seized with fear
And drowning at home.)

Contemporary accounts by Berkh and others had made much of the heroic participation of the military Governor-General of St Petersburg and the future chief of the Corps of Gendarmes in sailing unhesitatingly forth on the day of the disaster 'for the profferment of assistance and the encouragement of the inhabitants'.[41] For Pushkin to name them was perhaps no more than accuracy or even deferential propriety demanded; and though the two 'generals' were consigned to the relative obscurity of a footnote (in contrast to the senator and versifier Count Khvostov, who appears in the body of the poem at line 344), there was nothing here to which the imperial authorities (or Benkendorf himself) could reasonably have objected. A satirical element of deflationary bathos is nevertheless difficult to ignore. The poetic text amplifies a contrast between the Tsar's immobile contemplation of the 'evil calamity' (lines 207-9), and the resolute activity of his 'unleashed' generals. An impression of their dynamism is built up by the syntactic parallelism of three consecutive adverbial clauses, each introduced by prepositions, over the first three of the lines quoted above. Anticipation of the repeatedly delayed subject is heightened by the mild inversion of verb and noun which places генералы (generals) at the end of the fourth line, and at this climactic (but not conclusive) point of the sentence, the footnote reference is inserted. The note's disclosure that the generals are only two in number - fewer even than the number of adverbial clauses - cannot fail to appear at least mildly anticlimactic. So, too, must the verbal complement, which prolongs the sentence for a further two lines after the interruption of the note.

Although the absurdity is less overt than in the comic episode from the poem's drafts which showed Miloradovich sailing 'in a boat along Morskaia Street' past the window of an astonished Senator V.V. Tolstoi,[42] it is enough to allow Pushkin a satirical dig at two high officials who had each had a hand in determining his personal fate. (Benkendorf's long and baleful connection with Pushkin after his return from Mikhailovskoe in 1826 is too familiar to require comment; Miloradovich had summoned Pushkin to interrogation in 1820 and, though apparently more favourably disposed towards him than Alexander I, had overseen his dispatch into Southern exile.[43]) The satire arguably acquires darker overtones from the recollection that both generals were likewise 'unleashed' on to Senate Square against the Decembrist 'flood' of 1825; but here the issue becomes typically double-edged. Any inclination to detect a covert expression of pro-Decembrist sympathy must surely be tempered by awareness that Miloradovich was fatally wounded by the Decembrist rebel Kakhovskii. Such extra-textual association might lead in turn to consideration of the propriety of the footnote's satirical barb, apparently directed in equal measure against the dead 'general' (against whom Pushkin's grudge was presumably the lesser) as well as the living Benkendorf.[44] Just as Pushkin's reaction to news of the flood in 1824 was ribald amusement later followed by serious concern for the victims and consequences,[45] so elements of 'inappropriately' black humour are a component of Pushkin's contradictory creation at several points throughout the poem and notes.

The discrepancy between semblance of action and inadequate implementation to which the combination of text and note here directs attention might be taken to criticize not just the serio-comic failings of a flood-relief effort which - to conflate fiction with 'extra-textual reality' - cannot even reach Evgenii, not left 'to drown at home', but unrescued in the immediate proximity of Alexander's Winter-Palace balcony. It presumably reflects also on the failings of official versions of events. Despite numerous anecdotes recording the brave deeds of ordinary people,[46] Berkh, for instance, describes only Miloradovich's heroism during the flood, and singles out the actions of generals and government alone. Pushkin's mock-heroic tone, his implication that the generals reach the entire city, and that the 'people drowning at home' merely wait passively for their salvation, evidently parodies the glib satisfaction of Berkh-Bulgarin's 'documentary' account: 'Within twenty-four hours there was not a single person in the capital without food and shelter. The speed and efficiency of the government's measures averted the consequences of this disastrous event: poverty and disease'.[47] *The Bronze Horseman* refutes this propagandist version in points of detail[48] as in the entire, comfortless story of Evgenii's descent into poverty and death; and the note which identifies the generals is a signal component of Pushkin's sceptical subversion. But of course the anti-establishment stance of note four is (perhaps consistently!) inconsistent with the ostensibly pro-establishment viewpoint of the two notes which engage with Mickiewicz. Moreover, the source whose authority Pushkin chiefly subverts is in this instance precisely that which he invoked in the 'Foreword' as an authoritative measure of his own poem's authenticity.

It is therefore scarcely surprising that the 'greater realism' which Pushkin offers tends also to undermine the artificialities of literary realism. Although note one appears to do what a footnote should in identifying (albeit imperfectly) a literary source, the quotation from Algarotti's work of the late 1730s is incorporated not into authorial narrative, but into the thoughts attributed directly to Peter the Great as he contemplates the foundation of his city in 1703.

The very presence of the note, that is, tacitly underlines the implausibility of the real, historical Peter ever thinking the aphoristic formula derived from Algarotti. It draws indirect attention to the fictionality of Pushkin's Peter, and the relation of Pushkin as creator to Peter as creator. Pushkin's poem and his creation of meaning have precedence over Peter and his creation of history.

NOTE TWO

Though it would be misleading to promise resolution, several of the considerations described above come together beneath the innocent-seeming second note: 'Смотри стихи кн. Вяземского к графине З***'. ('See Prince Viazemskii's verses to Countess Z***'). Here again, a somewhat cryptic footnote apparently makes due acknowledgement of a literary source. Again this puzzles rather than elucidates. The lines indicated, and routinely cited in editions of *The Bronze Horseman*, are from Viazemkii's *Conversation of 7 April 1832* (*Разговор 7 апреля 1832 года*): 'Я Петербург люблю, с его красою стройной, / С блестящим поясом роскошных островов, / С прозрачной ночью - дня соперницей беззнойной - / И с свежей зеленью младых его садов'.[49] ('I love Petersburg, with its shapely beauty, / With its dazzling belt of luxuriant islands, / With its transparent night - unsultry rival of the day - / And the fresh verdure of its young gardens'.)

The poem was dedicated to Countess E.M. Zavadovskaia, and published just a few months before Pushkin began work on *The Bronze Horseman*. He, too, had dedicated a poem of 1832 to Zavadovskaia.[50] Although such compositional details might be expected to reinforce the implied affinity, Viazemskii's lines do not, however, bear very close thematic or stylistic resemblance to the relevant passage from Pushkin: 'И не пуская тьму ночную / На золотые небеса, / Одна заря сменить другую / Спешит, дав ночи   полчаса' (lines 55-8) . ('And not allowing night-time dark / Upon the golden heavens, / One dawn hurries to replace / Another, giving half an hour to night.')

In fact, the stanza from Viazemskii seems scarcely closer to Pushkin's quatrain than the following extract from the 'charming description of a Petersburg night' in N.I. Gnedich's idyll *The Fishermen* (*Рыбаки*) - which Pushkin had quoted at length in the footntoes to *Evgenii Onegin*,[51] and which, it could be argued, he reworks here in a different stylistic key:

Вот ночь: но не меркнут златистые полосы облак.
Без звезд и без месяца вся озаряется дальность.
… Сияньем бессумрачным небо ночное сияет,
И пурпур заката сливается с златом востока:

Как будто денница за вечером следом выводит
Румяное утро.[52]

(Night is here: but the golden strands of cloud do not darken.
Without stars and without moon the whole distance is illumined.
… The night sky shines its twilightless shine
And the crimson of sunset merges into the gold of the east:
As though dawn brings forth on the heels of evening
The rosy morning.)

The question therefore arises as to why Pushkin should choose to acknowledge a fleeting debt to Viazemskii - but not also, for instance, to Gnedich (as he had done in *Evgenii Onegin*), to K.D. Batiushkov (to whose 'Walk in the Academy of Arts' ['Прогулка в Академии художеств'] the 'Introduction' certainly owes more than to Viazemskii's poem), or to prominent and less prominent representatives of the Russian odic tradition from Lomonosov and Trediakovskii onward. His borrowings of course extend also to foreign sources (Joseph de Maistre, for one, was a comparably unacknowledged yet more substantial influence than Algarotti).[53] In this context, the minimal reference to Viazemskii - after the effort of expansion by the 'curious' reader, from single initial of dedicatee, to identity of dedicatee, to title, to 'relevant' lines - is liable to appear parodically inconsequential. Perhaps, however, by indicating a single tenuous source, Pushkin indeed draws attention by default to the many sources he fails to acknowledge through the meagre sequence of five footnotes. Such characteristic misdirection might be regarded as an assertion of creative independence broadly comparable to that which in note one implicitly elevates the creative personality over historical contingency: at issue here is the unconstrained liberty with which, nowhere more conspicuously than in *The Bronze Horseman*, Pushkin plunders from previous writers and traditions to create something uniquely his own.

In another respect, the reference to Viazemskii nevertheless prompts another indirect chain of association which returns us from creative liberty to political anxiety. (This is unrelated to possible echoes of other motifs from Viazemskii's poem, such as the city's green gardens and islands, elsewhere in Pushkin's 'Introduction'.)[54] Viazemskii's expression of 'love' for St Petersburg in the poem to Zavadovskaia ('Я Петербург люблю' ['I love Petersburg']: an assertion he repeats in the stanza following the one quoted above) is advanced in apologetic repudiation of his 'mad' invective *against* the city in the 'conversation' with the dedicatee to which his title refers. Pushkin, therefore, would doubtless have been mindful also of Viazemskii's poem of 1828, 'I do not love Petersburg' ('Я Петербурга не люблю').[55] This then unpublished (and unpublishable) piece was a vitriolic diatribe against the tense, inimical life of the imperial city, bureaucratically regimented under the eye of the Chief of Police.

Pushkin had in his papers a manuscript copy, written out for him by Viazemskii.[56] For anyone sufficiently well-informed - no longer, however, even the most conscientious of general readers, but only an intimate circle of friends familiar with Viazemskii's unpublished work - Pushkin's footnote hints once again at the possibility of a diametrically opposed, negative perception of St Petersburg present beneath, or in conjunction with, the overtly unclouded panegyric of the opening. It thereby serves once more to cast doubt on the reliability and/or sincerity of Pushkin's own text, and confirms the oblique subversion of outwardly unelusive sense as a persistent feature of *The Bronze Horseman*.

Pushkin's footnoted reference to Viazemskii may be misleading in another respect, too. If his 'Introduction' is indeed indebted to Viazemskii, it is less to the poem alluded to in the note, with its disingenuous repetition of 'люблю' ('I love'), than to the odic 'fragment' of 1818 entitled *Petersburg* (*Петербург. Отрывок. 1818 года*). This contains a lengthy eulogy of 'Peter's city', raised from the marshes as a glorious triumph of reason over the elements; and of Peter himself, who lives on in the 'eloquent bronze' of Falconet's monument, and guards his city-creation from its enemies. As in Pushkin's 'Introduction', there is considerable emphasis on the military and commercial aspects of St Petersburg, with its 'flocks of ships'.[57] But it seems probable that Pushkin's most significant debt to Viazemskii lay elsewhere again. Alongside the lines: 'Не так ли ты над самой бездной, / На высоте, уздой железной / Россию поднял на дыбы?' (lines 421-3) ('Have you not thus, over the very abyss, / On high, with iron bridle, / Raised Russia onto its hind legs?'). Viazemskii was afterwards to write in his edition of Pushkin's *Works*: 'My expression, uttered to Pushkin and Mickiewicz as we were walking past the statue'.[58] He also hinted as much in his published essay on Mickiewicz and Pushkin.[59] Pushkin's reference in note two to a tenuous and insignificant debt to Viazemskii might in other words mis- or re-direct to a more substantial, ideologically fundamental borrowing, relating instead to the material covered in note five. And if that is so, the misdirection of note five, which, we have argued, invokes Mickiewicz to convey instead something about Pushkin himself, also acquires a further twist. Pushkin's most significant source for the description at note five was not Mickiewicz or even Ruban, but Viazemskii (to whom explicit reference at that point would presumably have been politically compromising); and the Polish poet, too, was, after all, beholden to a Russian - although neither to 'Pushkin-as-bard', nor to Ruban, whom Pushkin's *fifth* note so implausibly identified.

Undoubtedly, this line of argument is as obscure as it is convoluted. The clues offered by the notes ultimately relate to an entirely private, potentially seditous conversation between author and two fellow poets, who alone could be relied upon to interpret appropriately. They fail to address fully the most knowledgeable reader, or even a circle of intimate friends. The inescapable inference in that case is that the material in question, given fresh focus by the publication of Mickiewicz's *Digression* in Paris in the year preceding *The Bronze Horseman,* indeed prompted Pushkin to troubled private reflection. His almost obsessive preoccupation with Mickiewicz reveals, in addition to ideological and æsthetic opposition, self-directed misgivings and perhaps, as Anna Akhmatova argued in a different context, a somewhat Salierian envy and sense of inadequacy.[60] But nor must the significance of Viazemskii be under-estimated. Pushkin's old friend had long-standing Polish sympathies, was a champion of Mickiewicz, and had reacted negatively to Pushkin's Polish poems of 1831 ('Why write nonsense and moreover against conscience and above all counter-productively?').[61] Relations were cool during the early 1830s.[62]

      Pushkin's second note nevertheless refers to a poem by Viazemskii which, from its opening line, treats the Petersburg theme in a context of authorial unreliability, inconsistency and dissimulation ('Нет-нет, не верьте мне: я пред собой лукавил': ['No, no, do not believe me: I dissembled before myself']), and which leads by association to a seemingly shared perception of the ambiguity of the central political symbol of the Bronze Horseman. Whereas Pushkin was at pains to distance himself from Mickiewicz, he sought instead to re-confirm his association with Viazemskii, whose recent cold disdain he challenges in a spirit contrary to that in which he approaches the author of 'To Russian Friends'. The private message of the note is that Viazemskii (more than the many authors not referred to, and for all his liberal political rectitude) is a distinguished predecessor[63] for the ideological and æsthetic inconsistency which is once more re-asserted as fundamental to Pushkin's masterpiece.

CONCLUSION

Pushkin's five footnotes to *The Bronze Horseman* create an initial impression of academic precision, but there is a sharp contrast between conventional appearance (foreign quotation, cross-reference to other texts, identification of referents) and unconventional function. Taken at face value, the information offered in the annotations is next to useless: it may seem inconsequential (notes two and four) or fragmentary (note five), and there is a bewildering randomness in what is referenced (Algarotti, Ruban …[!]) and what is not. The notes resist rather than assist interpretation, and thereby challenge the 'curious' reader (whom Pushkin so disparagingly invokes in the 'Foreword') to search for (or decode) their concealed meanings. In so doing, they reveal a self-conscious literariness such as critics willingly recognize in *Evgenii Onegin*, but which, as Andrew Kahn points out, is generally not associated with *The Bronze Horseman*.[64] In fact, the realism of Pushkin's poem, with its paradoxical intersections of 'documentary reality' and better authenticated fiction, involves a pre-realist acknowledgement of its own literary artifice; while the search for meaning which the notes invite is parodically thwarted by the extent to which they rely on information not merely withheld but inaccessible. There is a sense in which they were Pushkin's dialogue with a select few, rather than a general reader.

Certainly far more than in *Evgenii Onegin*, the footnotes in this work, lacking in such direct authorial participation, express serious personal preoccupations. At its very margins, Pushkin quite literally 'encodes' more of himself than he chooses to reveal in the central body of the poem; and the footnotes in which he does so serve less to elucidate the text than to expand it outwards, into Pushkin's complex private and ideological relations with fellow writers, imperial authority, and perhaps his own self. The obscurities of the notes confirm that extra-textual information is a legitimate and necessary component in the poem's interpretation. More than that, they imply something of the personal impetus behind the poem's creation,[65] and suggest behind the renowned ambivalence of the poem a mind more troubled than is usually acknowledged.

Though there is no single consistent meaning which unites the notes, there is a consistency in areas and type of preoccupation; and the creative and the ideological, aesthetic and political, largely coincide in the shifting contrarieties to which the notes draw attention, and which are fundamental to a reading of the whole. This may involve personal anxiety, but there is also creative autonomy; and the notes which persistently undermine stable meaning and are subversive, singly and collectively, even of the author's own positions, are nevertheless finally concerned with creation rather than negation of meaning: an analogue to Peter's creation from nothing, rather than Evgenii's descent into meaningless incoherence.

158   Michael Basker

NOTES

1. Andrei Belyi, *Ritm kak dialektika*, Federatsiia, Moscow, 1929, pp. 266-8.

2. S. Shvartsband, *Logika khudozhestvennogo poiska A.S. Pushkina: ot 'Ezerskogo' do 'Pikovoi damy'*, Magnes Press, Jerusalem, 1988, p. 83. The essence of the argument is set out on pp. 82-9.

3. A.S. Pushkin, *Mednyi vsadnik*, ed. N.V. Izmailov ('Literaturnye pamiatniki'), Nauka, Leningrad, 1978, p. 24 (hereafter *Mednyi vsadnik*). All quotations are from this edition of the poem; subsequent references will be indicated in the text of the article by line or footnote number. Translations of all Russian texts are my own.

4. See the contemporary accounts reproduced in ibid., pp. 104, 110.

5. Ia.L. Levkovich, 'Perevody Pushkina iz Mitskevicha', in *Pushkin: Issledovaniia i materialy*, VII, Nauka, Leningrad, 1974, pp. 157-8.

6. *Oleszkiewicz* is cited in the English translation by W. Lednicki, *Pushkin's 'Bronze Horseman': The Story of a Masterpiece. With an Appendix Including, in English, Mickiewicz's 'Digression', Pushkin's 'Bronze Horseman', and Other Poems*, University of California Press, 1955; repr. Greenwood Press, Westport, Connecticut, 1978, pp. 134-7.

7. The source is the Book of Jeremiah: see Wiktor Weintraub, *The Poetry of Adam Mickiewicz*, Mouton, 'S-Gravenhage, 1954, p. 189.

8. E.N. Stroganova, 'Otgoloski dekabristskoi temy v primechaniiakh k poeme *Mednyi vsadnik*' in *Pushkin: problemy poetiki*, Tverskoi gosudarstvennyi universitet, Tver', 1992, p. 115.

9. See Lednicki, op.cit., p. 21. The translation of Mickiewicz's *Petersburg* is cited from ibid., pp. 117-18.

10. Shvartsband, op. cit., p. 84.

11. On the authorship and composition of the various sections of Berkh's pamphlet, see Izmailov's commentary in Pushkin, op. cit., pp. 105, 106.

12. For a possible reflection on the contemporary, anti-Romantic-exotic, unheroic connotations of Pushkin's subtitle, see A.L. Ospovat and R.D. Timenchik, *'Pechal'nu povest' sokhranit'': Ob avtore i chitateliakh 'Mednogo vsadnika'*, Kniga, Moscow, 1985, pp. 13-14.

13. Charles Robert Maturin, *Melmoth the Wanderer: A Tale*, Oxford University Press, London, 1968, p. 27 (volume I, chapter 2). On Pushkin's enthusiasm during the 1820s for Melmoth's 'novel of genius', to which he alluded in the opening stanza of *Evgenii Onegin*, and made part of Onegin's and even Tatiana's reading, see, for example, Iu.M. Lotman, *Pushkin: Biografiia pisatelia; Stat'i i zametki 1960-1990; 'Evgenii Onegin': Kommentarii*, Iskusstvo-SPB, Sankt-Peterburg, 1995, pp. 342, 547, 690.

14. Cf., for example, the lines from *The Gypsies* (*Tsygany*): 'Идет ... и вдруг ... иль это сон? / Вдруг видит близкие две тени' ('He walks on ... and suddenly ... or is it a dream? / He suddenly sees two shadows nearby'). (A.S. Pushkin, *Sobranie sochinenii v desiati tomakh*, Khudozhestvennaia literatura, Moscow, 1974-8, III, p. 156).

15. Maturin, op. cit., p. 60.

16. Cf. in particular lines 353-5: 'Ужасных дум / Безмолвно полон, он скитался. / Его терзал какой-то сон' ('Full of dreadful thoughts / In silence he wandered / Some sort of dream was tearing him apart'). The title of Maturin's novel in Russian is of course *Мельмот-скиталец*.

17. On the 'demonic substratum' beneath Pushkin's depiction of Peter in *The Bronze Horseman* see B.M. Gasparov, 'Poeticheskii iazyk Pushkina kak fakt istorii russkogo literaturnogo iazyka', *Wiener Slawistischer Almanach*, 27, Vienna, 1992, pp. 312-16.

18. Maturin, op. cit., p. 60. The thematization of 'horror' is maintained in *The Bronze Horseman*: 'Ужасен он в окрестной мгле' etc. (line 414). ('He is dreadful in the surrounding gloom'.)

19. Pushkin's 'Messianic-eschatological' and apocalytpic imagery is a main focus of B.M. Gasparov's stimulating analysis of the poem: op. cit., pp. 287-319.

20. For the full text of Ruban's poem, see Pushkin, *Mednyi vsadnik*, p. 270.

21. See M.P. Alekseev, *Pushkin i mirovaia literatura*, Nauka, Leningrad, 1987, p. 58.

22. On Nicholas' well-known attitude to his grandmother Catherine II, see Ospovat and Timenchik, op. cit., pp. 33-5.

23. Nicholas took censorial exception to the four lines of text, and evidently did so without troubling to consult Pushkin's footnotes, which he left unannotated (see the description of his censorship of Pushkin's manuscript in *Mednyi vsadnik*, pp. 220-1).

24. Lednicki, op. cit., p. 122.

25. Ibid., p. 121, slightly amended (the original reads 'Drugi był wieszczem rusjkiego narodu, / Sławny pieśniami na całej północy').

26. 'Mitskevich o Pushkine' (1873), in P.A. Viazemskii, *Estetika i literaturnaia kritika*, Iskusstvo, Moscow, 1984, p. 280.

27. See Weintraub, op. cit., pp. 186-7.

28. Lednicki, op. cit., pp. 138-9. A detailed note on Pushkin's self-identification appears on p. 138.

29. Shvartsband, op. cit., pp. 88-9.

30. Cf. *The Monument of Peter the Great*, in Lednicki, op. cit., pp. 120-2.

31. Viazemskii, loc. cit.

32. Lednicki, op. cit., p. 122.

33. Ibid., p. 121.

34. See Belyi, op. cit., pp. 207, 275-6.

35. Alekseev, op. cit., p. 57; see also R. Jakobson, *Pushkin and His Scupltural Myth*, translated by J. Burbank, Mouton, The Hague and Paris, 1975, p. 29.

36. For further details see Izmailov's note in *Mednyi vsadnik*, p. 266.

37. See S.G. Bocharov, 'Stilisticheskii mir romana (*Evgenii Onegin*)', in his *Poetika Pushkina: ocherki*, Nauka, Moscow, 1974, pp. 26-104. Bocharov vigorously expounds the view that a process of stylistic 'translation' is the 'creative force of Pushkin's novel' (ibid., p. 71). He deals with the special case of bilingual translation on pp. 77-85.

38. Cf. the incisive summary of such polarities in J.B. Woodward, 'The "Principle of Contradictions" in *Yevgeniy Onegin*', *The Slavonic and East European Review*, XL, 1, 1982, p. 34.

39. As Pushkin recalled in *Moia rodoslovnaia* ([1830]: *Sobranie sochinenii*, II, p. 260), Peter had in 1697 also condemned Pushkin's own paternal ancestor to the gallows for plotting against him - and seeking to enlist *Streltsy* support. For details of the cruelty attendant upon Fedor Pushkin's gory execution, carried out to instructions from Peter which included the exhumation and desecration of Ivan Miloslavskii's corpse, see Lindsey Hughes, *Russia in the Age of Peter the Great*, Yale University Press, New Haven and London, 1998, p. 453. On Peter's role in the execution of the *Streltsy*, see ibid., p. 371.

40. It is perhaps further oblique commentary on Peter's project that, though the narrator is able to read without a lamp (lines 50-1), the only 'Petersburg window' subsequently mentioned in the text is Evgenii's (line 162), where the association is not with European light, but with harsh November rain and darkness.

41. Berkh, *A Detailed Description*, reproduced in *Mednyi vsadnik*, p. 107. Cf. also p.109, and the account of S.A. Aller, ibid., p. 115.

42. *Mednyi vsadnik*, pp. 67-8. On the source for this episode, see ibid., p. 204. It might be added that Pushkin's use of 'boat' (*lodka*) involved a further deflationary comic twist by comparison with Berkh's version, which placed Miloradovich in a twelve-manned cutter (ibid., p. 107).

43. See the memoir of F.N. Glinka in *A.S. Pushkin v vospominaniakh sovremennikov*, Khudozhestvennaia literatura, Moscow, 1974, I, pp. 206-8.

44. It is not impossible that Pushkin's jibe against Benkendorf implicitly involved the issue of rank. By 1833 Benkendorf was, like Miloradovich in 1824, both full General and Count; but he was only recently promoted to these distinctions, in 1829 and 1832 respectively.

45. See Izmailov's commentary in *Mednyi vsadnik*, pp. 149-51.

46. Thus, for example, the newspaper *Russkii invalid, ili Voennye vedmosti* reported on 13 November 1824 that 'with noble fearlessness citizens of all estates placed their own lives in danger in order to save the drowning and their property. These features of courage, magnanimity and devotion are so numerous that we learn of new ones almost every day' (reprinted in *Mednyi vsadnik*, p. 104). Cf. also the private accounts of S.M. Saltykova (ibid., p. 122) and of A.S. Griboedov, who evidently shared something of Pushkin's scepticism towards the 'generals' (ibid., p. 118).

47. Reproduced in Pushkin, *Mednyi vsadnik*, pp. 108-9.

48. Lines 201-2 ('Увы! Все гибнет: кров и пища! / Где будет взять?' ['Alas! All perishes: food and shelter / where will they be found?']) appear, for instance, to be a direct, satirical echo of the passage from Berkh just quoted.

49. P.A. Viazemskii, *Stikhotvoreniia*, Sovetskii pisatel' (Biblioteka poeta, bol'shaia seriia: izdanie tret'e), Leningrad, 1986, p. 241. First published in A. Smirdin's *Novosel'e*, St Petersburg, 1833.

50. *A Beautiful Woman (Красавица)*: Pushkin, *Sobranie sochinenii*, II, p. 284.

51. Pushkin, *Sobranie sochinenii*, IV, pp. 163-4.

52. The lines are from an early draft which was somewhat condensed in the final published version: cf. N.I. Gnedich, *Stikhotvoreniia*, Sovetskii pisatel' (Biblioteka poeta, malaia seriia: izdanie tret'e), Leningrad, 1963, pp. 212, 449. As N.V. Izmailov has pointed out (*Mednyi vsadnik*, p. 126), the footnote referring to Gnedich appeared for the first time in the first full edition of *Evgenii Onegin*, published in March 1833, just a few months before Pushkin began work on *The Bronze Horseman*.

53. For a broad summary of Pushkin's main literary sources, see for example, Iu. Borev, *Iskusstvo interpretatsii i otsenki: Opyt prochteniia 'Mednogo vsadnika'*, Sovetskii pisatel', Moscow, 1981, pp. 184-202.

54. See ibid., p. 199. Of more tangential relevance to Pushkin's footnote is Lednicki's interesting observation that Pushkin's line 'И пунша пламень голубой' ('And the blue flame of punch') (line 66) might seem to echo 'И пламень голубой их девственных очей' ('And the blue flame of their virginal eyes'), from the closing section of Viazemskii's *Conversation* ... (Lednicki, op. cit., p. 89 n.).

55. Viazemskii, *Stikhotvoreniia*, pp. 220-1.

56. G.M. Fridlender, 'Poeticheskii dialog Pushkina s P.A. Viazemskim', in *Pushkin: Issledovaniia i materialy*, XI, Nauka, Leningrad, 1983, p. 168.

57. Viazemskii, *Stikhotvoreniia*, pp. 118-21. Fridlender (op. cit., p. 167) claimed to provide the first brief description and analysis of some of these textual correspondences (previously noted in passing in, for example, Lednicki, op. cit., p. 20; see also, however, Jakobson, op. cit., p. 35); but the relationship of Viazemskii's lengthy poem (almost 150 lines of iambic hexameter) to *The Bronze Horseman* still merits closer investigation. Among the more intriguing (near-)coincidences is that of Viazemskii's 'Чей повелительный, *назло природе*, глас / Содвинул и повлек ...' (with reference to Peter) ('Whose imperious voice, *spiting nature* / Moved and drew after it ...') and Pushkin's '... На зло надменному соседу. / *Природой*

здесь нам суждено / В Европу прорубить окно' (lines 14-16; my emphasis) ('… *To spite* our haughty neighbour / We are here destined *by nature* / To cut a window into Europe'.) A subtextual echo of Viazemskii at precisely the point where the first footnote cites Algarotti would of course entail a further characteristic subversion of that note's comprehensive authority.

58. Viazemskii, *Estetika i literaturnaia kritika*, p. 427.

59. 'Incidentally, the observation that the horse beneath Peter is rather raised on its haunches than galloping forward belongs neither to Mickiewicz nor Pushkin': ibid., p. 280.

60. For a detailed exposition of Akhmatova's view, see N. Mandel'shtam's essay 'Motsart i Salieri' in her *Kniga tret'ia*, YMCA Press, Paris, 1977, pp. 19-75, especially pp. 22-4, 30-2. Akhmatova also discerned sexual jealousy in Pushkin's attitude to Mickiewicz during 1828 (A. Akhmatova, *O Pushkine: Stat'i i zametki*, Sovetskii pisatel', Leningrad, 1979, p. 214), which was almost certainly the year of his Petersburg meeting with Viazemskii and Mickiewicz (cf. Shvartsband, op. cit., p. 86; Viazmeskii, *Stikhotvoreniia*, p. 493).

61. For a summary of Viazemskii's Polish activities and sympathies, with particular reference to Mickiewicz, see M.I. Gillel'son's long note in P.A. Viazemskii, *Sochineniia v dvukh tomakh*, Khudozhestvennaia literatura, Moscow, 1982, II, pp. 332-4. Viazemskii's reaction in 1831 to Pushkin's *To the Slanderers of Russia* (*Klevetnikam Rossii*) is quoted from R. Edmonds, *Pushkin: The Man and His Age*, Macmillan, London, 1994, p. 149.

62. Clear testimony to this is the drastic falling off of their correspondence after summer 1831.

63. Cf. Lidiia Ginzburg's observation on the unequal relationship between Pushkin and Viazemskii, which continued to endow the latter with a certain 'pedagogical authority' (L. Ginzburg, 'P.A. Viazemskii', in Viazemskii, *Stikhotvoreniia*, p. 30).

64. A. Kahn, *Pushkin's 'The Bronze Horseman'*, Bristol Classical Press, London, 1998, pp. 74-5.

65. Cf. Nadezhda Mandel'shtam's observation: 'No-one will doubt that every work by Pushkin has a personal basis, something reflecting the inner condition of his spirit. To find this "something" means to penetrate the prime cause for the creation of the work, to disclose … the concealed inner theme' (op. cit., p. 30).

How *The Bronze Horseman* Was Made

by

PRISCILLA MEYER

We are always fascinated by genius, and try to get closer to its mystery by taking it apart. Pushkin's letters, diaries, articles, notebooks, epigrams; his friends' letters and memoirs; and the huge literature in Italian, French, Russian and English that he is known to have read make us feel it must be possible to penetrate his creative process. But *The Bronze Horseman* has posed an exceptional problem because the manuscripts provide little insight into the poem's genesis.[1] Some of the finest critical literature identifies sources for particular themes: Wacław Lednicki examines Pushkin's ambivalent assessment of Peter the Great and his implied dialogue with Mickiewicz about Peter in *The Bronze Horseman*;[2] Roman Jakobson reveals the continuity from the Boldino autumn of 1830 to the next one in 1833.[3] New insight into the genesis of *The Bronze Horseman* may be provided by a hitherto unremarked work, *The Flood at Nantes* (*L'inondation à Nantes*), published in 1832 by Madame Aimée Harelle.

We know the history of Pushkin's involvement with many of the components that were to go into *The Bronze Horseman*: Peter the Great; the Decembrist uprising; the flood of 1824; the sources he himself cites in his notes to the poem; his own characters Evgenii and Parasha. Commissioned by Nicholas I, Pushkin started research in the State Archives for a history of Peter the Great in 1831, but was also covertly researching the Pugachev rebellion in the summer of 1833,[4] a juxtaposition of both Pushkin's circumstances and the two histories he was writing that is suggestive of the *Horseman*'s drama between Peter and Evgenii.

The salient elements incorporated into *The Bronze Horseman* have been discussed by a battalion of Pushkin scholars; here a simple list will suffice. These include:

1. Pushkin's complex understanding of the role of Peter the Great in Russian history as both bearer of enlightenment and destroyer of the old boyar nobility. His discussions with Mickiewicz of both the historical Peter and his mythic representation in Falconet's monument led to a dialogue between the Polish poet's *Digression* - especially *The Day Preceding the Inundation of St. Petersburg in 1824: Oleszkiewicz* and *The Monument of Peter the Great* in which Mickiewicz calls Peter a 'bronze tsar'- and *The Bronze Horseman*. Pushkin copied Mickiewicz's poems into his notebook some time after the end of 1832.[5]

2.   The Decembrist uprising of 1825, which is encoded in *The Bronze Horseman*.[6] Evgenii sits astride the lion in front of the house from which they fired on the Decembrists on what is now Decembrists' Square, and Pushkin gives the names of the generals sent out by the tsar to help the drowning (Count Miloradovich and Adjutant-General Benkendorf) because of their role in the suppression of the revolt the following year.[7] Even Pushkin's particular use of the Neva shore (взморье), as Anna Akhmatova has shown, refers to the unidentified burial place of the five executed Decembrists.[8] Pushkin's notes to his poem themselves hint at the Decembrist theme.[9]

3.   Pushkin's characters Evgenii and Parasha evolve out of his earlier work. The hero of the unfinished poem *Ezerskii* (1832), a fragment of which became *My Hero's Genealogy* (1836), has been taken to be a first draft of the character that will become Evgenii, stripped of Ezerskii's aristocratic trappings and defiance.[10] Evgenii's musings on his humble future resemble some of Pushkin's own that he had given to Evgenii Onegin in chapter 8 (later destroyed), but in *The Bronze Horseman*, Pushkin omits them in order to emphasize Evgenii's ordinariness and initial humility.[11] Pushkin's implied identification with Ezerskii is instead taken up by the figure of the poor poet in *The Bronze Horseman* who inherits Evgenii's abandoned apartment. Perhaps he will tell Evgenii's tale and in so doing, somehow reconcile the conflicts between nature and culture, citizen and state, thereby redeeming Evgenii and Parasha from oblivion.

Parasha is clearly connected to the Parasha of *The Little House in Kolomna* (1830). The earlier Parasha and her widowed mother live in a little house that the narrator tells us has disappeared.[12] In *The Bronze Horseman* it is Evgenii who lives in Kolomna (as Pushkin had until his exile in 1820), while the widow and her daughter live on an island in the Neva. The action of *The Little House* takes place 'eight years ago' writes the narrator of the tale written in 1830, therefore in 1822. This is two years before the beginning of the action of *The Bronze Horseman*. If we connect the two poems, as it appears Pushkin must have done, the house could have vanished by 1830 because it was swept away in the flood of 1824, but there is no hint of this in the poem; the narrator asks at the opening of the poem, 'Are they alive?', but Parasha's story is a playful farce.

       Pushkin appears to have consciously chosen only to hint at the flood but not to address it. Another tale, *The Lonely Little House on Vassilevskii Island*, is said to have been taken by V.P. Titov from an anecdote Pushkin told in 1828 about a poor Petersburg clerk who lost his fiancée during a flood. Even if the later *Little House* is the germ of the tale of Evgenii and Parasha,

Pushkin still waited five years to incorporate it into the constellation of features that comprise *The Bronze Horseman.*

But *The Bronze Horseman* is the tale of the conflict of three agents,[13] Peter, Evgenii and the Petersburg flood of 1824, and we have only accounted for the first two. How did Pushkin's deep interest in Peter, in uprisings from Pugachev to the Decembrists, and his earlier characters Evgenii and Parasha, all occupying him in the early 1830s, become connected to and merge in the fact of the flood of 1824? Was the flood the missing element that united all the aforementioned components for the first time to produce 'the greatest work ever penned in Russian verse', as Mirsky calls it?[14] Mickiewicz's poem, *Oleszkiewicz*, treats the day preceding the inundation quite briefly, devoting only four lines to a description of the ocean.[15] In a variant of the Introduction of *The Bronze Horseman* Pushkin says that since 1824 he had felt it an obligation to the 'mournful hearts' of his contemporaries to describe the flood;[16] Andrew Kahn, on the other hand, says there is nothing else to link the theme of the flood to an early version of the work, nor was it an event Pushkin dwelled upon.[17] No one has suggested how this historical event, connected neither to Peter nor Catherine, whose reigns Pushkin had been studying so exhaustively, came to be the subject of his 'Petersburg tale'. Why, then, at the end of a six-week trip researching the Pugachev rebellion in Uralsk and Berdy, did Pushkin, having reached Boldino on 1 October 1833, start writing *The Bronze Horseman* on 6 October, completing it on 30 October?

Jakobson mentions an implied connection between Catherine's monument to Peter and the flood of Catherine's time: in Pushkin's lyceum poem *Recollections in Tsarskoe selo* (1814) (*Воспоминания в Царьском селе*) Pushkin describes a monument in Tsarskoe selo to the Battle of Chesma as 'surrounded by waves' with 'grey billows lapping its base with shining foam'.[18] Although the elements of statue, waves and foam do link the description of the Chesma monument to that of the Bronze Horseman, the connection to the flood of Catherine's time is only indirect. In any case, this conjunction of statue, monarch and water and/or flood did not inspire a poem until a full nineteen years later.

In the absence of clues to the stages of the poem's development, I propose that Pushkin read Madame Harelle's *The Flood at Nantes* some time between its publication in January 1832 and September 1833, and that this may have precipitated the conjoining of the compositional elements of *The Bronze Horseman,* many of which Pushkin had been actively assembling in 1832. As Lednicki suggests, the poem is so rich in precise citations that Pushkin must have brought materials for the poem with him from Petersburg.[19] *The Flood at Nantes* could have been among them.

The Flood at Nantes appeared in the very first issue of the journal *The Foreign Review of Literature, Science and the Arts* (*Revue étrangère de la littérature, des sciences et des arts*) in January, 1832. It is an unusual journal, in that it was published in Petersburg entirely in French. The review was a kind of digest that contained articles on popular science (life vests, lighting agents, the instincts of spiders), current socio-historial topics (penal colonies in England, the financial situation in the United States), theatre reviews, travel notes, sketches of mores ('The Physiology of the Cigar', 'Gastritis'), anecdotes and works of French literature. The *Review* published stories, poems, or chapters from novels by Victor Hugo, Honoré de Balzac, Alexandre Dumas, Eugène Sue as well as by less well-known writers. That the review was popular is attested to by the fact that it appeared four times yearly up until 1864. Oddly, however, there are almost no references to it even in the critical literature dealing with Russian writers' reading of French literature.

Given Pushkin's life-long avid interest in everything French, especially literature, and even more so French prose of the 1830s as Vera Milchina has shown,[20] as well as his active participation in the world of Petersburg journalism both as contributor and as publisher, it is not surprising that his library contains the first eight volumes of the *Review*.[21] He is likely to have read right away the first issue of this new journal that appeared in Petersburg, where he was in residence that year until mid-September, as his letters attest. His last letter from Petersburg in 1832 in fact contains a critique of French critics, journals, and poetry of the period: 'Their prose barely manages to redeem the vileness of what they call poetry',[22] he writes to Pogodin, in a letter discussing his programme for the contents of his 'own' newspaper, *The Literary Gazette* (*Литературная газета*).

What would Pushkin have found in *L'inondation à Nantes* that would inspire his own *Inondation à Petersbourg*? Madame Harelle's tale is a chapter from her novel, *The Accursed, or an Episode from the Wars of the Vendée*, of which the editors say: 'the main characters are marked with a seal of verisimilitude that raises the suspicion that they are far from fictitious'. *The Flood* opens with a realistic description of the Nantes harbour, where the Loire flows into the Atlantic (see Appendix). Of course, flood conditions have general similarities, but these are reasonably specific; the setting of a river delta with its islands, the everyday detail, and the descriptions of the effects of the flood are close to Pushkin's:

> The river ... *rolls its troubled waters impetuously*. It overflows everywhere.[23]

> Нева всю ночь
> Рвалася к морю против бури
> Не одолев их буйной дури ...
> Теснился кучами народ,
> Любуясь брызгами, горами
> И пеной *разяренных вод*.

(All night the Neva
Surged toward the sea against the storm,
Not taming its stormy folly ...
People crowd in heaps
Admiring the splashes, the mountains
And foam of the *infuriated waters*.)[24]

Naturally the islands at the conjunction of rivers and oceans are most vulnerable:

> *Charming islands*, rich plains, which, just yesterday, covered with numerous flocks, offered on its left bank gracious scenes today are no more than *a surging sea from which stick out here the tops of trees filled with tufts of foam, there a group of houses against which the waves surge and break.*

> Но силой ветров от залива
> Перегражденная Нева
> Обратно шла, гневна, бурлива,
> *И затопляла острова.*

> (But by the force of the winds from the gulf
> Fenced off, the Neva
> Angry, stormy, went backward
> *And flooded the islands*.)

And naturally the lowest places are the first to flood:

> From moment to moment the flood makes frightening progress: it has already *penetrated several low quarters of the city...*

> Воды вдруг
> Втекли в *подземные подвалы*

> (The waters suddenly
> Flowed into the *underground cellars*)

Both writers describe the people's desperation at the loss of all they've laboured for and depend upon:

> However much a crowd of arms hastens to remove from riverside houses *objects that the water could take off or destroy*, the river mounts so rapidly that it seems impossible to save everything. *And every owner*

*is distressed thinking about the ruinous damage that he tries in vain
to prevent.*

Pushkin uses a metaphor of theft on the one hand and God's anger on the other
to paint the same picture:

> Осада! Приступ! Злые волны,
> Как воры, лезут в окна ...
> Лодки под мокрой пеленой,
> Обломки хижин, бревна, кровли,
> Товар запасливой торговли,
> Пожитки бледной нищеты,
> Грозой снесенные мосты,
> Гроба с размытого кладбища
> Плывут по улицам.
> Народ
> Зрит божий гнев и казни ждет.
> *Увы! Все гибнет; кров и пища!*
> *Где будет взять?*

> (Siege! Attack! The angry waves
> Like thieves crawl in the windows ...
> Boats under soaked canvas,
> Pieces of huts, wood, roofs.
> *The wares of thrifty trade,*
> *The chattels of pale poverty,*
> Bridges swept away by the storm,
> Coffins from the swamped graveyard
> Float along the streets.
> The people
> Sees God's anger and awaits punishment.
> *Alas! All's ruined, roof and food!*
> *Where will we get them?*)

As Vernadsky has noted, the waves of the Neva 'attacking the lofty buildings
of Petersburg, were for Pushkin symbolic of human crowds in revolt against
peace and order', close to his own description of the Pugachev uprising.[25]
The Flood at Nantes also contains a hidden political commentary. The
description of the flooded Nantes harbour introduces the tale of a sixteen-year-
old girl, Hélène, who is trapped in a collapsing house. Workers are trying
to save her under the direction of a Marquis and his son the Vicomte, who is
apparently in love with Hélène. He is 'pale and agitated', 'trembling with
emotion' and experiencing 'extreme anxiety' as she sits on a beam over a

large hole. 'Her feet, deprived of a point of support, are bathed by the steadily rising water'.

Hélène is saved, as Parasha is not, but several elements of her story relate to *The Bronze Horseman*: the beloved girl drowned (or not) in a house destroyed by a flood, her anxiety-filled lover, and the detail of the waves mounting beneath dangling feet, which in *The Bronze Horseman* describes the 'terrifyingly pale' Evgenii as he sits astride the stone lion:

> Он страшился, бедный,
> Не за себя. Он не слыхал,
> *Как подымался страшный вал,*
> *Ему подошвы подмывая ...*

> (He feared, poor man,
> Not for himself. He did not hear
> *How the terrifying billow rose,*
> *Washing his soles ...*)

The development from the *The Little House in Kolomna* and *Ezerskii* to *The Bronze Horseman* is from classicism and romanticism toward 'the poetry of everyday life and of the little man'.[26] The juxtaposition to the Vicomte in *The Flood at Nantes* heightens our appreciation of Pushkin's choice of the 'little man' as the one to suffer tragic loss of his beloved. Pushkin presumably demoted Ezerskii to Evgenii, lowering his social status, in order to have him represent everyman. This concern must be somehow connected to the Decembrist material in the poem. *The Flood at Nantes* provides insight into this question.

From the opening paragraph we learn that *The Flood* takes place in 1789. At the quay we meet the young captain of an American ship, *L'indépendence*, who is to be the heroic rescuer of Hélène. He 'has undergone more than one combat to assure America's liberty'[27] and now his former warship has been converted to commerce. On an errand, the captain arrives at the scene of the collapsed building, where someone has proposed that the only way to rescue Hélène is to swim under the building and take her out through the raging river. The Vicomte offers ten thousand francs to anyone who will make this dangerous attempt. A pale, thin man dressed in miserable clothing offers to try, although he is clearly too weak to succeed. He is willing to die in the attempt if the money will go to his starving wife and children. Overhearing this, the captain hands him his own purse and volunteers to undertake the rescue himself.

> 'You?' replies the Marquis ...'No, monsieur, I won't permit it.'
> 'My life is not any more precious than that of this unfortunate man', the sailor interrupts with some severity.[28]

The implied discourse on the equality of man is further underscored when the Marquis regrets that he is 'only the useless witness of your generous action!' and the captain responds, 'You or me, what's the difference?'[29] *The Flood at Nantes* thus hints at both the French and the American revolutions and the ideals they represent.

Pushkin's political views, as Eidelman emphasizes, cannot be neatly classified,[30] which has given rise to debate among a variety of scholars. Semen Frank distorts the evidence in demonstrating Pushkin's profound conservativism when he quotes only the second paragraph of *John Tanner*, which gives a negative view of America[31] and which was in any case written in 1836, at the end of Pushkin's life. Presumably the first paragraph of Pushkin's essay reflects his earlier views:

> For some time the North American States have been attracting the attention of the most thoughtful people in Europe. This is not the result of political events: America peacefully goes about its business, up to now harmless and blooming, strong in its peace, assisted by its geographic position, proud in its institutions.[32]

This is not to say that Pushkin was not 'firmly convinced of the futility of revolutions,'[33] afraid of a repetition of the French terror in Russia. But while Pushkin cherished the Russian aristocracy and was ambivalent about tsardom, he was also a Decembrist sympathizer who opposed serfdom and despotism, and whose poetry continued to inspire liberal thought after 1825.[34] He attributed the failure of the Decembrist uprising to the absence of a third estate in Russia, that is, as is clear in *André Chénier* (1825), he drew a parallel between the Russian uprising and the French Revolution,[35] which he studied in the 1820s, getting books from Eliza Khitrovo in order to write a (never completed) history of it.[36] In *André Chénier*, 'равенство' ('equality') is twice rhymed with 'блаженство' ('blessedness'), even if Pushkin then deplores the absence of Law that leads to regicide. 'Holy freedom' is nonetheless a 'pure goddess', not to be blamed for the madness of the people, who 'In the shade of equality / In your embrace will rest sweetly.'[37] The egalitarian sentiments of *The Flood at Nantes*, the 1789 (not 1792) setting and the glowing treatment of the American revolution with its heroic, victorious representative, would provide *The Bronze Horseman* with a hidden positive variant of 1825, a happier resolution than is achieved in Russia or by Evgenii and Parasha. That Evgenii's humble rank resonates with Pushkin's thoughts about the French revolution is clear from a line of the eighth stanza of *Ezerskii*: 'from gentry we crawl into the third estate',[38] even though in this line Pushkin is regretting the decline of the Russian aristocracy. *The Flood at Nantes* can be read at least as the basis for a bitter comparison with the situation in Russia, in which the American captain embodies individual freedom and self respect of the sort Pushkin considered attributes of an ideal member of the Russian aristocracy.

Besides the thematic points of contact between the two poems - the flood, the love story, the revolution - there are two other suggestive correspondences. The American captain passes through the humble and chaotic dwellings of the poor part of Nantes - a 'sad, miserable scene' and reaches the Stock Exchange: 'This was not the beautiful building of which Nantes is proud today, but a wooden barracks of pitiful aspect'.[39] Past poverty and disorder is replaced by present beauty, as in Pushkin's Introduction.

What of the essential aspect of *The Bronze Horseman*, the statue's pursuit of Evgenii? Pushkin's sources for the animated statue have been found in Molière's Commander, Washington Irving and even Lemercier.[40] But Evgenii is clearly not Don Juan; his madness does not derive from those sources. There has been some disagreement over what precisely drives Evgenii mad - the loss of Parasha, the flood itself, or his helplessness before the all-powerful Peter[41] - but clearly it is when he discovers that Parasha's house has been swept away that he goes mad: 'he burst out laughing'... His traumatic experience leads him to hallucinate pursuit by the statue. There is a parallel moment at the end of *The Flood at Nantes*. Although it is used only for a kind of lyrical closure rather than as a thematic line, the hero re-experiences his adventure in a brief hallucination.

The Captain is hastening back to his ship in order to set sail at high tide after rescuing Hélène:

> Arriving before the place of the ruin, he stops, his heart beats violently ... A trick of his imagination presents to him the young girl still placed on that wobbling beam whence he had removed her. This vague airy form, this pale and gracious face that he had only managed to glimpse, seemed at this moment to lean towards him, to implore his help. He extends his arms, crosses them on his chest, as if he were again clasping the charming being he thinks he sees ...[42]

But the captain is sane, and the adventure was successful; he comes to himself. 'Sweet and cruel mirage, he says, should I fear or desire to see you reappear?' The mirage can be connected to Evgenii's madness: Evgenii's challenge to the Horseman relates to the captain's role in the American revolution. The captain hallucinates Hélène imperilled by the flood shortly after rescuing her, but Evgenii's hallucination comes a year after Parasha's disappearance in the flood, 1825, which clearly relates Evgenii's challenge to the Decembrist uprising.[43] Pushkin endows the events of December as well as of the flood with a 'Shakespearean' historical perspective by having Evgenii trace Parasha's fate to its source in Peter, and by implicitly comparing that conflict with those of other countries through his subject.

With so many points of contact between *The Flood at Nantes* and *The Bronze Horseman* - the realistic descriptions of the flood; the indirect allusions to revolutionary ideas; a girl in a house swept away by the flood; the city setting that emphasizes the gulf between rich and poor; and the hero's hallucination - we can hypothesize that the French tale served as a catalyst for Pushkin, bringing together elements he had not hitherto combined: his archival work on Peter the Great, the bitter experience of his Decembrist friends, the poems of Batiushkov, Mickiewicz, Viazemskii, his own work from the 'freedom poems' such as *Freedom* and *André Chénier* to the less obviously civic works *Ezerskii* and *The Little House in Kolomna*, and an array of other subtexts (*Genesis, The Aeneid, The Tempest, Don Juan*). The shift from the odic Introduction to the prosaic part of the poem may have been triggered by French prose;[44] Pushkin's poem becomes a 'Petersburg *tale*' when he introduces the story of Evgenii and Parasha into the scene of the flood. The story of Hélène's plight may have allowed Pushkin's rich materials to crystallize, causing him to recreate the Petersburg flood of 1824 in the Boldino autumn of 1833.

APPENDIX

The Flood at Nantes

Madame Aimée Harelle

The wind turns to the west, and presses from the Ocean rain clouds which for three weeks have torn the grey veil of a harsh winter. The sky has regained all its brilliance, it is under the influence of a pure sun, of a warm and balmy air which opens the month of March of the year 1789. It is about seven o'clock in the morning; great activity reigns in the port of Nantes: and yet, an extraordinary thing, none of its numerous dockyards contains a song, nor the blows of carpenters' hammers. The caulkers no longer smoke their tar by the quayside filled with ships leaning against the piers. The sailmaker has stopped assembling large bands of canvas along which just yesterday his hand ran so hastily. Construction, repairs, rope making is all suspended: these are unaccustomed labours which at this moment are occupying a crowd of workers of all classes; and while they are occupied, distress is imprinted on each face. All movements are precipitous. No joyous words are exchanged; voices aren't raised except for mutual advice about what is urgent to do.

Take a look at the Loire, and you will learn the cause of this sad agitation. The river, suddenly enlarged by the melting of the snow and by long rains, *roils its troubled waters impetuously*. It overflows everywhere. Charming islands, rich plains, which, just yesterday, covered with numerous flocks offered on its left bank gracious scenes are today no more than *a surging sea from which stick out here the tops of trees filled with tufts (flocons) of foam, there a group of houses against which the waves surge and break*. From moment to moment the flood makes frightening progress: it has already *penetrated several low quarters of the city*, and will not hesitate to cover the quays. However much a crowd of arms hastens to remove from riverside houses objects that *the water could take off or destroy*, the river mounts so rapidly that it seems impossible to save everything. *And every owner is distressed thinking about the ruinous damage that he tries in vain to prevent*.

Equally as active as the nervous inhabitants of Nantes, but animated by a different motive, the sailors *of all countries* move along the shore and make preparations for a departure too long delayed by contrary winds. At the command of the captain, *the national flag is deployed on each ship*: the cables are unfurled, the masts are covered with sails; and the anchor is at last weighed (my italics).

NOTES

I am grateful to Alexander Schenker, Susanne Fusso and Vera Milchina for their valuable comments on my manuscript, to which I have inadequately responded.

1. See Andrew Kahn, *Pushkin's 'The Bronze Horseman'*, Bristol Classical Press, London, 1998, pp. 3-8.

2. Wacław Lednicki, *Pushkin's 'Bronze Horseman'*, Greenwood Press, Westport, Connecticut, 1978.

3. Roman Jakobson, *Pushkin and His Sculptural Myth*, Mouton, the Hague and Paris, 1975, p. 26.

4. Natan Eidelman, *Pushkin: istoriia i sovremennost' v khudozhestvennom soznanii poeta*, Sovetskii pisatel', Moscow, 1984, pp. 142-8.

5. Lednicki, op. cit., chapter 3, pp. 25-42. On the importance of Mickiewicz see chapter 8.

6. G. Vernadsky, 'Pushkin and the Decembrists', *Centennial Essays for Pushkin*, ed. Samuel H. Cross and Ernest J. Simmons, Russell and Russell, New York, 1937, pp. 45-76; D. Blagoi, *Sotsiologiia tvorchestva Pushkina. Etiudy*, Federatsiia, Moscow, 1929, pp. 263-328; Jakobson, op. cit., p. 25.

7. A.D.P. Briggs, *A Comparative Study of Pushkin's 'The Bronze Horseman', Nekrasov's 'Red-Nosed Frost,' and Blok's 'The Twelve'*, The Edwin Mellen Press, Lewiston/Queenston/Lampeter, 1990, pp. 106-7.

8. Anna Akhmatova, *Sochineniia*, 2 vols., Khudozhestvennaia literatura, Moscow, 1986, 'Pushkin i nevskoe vzmore', II, pp. 119-26.

9. The scholarship discussing the presence of the Decembrist material in *The Bronze Horseman* is catalogued by Andrew Kahn, op. cit., pp. 16-17.

10. D.S. Mirsky, *Pushkin*, Dutton, New York, 1963, pp. 209-10; Lednicki, op. cit., pp. 13-14. Kuleshov, *Zhizn' i tvorchestvo A.S. Pushkina*, Khudozhestvennaia literatura, Moscow, 1987, p. 331.

11. Jakobson, op. cit., p. 26.

12. William Harkins, 'The Place of *Domik v Kolomne* in Pushkin's Creation' in *Alexander Pushkin: A Symposium on the 175ᵗʰ Anniversary of his Birth*, ed. Andrej Kodjak and Kiril Taranovsky, New York University Press, New York, 1976, pp. 196-205, pp. 201-2.

13. In keeping with Lotman's observation that Pushkin's thinking about the historical process in the 1830s took the form of a tri-partite paradigm. See Iurii Lotman, 'Zamysel stikhotvoreniia *O poslednem dne Pompei*' in *Pushkin*, Iskusstvo-SPB, St Petersburg, 1995, pp. 294-9.

14. D.S. Mirsky, op. cit., p. 212.

15. Lednicki, op. cit., p. 137.

16. Quoted in Lednicki, op. cit., p. 12.

17. Kahn, op. cit., p. 5.

18. Jakobson, op. cit., p. 25.

19. Lednicki, op. cit., pp. 11-12.

20. Vera Milchina has shown the degree to which Pushkin incorporated French prose works into his poetry and prose in 'Frantsuzskaia literatura v proizvedeniiakh Pushkina 1830-x godov', *Izvestiia akademii nauk SSSR: seriia literatury i iazyka*, LXV, 3, Moscow, 1987, pp. 244-54.

21. B.L. Modzalevskii, 'Biblioteka A.S. Pushkina', *Pushkin i ego sovremenniki. Materialy i issledovaniia*, Vypuski IX-X, Akademiia nauk, St Petersburg, 1910, otdel IV, p. 369.

According to Evgenii Belodubrovskii, the pages are cut in the issues that appeared during Pushkin's lifetime.

22. A.S. Pushkin, *Polnoe sobranie sochinenii v desiati tomakh*, Akademiia nauk, Moscow, 1962-1966 (hereafter *Pss*), letter 495, first half of September, 1832, X, p. 416.

23. Madame Aimée Harelle, *L'inondation à Nantes, Revue étrangère de la littérature, des sciences, et des arts*, 1832, I, pp. 24-41 (hereafter *The Flood*). All translations from the French are mine.

24. *Pss*, IV, pp. 377-98.

25. Vernadsky, op. cit., p. 74.

26. Harkins, op. cit., p. 205.

27. *The Flood*, p. 26.

28. Ibid., p. 37.

29. Ibid., p. 38.

30. Natan Eidel'man, *Pushkin, Istoriia i sovremennost' v khudozhestvennom soznanii poeta*, Sovetskii pisatel', Moscow, 1984, p. 111.

31. Semen Frank, 'Pushkin kak politicheskii myslitel'', *Pushkin v russkoi filosofskoi kritike*, Kniga, Moscow, 1990, pp. 396-422.

32. A.S. Pushkin, *Dzhon Tenner*, *Pss*, VII, pp. 434-69; 434-5. Translation is mine.

33. Michael Karpovich, 'Pushkin as an Historian', *Centennial Essays for Pushkin*, ed. S.H. Cross and E.J. Simmons, Russell and Russell, New York, 1937, pp. 181-200 (196). I am grateful to Dr Tim Binyon of Wadham College, Oxford and Vera Milchina for their remarks on this topic.

34. B. S. Meilakh, 'Pushkin i dekabristy posle 1825 goda' in *Pushkin: issledovaniia i materialy*, 15 vols., Akademiia nauk, Moscow, 1956-1995, II, pp. 196-213.

35. Dmitrii Blagoi, *The Sacred Lyre*, Raduga, Moscow, 1982, p. 307.

36. Kuleshov, op. cit., pp. 312-4.

37. A.S. Pushkin, *Pss*, II, pp. 259-60; Natan Eidel'man, *Pushkin i dekabristy*, khudozhestvennaia literatura, Moscow, 1979, p. 312.

38. A.S. Pushkin, *Pss*, IV, pp. 344.

39. *The Flood*, p. 28.

40. Jakobson, op. cit., p. 10; Robert Belknap, 'A Likely Story, Pushkin's *Bronze Horseman*: A Study in Verisimilitude', in *The Supernatural in Slavic and Baltic Literature: Essays in Honor of Victor Terras*, ed. Amy Mandelker and Roberta Reeder, Slavica, Columbus, Ohio, 1988, pp. 26-33; Catharine Theimer Nepomnyashchy, 'The Poet, History and the Supernatural: A Note on Pushkin's "The Poet" and *The Bronze Horseman*', in *The Supernatural* etc., pp. 34-46. See also chapter 6 of this volume.

41. Gleb Zhekulin, 'On Rereading the *Bronze Horseman*', *Canadian Slavonic Papers*, 29, 1987, pp. 228-40 (230).

42. *The Flood*, p. 41.

43. Nepomnyashchy, op. cit., p. 37.

44. A.N.Arkhangel'skii (*Stikhotvornaia povest' A.S. Pushkina 'Mednyi vsadnik'*, Vyshaia shkola, Moscow, 1990, p. 8) notes that prose is the source of the realism of *The Bronze Horseman*.

Pushkin's *History of Pugachev* and the Experience of Rebellion

by

WILLIAM MILLS TODD III

'Peindre, non la chose, mais l'effet qu'elle produit.'
Mallarmé, letter to Henri Cazalis, 30 October 1864[1]

Pushkin's *History of Pugachev* challenged its first readers - and subsequent ones - in ways that they do not encounter in his subtly self-conscious, often parodic artistic texts. In his other nonfictional prose works, such as *A Journey to Arzrum*, they could find poets and poetry, including the author's own. In this text they do meet three great Russian poets, Krylov, Dmitriev, and Derzhavin, but not on Mount Helicon. The first nearly starves to death, the second bears witness to the brutal execution of the rebels, the third is an agent of harsh reprisals. The text is striking, even in Pushkin's œuvre, for its starkness and lack of literary playfulness.

Pushkin's use of epigraphs immediately signals a different way of writing. Pushkin generally provided his artistic texts, such as *The Captain's Daughter*, with epigraphs. In that historical novel, the contrasting chapter epigraphs are taken from gentry and Cossack or folk culture; Pushkin invents some as parodies or stylizations of these cultural levels. In contrast *The History of Pugachev* offers only one sober epigraph, taken from an account by the archimandrite of the Spaso-Kazanskii Monastery, Platon Liubarskii, who witnessed the events of the Pugachev uprising:

> To describe properly all the plots and adventures of this traitor would, it seems to me, be beyond not only an average historian, but even an excellent one, for all his escapades depended not on reason or on military order, but on daring, chance and luck. For this reason I think that Pugachev himself would be in no condition not only to relate the details of these ventures, but also to remember the deliberate part of them, since they did not depend upon him directly, but rather proceeded from the complete liberty and reckless daring of his accomplices in several places at once.[2]

Here the archimandrite captures, in the convoluted prose of an eighteenth-century churchman, the challenges which the events and agents posed to Pushkin, their first historian. Pushkin accepted these challenges and passed them on to his readers, offering however, more pattern and guidance than his pious predecessor. Pushkin showed them Russian civilization brought to the brink of

destruction and to the confused surrender of explanation expressed in the
archimandrite's overview. *The History of Pugachev* proved a work his
contemporaries did not want to read, especially in the stark way Pushkin narrated
it. I will outline their critical response in order to highlight Pushkin's
innovations, then analyse the claims the narrative made upon his readers. My
point will be that it made too many claims, and that they were too difficult and
unconventional. Pushkin had himself described the trivial stylistic quibbles
which had greeted the first volumes of Karamzin's magisterial *History of the
Russian State* in 1818, and he had himself joined the chorus of young people
who forgot that the circumstances of its publication under the monarch's
protection had obliged Karamzin to be moderate in his judgments.[3] Pushkin
knew that his own works had from the late 1820s on been met with generally
mindless criticism. He should, therefore, have known better than to anticipate
that his *History of Pugachev* (published in two volumes in 1834) would be both
a critical success and a sorely needed financial one. Still, he had grounds for
optimism. It was, after all, the very first account of the astonishing rebellion
which had swept across Eastern Russia a scant sixty years previously and 'had
rocked the state from Siberia to Moscow, from the Kuban River to the forests of
Murom'.[4] 'Tis sixty years since' had been a successful formula for Sir Walter
Scott, and Russian readers of the twenties and thirties had eagerly snapped up
histories and historical novels, translated and native. Pushkin had read the best
European examples of the historian's craft and sought to make his new work the
embodiment of dispassionate, judicious scholarship.[5] At first Fortune smiled
upon him; he had obtained access to most of the relevant state archives.
Moreover, unlike other works he wrote during the thirties, such as *The Bronze
Horseman*, *The History of Pugachev* had been virtually uncensored; N.N.
Petrunina has persuasively argued that only the narrative body of the text was
lightly edited by the Emperor, who - to give one example of these alterations -
changed the title to *The History of the Pugachev Rebellion*. Pushkin's extensive
endnotes and the entire second volume were untouched by any censor, imperial
or bureaucratic.[6] Pushkin had three thousand copies printed and he was sure that
the history would be appreciated if only for the second volume,[7] which contained
the unpublished archival and eyewitness sources from which he had, in part,
crafted his narrative: government decrees and manifestoes, the reports of military
commanders, Academician Rychkov's account of the siege of Orenburg, the
solemn narration of the uprising by Platon Liubarskii.

The immediate fate of the book, however, frustrated all of Pushkin's
expectations. Not only was it a financial disaster - only a thousand copies were
sold - it was also a critical one. Bulgarin and Senkovskii were, at best, lukewarm
in their assessment of the project, although Senkovskii at least recommended the
documents and several of the episodes to potential readers. The longest review,
by Bronevskii in *The Son of the Fatherland*, took Pushkin to task for a few
alleged mistakes and a shoddy map, then reproached him for not having painted

his picture of Pugachev with 'the brush of Byron' and for not having viewed him from 'the appropriate point of view', by which Bronevskii meant a moralizing one.[8] Critics closer to Pushkin - A.F. Voeikov and Baron Rozen - gave Pushkin the benefit of the doubt, but in their very brief reviews praised *The History of Pugachev* as a step toward some future larger history.[9] They praised its literary and historical qualities without really specifying them; Rozen went out of his way to find liveliness in the exposition, focusing on Pushkin's most vividly novelistic episode, the brutal murder of Elizaveta Kharlova and her young brother. It is indicative of the book's ill fortune that the most intelligent review, by the historian M.P. Pogodin, was rather casually sent off to the *Moscow Observer* and somehow was not published until 1865. Pogodin's review places the literary qualities of the *History* above its historical ones, but still finds it a landmark in Russian historical writing, Russia's first non-oratorical history and a significant departure from Karamzin's achievement. Despite Pogodin's sympathy for Pushkin's style, choice of subject, and general approach to Pugachev, he nevertheless devotes most of his review to listing nineteen questions the text begged but did not answer.[10] Subsequent historians, such as Kliuchevskii, were more critical, mainly faulting Pushkin for not using sources to which he had no access.

Pushkin is by now a canonical author, as he was not in 1835. Among the privileges of canonicity, as Frank Kermode has argued, is that all the works of a canonical author are taken seriously: what might otherwise be read as a boring 'muddle' becomes, with canonical status, an 'enigma' to be resolved with the full resources of sophisticated interpretation and commentary.[11] Nevertheless, *The History of Pugachev,* as a text, has still not acquired this aura of reverence. Mark Raeff salutes Pushkin as the first historian of the rebellion and as a collector of materials, but he much prefers Pushkin's novel *The Captain's Daughter* for its insights into contemporary Russian social relations, and he dismisses *The History of Pugachev* abruptly: 'by today's standards and tastes it is pretty boring'.[12] His judgment differs little from those of Bulgarin, Senkovskii, and Bronevskii. As Maria Langleben has shown, historians are more likely to cite *The Captain's Daughter* than *The History of Pugachev*.[13] Although Soviet and Russian Pushkin scholars have given us many valuable studies of the process by which Pushkin conducted his historical research, literary scholars leave tended to join Professor Raeff in looking past the history to the novel, which appeared over a year later.[14] Indicative of this general neglect of the poetics and pragmatics of Pushkin's history is the title of Petrunina's useful article, 'Around *The History of Pugachev*'.

That professional historians, modern or otherwise, should not have provided a complete assessment of Pushkin's work is not surprising. Aside from a few renegades, such as Hayden White or Robert Berkhofer, who have strayed into historiography, historians are unlikely to assess how a story is told. As Berkhofer puts it in his recent book, *Beyond the Great Story: History as Text and Discourse,* historians tend to review the way other historians create facts from evidence, the science of history, not the way they create narrative exposition from facts, the art of history.[15] That a history might make its argument through its style, emplotment, modes of characterization, and treatment of point of view - that is, through the totality of its narrative aspects - and, moreover, that these aspects might creatively be at odds with each other, is not a possibility raised by normal historians but rather by philosophers, deconstructionists, discourse analysts, and literary theoreticians. What I would like to do in this chapter is to examine what Pushkin did with his narrative, the patterns he established, and the demands he placed upon his readers, demands which, as we have seen, they were unwilling or unable to fulfill as they made their own demands on it. I will argue that it is precisely where Pushkin's text seems to be most dry, factual, or seemingly disorganized, that it is, on the contrary, most artful and most subtle in making its pragmatic claims upon its readers: that they appreciate the role of chance and chaos in the uprising, that they see the social forces at work in the conflict, that they understand the triviality and inconclusiveness of the government's actions. As Pope observed 'Those oft are *Stratagems,* which *Errors* seem, / Nor is it *Homer nods,* but *We* that *dream'*.[16]

The first aspect of the history which might have confused its readers was its very genre. Entitled a 'history', it shaded into two other types of writing, the historical article, and the memoir, as in Karamzin's 'Memoir on Ancient and Modern Russia' (1837), which Pushkin and Zhukovskii published in *The Contemporary.*[17] This set of multiple possibilities, seized upon by Senkovskii, who labelled the book an 'article', not a history proper, arose because Pushkin, in the preface to his history, called it a 'fragment of a work', a 'page of history', part, that is, of a larger story which some future historian might take up, but which he had broken off. A fragment can, of course, fit into multiple wholes - universal history, for instance, or a grand national history. Both of these types of historical writing were fresh in the memories of Pushkin's readers. But Pushkin makes his underlying 'great story' more specific, as his narrative begins and ends with specific incidents: the imperial government's repression of Cossacks and indigenous non-Russian peoples in the first chapter and trivial government attempts to heal the wounds in the concluding chapter. Pushkin's narrative, in this sense, became social and administrative history.

Pushkin engaged the other generic possibility, the memoir, when he delivered to Nicholas I not only the *History of Pugachev*, but also a special set of notes, which were published for the general public in an accurate form only 35 years later.[18] These 'Comments on the Rebellion' are included with *The History* in modern editions and, like the appended materials, they should be considered integral to the text. They move the *History* in the direction of a memoir or policy paper, by making much more explicit Pushkin's otherwise implicit analysis of the rebellion in terms of class antagonisms and government incompetence.

In the absence of this summation for the less than perspicacious reader, Pushkin's contemporary reviewers felt free to treat his history as a fragment of their own historical understandings, as I will attempt to show with each element of the *History's* poetics that I discuss.

In Pushkin's *History of the Village of Goriukhino* (written 1831, published 1837), the would-be writer, Belkin, is seduced by the charms of rhetorical historiogaphy: 'To be the judge, observer, and prophet of ages and peoples seemed to me the highest achievement, attainable to a writer' opined Belkin.[19] In crafting the persona of his own first historical writing, Pushkin made it his first principle to reject such grandiloquence, whether it be the solemn archaism of Karamzin's narration or the bolder, more colourful touches of French and Russian romantic historians. Pushkin usually observes the self-effacing conventions of normal history: third-person, past tense, active voice, non-figural narration. His evaluations and generalizations proceed from the events and situations he has narrated (as, for example, when he writes on the last page of the 'unforgivable negligence of the authorities'),[20] they do not relate the events to some nebulous sense of human nature or divine Providence. Such reticence, such anti-figuralism required intense stylistic self-discipline in the 1830s, when normal prose called for heavy ornamentation. Pushkin's reviewers, in presenting passages from *The History of Pugachev*, tended to add what they, and their readers, felt missing. Thus Bronevskii called for Byronic touches, and Senkovskii, noting that Pushkin's unadorned narration of the Kharlova episode might constitute an entire novel, nevertheless takes the liberty of adding epithets where Pushkin's account had none, and we find in his review such locutions as 'the savage friend of the unfortunate victim' and 'gave in to the attraction of a new, even more tender passion' and 'the lamentable demise of Kharlova'.[21]

Pushkin crafted other aspects of the *History's* poetics in concert with this narratorial reticence. His treatment of character and agency, for instance, emphasizes boundaries and constraints. Pugachev is introduced to the reader only in the second of eight chapters, after a long and systematic account of how the government had repressed the Iaik Cossacks and cruelly put down their rebellions for nearly two centuries. The reader learns of Pugachev only when social and political forces have made it possible for him to appear: 'Everything portended a new rebellion. A leader was missing. A leader was found'.[22] The *History* subsequently presents Pugachev as the government gradually came to know him, through accounts obtained under torture, through his sudden appearances and disappearances throughout the vast territory that the rebellion occupied. The *History* shows how the government is compelled to discover that Pugachev is, in capability, more than the farm hand and horse thief it proclaims him to be, and that he is something more than the creature of 'daring, chance, and luck' we meet in the Archimandrite's account or the 'stuffed animal', the Cossacks' plaything which the Russian commander, Bibikov, describes in a letter to Fonvizin.[23] These descriptions function as symptoms of the government's ineptness. Pugachev emerges from Pushkin's narrative as a skilled tactician, if not strategist, and as sensitive to the religious and social life of Cossacks and peasants. His personal qualities - daring and timidity, wit, casual brutality, fondness for drink and revelry - are less important to the narrative and receive comparatively little attention. This, too, frustrated reviewers, who looked in vain for a bolder personality and a more despicable villain. Pushkin chose not to tell the tale in these romantic or moralizing terms, and he treats the other principal characters in similar fashion. The mid-level commanders - such as Captain Krylov, Lt.-Col. Mikhelson, or the commander in Saratov, Boshniak - are capable, on a local level, of bravery, energy, honour, and tactical ability. At the highest level of command the leaders are at best capable of fine phrases - Catherine's witty exchange with Voltaire, for instance - but fail to effect the course of events. At their worst they are capable of brutality as harsh as that of the rebels. In general, the higher the rank of the government official, the less his (or her!) ability to put out the wildfires.

The aspects I have been analysing so far - genre, narratorial style, characterization - puzzled Pushkin's contemporaries, but at least the reviewers were able to articulate Pushkin's techniques. The final aspect of narration I shall discuss - point of view -   escaped their techniques of narrative analysis altogether. Here the insights of Mikhail Bakhtin into heteroglot discourse, or Iurii Lotman's treatment of event as a perspectival phenomenon, or the analytic tools of Boris Uspenskii, who treated narrative in terms of a succession of viewpoints, help sensitize us to what Pushkin's *History of Pugachev* tried to accomplish. Pushkin's narratorial reticence was not merely stylistic, when `style' is viewed in the traditional sense of word choice and arrangement. Pushkin, beyond this, opened his text by way of emplotment to a variety of points of view, both in the metaphoric sense of the word, where 'point of view' signifies worldview or experience, and in the literal sense, where it signifies visual perspective.

In these instances Pushkin surrenders the historian's normally synoptic, omniscient overview to contrast the over-confidence and ignorance of the high government officials in Petersburg and Kazan, the horrifying experience of soldiers and civilians in the small forts and cities overrun by the rebels, and the simmering resentment of Cossacks, Kalmyks, Bashkirs, and other groups, as they find themselves increasingly crushed by harsh government measures. Chapter 1, for instance, is recounted from this last viewpoint, which is less visual than conceptual, as the nomad peoples are seen to have built their cultures, only to have them constrained to breaking point. The ensuing chapters shift the perspective, in turn, to that of the government, as it tries to learn about Pugachev and to counteract his spreading influence, to that of the besieged populations of Orenburg and Iatskii Gorodok as they see the rebels approach with impunity, and to that of individuals in the smaller posts. The narration foregrounds confusion and the play of rumour and surprise. When the narration again becomes synoptic, it maintains the sense of desperation by stressing speed and range and the numerical superiority of the rebels. Maps provided by Pushkin and by some modern editions make it possible to appreciate that the story space covers many hundreds of square miles. A reader who follows the action carefully will fully appreciate the shocking spread of the rebellion.

Midway through chapter 4 Bibikov writes a despairing letter to his wife, in which he admits he cannot describe the conditions he has found. The narrator follows it with a paragraph which takes up Bibikov's points but compresses the sentences to increase that sense of despair and to provide the description that had eluded Bibikov:

> The situation was indeed horrible. A general uprising by Bashkirs, Kalmyks, and other peoples scattered about the region cut off communication from all sides, The army was small and unreliable. Commanders deserted their posts, fleeing at the sight of a Bashkir with a bow and arrow or a factory serf with a club. Winter exacerbated the difficulties. The steppes were covered with a deep snow. It was impossible to move forward unless one had a good supply not only of bread, but of firewood. Villages were deserted, major cities were either besieged or occupied by bands of rebels, the factories were plundered and burned. The rabble rioted and wreaked havoc everywhere. Troops dispatched from different regions approached slowly. The evil, unimpeded, spread far and wide with great speed.[24]

The narrator picks up the words 'horror' and 'evil' from Bibikov himself, thereby retaining his evaluation and worldview. The narrator's choice of verbs and grammar (passive/active voice) elegantly captures the relative strength of forces. The agents here are the rebels, the hostile winter conditions, and 'the evil'. The forces of government and civilization are, by contrast, passive, slow, or absent altogether.

There is no better prolonged example of this effective arrangement of point of view than in Pushkin's treatment of the siege of Kazan in chapter 7. Pushkin's notes show that he had carefully constructed a chronology for his book, a *fabula*, in effect, and creatively worked his plot, his *siuzhet*, to show the siege from the perspective of Kazan's horrified citizens. As the fortified part of the city seems about to fall to the rebels, who have already plundered the outlying districts, Pugachev's forces suddenly break off the siege. Why? How? Pushkin's narrative has given us a series of events, linked paratactically with such adverbs as 'suddenly'. It has given us the perspective of the anxious archbishop, with his hymns and miracle-working icons.[25] But only at the end do we find out what had chronologically occurred first, namely Mikhelson's careful advance toward Pugachev, which caused Pugachev to pull back his forces.

What we subsequently learn was a considered military manœuvre; we have seen as the people of Kazan saw it, as Pushkin's narrative seeks to render the experience of the events from their point of view. In schematic terms, the narrative gives us five principal events: 1. Mikhelson approaches, 2. Pugachev learns of this threat, 3. Pugachev suddenly retreats, 4. Mikhelson defeats Pugachev and 5. Mikhelson's hussars enter Kazan. But the *History* presents them in the order 3, 5, 1, 2, 4.

The narrative section of *The History of Pugachev* concludes from the perspective of the seemingly triumphant government: the Cossacks betray Pugachev and the rebels are punished, in a fashion strikingly parallel to the rebels' execution of captured military officers. In conventional terms, the main plot is completed, although the narrative informs us that it took Suvorov and Panin a year to restore order. But Pushkin's polyperspectivalism and arrangement of his plot lend *The History of Pugachev* an ironic and troubling lack of conclusion. The history proper begins and ends with accounts of Catherine's renaming of the Iaik Cossacks, as if this war of words could erase the memory of the uprising.[26] Even this government measure proved fruitless. The last word of the *History* is '*Pugachevshchina*' - and it belongs to the people, who have not forgotten that bloody time. The 'General Comments' which Pushkin appended to the *History* for Nicholas I conclude in an even more ironic fashion. After cataloguing the extreme social divisions in Russian society, Pushkin lists the government's measures which arose as supposedly positive consequences from the evil of the uprising: the government had reduced the size of the provinces and communications had become faster. Pushkin's last word in the 'General Comments' is a dismissive 'etc.'.[27]

We recall that Pushkin's preface labelled *The History of Pugachev* a fragment of an unfinished work. We recall that shortly before this book was written, Russia had faced a Polish uprising and rebellions in the military colonies, as well as urban unrest occasioned by a cholera epidemic. Similar conditions had obtained in 1773-4. The pseudo-finality of Pushkin's ending is, I would argue, a closure that continues the book's thematics of perpetual unrest.

Of all explanations for the book's lack of popularity, Ivan Dmitriev, himself a witness to the execution of Pugachev, had perhaps the best. He reported to Pushkin that people found his *History* insufficiently ornate and that it told a story they wished could be forgotten.[28] Even sixty years later, a Russian rebellion was too close to have been anything but 'senseless and merciless', in the famous phrase from *The Captain's Daughter*.

I will add a third explanation to Dmitriev's two. It may be that the readers of a history cannot be expected to read it as a cognitive and æsthetic adventure in the way they would read, say, the different perspectives on love in chapters 3-5 of *Evgenii Onegin,* or the way they would read the different temporal and ideological perspectives at play in *The Captain's Daughter.* Fiction and poetry may demand cognitive effort (the inference of meaning from juxtaposition, absence, or repetition), a non-fictional work of history may not. The conventions of historical writing require a more explicit narration, straightforwardly articulated conclusions, and, on the reader's part, less reading between the lines than a work of imaginative literature. Pushkin demanded too much, cognitively speaking, and his readers have not met his challenge.

NOTES

1. Carl Paul Barbier and Lawrence A. Joseph, eds, *Documents Stéphane Mallarmé VI: Correspondance avec Henri Cazalis*, Librairie Nizet, Paris, 1977, p. 239.

2. A.S. Pushkin, *Polnoe sobranie sochinenii* (hereafter *Pss*), ed. Maksim Gor'kii, D.D. Blagoi, S.M. Bondi et al., Nauka, Moscow-Leningrad, 1937-59, IX, p. 4.

3. Ibid., XI, p. 57.

4. Ibid., VIII, p. 80.

5. Alexander Dolinin argues persuasively that Pushkin worked against the tendency of contemporary western historians, particularly French Romantic ones, to find order and progress in history; see 'Historicism or Providentialism? Pushkin's *History of Pugachev* in the Context of French Romantic Historiography', *Slavic Review*, LVII, 2, 1999, pp. 291-308.

6. N.N. Petrunina, 'Vokrug *Istorii Pugacheva*' in *Pushkin: issledovaniia i materialy,* VI, 1969, pp. 233-47.

7. Pushkin, *Pss.*, IX, p. 390.

8. [V.B. Bronevskii], '*Istoriia Pugachevskogo bunta*', *Syn otechestva*, 1835, 3, pp. 177-9. Bronevskii was identified as the author of the anonymous review by F.V. Bulgarin, 'Mnenie o literaturnom zhurnale *Sovremennik*', *Severnaia pchela,* 129, 9 June 1836, p. 516.

9. A.F. Voeikov, '*Istoriia pugachevskogo bunta*', *Russkii invalid*, 104, 27 April 1835, p. 416; Baron Rozen, '*Istoriia pugachevskogo bunta*', *Severnaia pchela*, 38, 2 February 1835, pp. 149-52.

10. M.P. Pogodin, 'Neskol'ko slov ob *Istorii Pugachevskogo bunta* A.S. Pushkina', *Russkii arkhiv,* 1, 1865, pp. 103-7.

11. Frank Kermode, *The Genesis of Secrecy: On the Interpretation of Narrative*, Harvard University Press, Cambridge, Massachusetts, 1979, pp. 10, 49, 66.

12. Marc Raeff, 'Pugachev's Rebellion' in Robert Forster and Jack P. Greene, eds., *Preconditions of Revolution in Early Modern Europe*, The Johns Hopkins University Press, Baltimore and London, 1970, p. 200. The best recent study of the historiography of the rebellion ignores Pushkin's work altogether: Alan Bodger, 'Nationalities in History: Soviet Historiography and the Pugachevshchina', *Jahrbücher für Geschichte Osteuropas,* 39, 1991, pp. 561-81.

13. Mariia Langleben, 'Nakazanie miatezhnoi prirody: chetyre fragmenta iz "Istorii Pugacheva" A.S. Pushkina', *Russian Literature*, XXIX, 1991, pp. 177-203 (198).

14. Svetlana Evdokimova, *Pushkin's Historical Imagination,* Yale University Press, New Haven and London, 1999, pp. 13-14, takes Andrew Wachtel to task for his insistence on reading the two accounts of the rebellion in 'intergeneric dialogue', but she herself slights the history by paying virtually no attention to it in her substantial and intelligent book. See Andrew Wachtel, *An Obsession with History: Russian Writers Confront the Past*, Stanford University Press, Stanford, 1994, pp. 66-84. Wachtel does, however, make a number of perceptive observations on the structure of Pushkin's history and on the varieties of historical writing in Pushkin's time. Evdokimova's thesis that Pushkin 'did not believe in Truth, but in truths', p. 14, is well supported by the polyperspectivalism of *The History of Pugachev.*

15. Robert F. Berkhofer, Jr., *Beyond the Great Story: History as Text and Discourse*, Harvard University Press, Cambridge, Massachusetts, 1995, p. 62.

16. Alexander Pope, 'An Essay on Criticism' in *The Poems of Alexander Pope*, ed. John Butt, Yale University Press, New Haven, 1963, p. 150.

17. On the publication history of Karamzin's text, see Richard Pipes, transl., *Karamzin's Memoir on Ancient and Modern Russia: A Translation and Analysis,* Harvard University Press, Cambridge, Massachusetts, 1959. It should be noted that Pushkin had finished his text before Karamzin's, written in 1811, had become available. Dolinin draws persuasive distinctions

between Karamzin's construction of 'Providence' and Pushkin's, 'Historicism or Providentialism' (op. cit., p. 306).

18. *Zaria*, 12 (December), 1870, pp. 418-22.

19. Pushkin, *Pss*, VIII, p. 132.

20. Pushkin, *Pss*, IX, p. 80.

21. Osip Senkovskii, 'Kritika', *Biblioteka dlia chteniia*, X, 113-14, 1835, pp. 26-7.

22. Pushkin, *Pss*, IX, p. 12.

23. Pushkin, *Pss*, VIII, pp. 2, 45.

24. Pushkin, *Pss*, IX, pp. 39-40.

25. Dolinin shows that Pushkin invents these traditional religious details which are not attested in his documentary sources: op. cit., p. 303.

26. Maria Langleben persuasively links the renaming of the Cossacks and the river, the execution of Pugachev, and the burning of Pugachev's home as elements of magic ritual: op. cit., pp. 190-1.

27. Pushkin, *Pss*, p. 376.

28. A.S. Pushkin, *Pss*, XVI, p. 18: Letter from I.I. Dmitriev to A.S. Pushkin, 10 April 1835.

'A Hundred Years Have Passed ...': A Diltheyan Approach to Time in Pushkin

by

ROBERT REID

The philosopher Wilhelm Dilthey is probably best known for his prototypical contribution to the theory of the history of culture. However, it is not my intention to use his ideas on history as such as the basis of an approach to Pushkin the historian. I am, in fact, much more interested in one of his asides to the larger historical theme which intriguingly equates the grand categories of time with specific human psychological states. The literary-critical potential of these ideas struck me particularly forcibly when I was writing on the metaphysics of Lermontov's *The Demon*, a work which, it seems to me, foregrounds temporality and its relationship to the hero's psychology in a particularly powerful way.[1] The poet constructs for the Demon a rarefied cosmic environment in which his only points of reference are temporal (rather than spatial). The discrete temporal categories of past and future are charged with emotionality in such a way that there is a consistent equivalence between, respectively, futurity and hope; past and regret. There is this kind of psychic equivalence in Dilthey too, but with the stress on the intellectual rather than emotional process: 'Looking at *the past* in memory we see the connections between the parts of life in terms of the category of *meaning*' while 'as we look towards *the future*, the category of *purpose* arises'[my italics].[2] Memory and anticipation, then, two important conditions of psychic awareness, interact with the intellectual processes of understanding and purpose respectively to create our consciousness of past and future. The components of this model are not in themselves peculiarly original, it is true. However the notion that time is not merely a mental construct in the Kantian tradition but also articulates discrete psycho-mental faculties is one which bears closer scrutiny, particularly in relation to literary criticism: it has the potential to emancipate temporality, at least partially, from its traditional associations with narrative process, with the production of events, and to link it instead to subjective dynamics, to character and characterization.

It is not only Dilthey's psychologization of past and future which has literary critical relevance; of equal importance is the equation he makes for the third temporal category: 'In *the present* we feel the positive or negative *value* of the realities which fill it' [my italics].[3] The equation of presentness with value seems enigmatic at first glance, but Rudolf Makkreel, the leading authority on Dilthey, understands him to be arguing that 'immediacy of felt apprehension is the hallmark of values ...'.[4] However, it is obvious that the fundamental problem with this equation lies in the difficulty of defining its two terms in such a way that they will relate to each other within a common epistemological context: valuation and presentness; we will return to this topic in due course. Suffice it to say that in the specific terms of Lermontov's *Demon*, I again experienced no difficulty in accepting the validity of the Diltheyan formula: in the *present* moment of his looking (the first significant *moment* that he has experienced) the Demon makes instantaneous and fundamental acts of evaluation: 'For a moment / He suddenly felt within himself / Inexpressible agitation /... and once again he grasped the sacredness / Of love, goodness and beauty'.[5] The temporal markers of instantaneous presentness are prominent here and the word which I translate as 'grasped' is 'постигнул', suggestive of a more spontaneous mental action, perhaps, than 'понял'.

My aim in the present chapter is to examine the relationship between temporality and psychology as it manifests itself in Pushkin's shorter narratives, particularly *The Bronze Horseman*. I have chosen Pushkin's shorter narratives because a number of them manage to accommodate striking lapses of represented time in what is arguably a restricted representational space, as Steinberg puts it[6] and thus run counter to the view, not infrequently met with, that short works cannot broach themes requiring a large time-span.[7] In these works, then, the presence of time-lapse and juxtaposition of time segments is all the more striking, given the structural economy of the whole. *The Shot*, *Mozart and Salieri*, *The Blizzard* and *The Station-Master* are all remarkable for building significant time-lapses not merely into the structure of the work but into the characterization system. However, the most striking from this point of view, in the sheer ambitiousness of its scope, is *The Bronze Horseman* wherein the use of time is quantitatively, if not qualitatively different from that employed in the other works mentioned.

In my search for the psycho-temporal nexus in these shorter narratives of Pushkin, I am encouraged by two quite separate insights by Caryl Emerson and Savelij Senderovič relating to *The Queen of Spades* and *The Bronze Horseman* respectively. Emerson, who concludes that there is a 'philosophy of history' in *The Queen of Spades*, locates Hermann's psychological flaw in 'blindness to the present'; he is undone because he cannot live in a world of contingency 'once the promise of code has been offered to him'.[8] Senderovič, writing of the importance of the retrospective or elegiac principle in Pushkin's work, equates Evgenii's loss of his past in *The Bronze Horseman* with an absence of the elegiac perspective in that work (and in Evgenii's mental make-up in particular).[9] Both commentators draw attention to the centrality of time in the profiles of these fictional characters, though significantly from a negative point of view: what defines them, almost as a *dominanta*, is the absence of (to use Heidegger's terminology) one of the three temporal *ecstasies* of past, present and future. This temporal circumscription of fictional characters may be regarded as the outcome of the natural process of selection which Doležel sees (along with the formative principle of siuzhetization) as essential to the creative process or poesis.[10] However it is equally a reflection of anthropological reality: to be human is to be temporally selective. Conversely, as Dilthey notes, a being, who, like Laplace's demon, was omnipresent and omniscient, would scarcely also be human.[11] Temporal deixis, then, is a basic psychic condition, not because it is necessarily a property of temporality *per se*, but because, as Strawson points out, a demonstrative element is fundamental to all thought: the privileging of *this* over *that* or, in temporal terms, *then* over *now* or *vice versa*.[12] Deictically privileged time is basic, therefore, both to the structure of human thought and also to narrative coherence. Thus, when Lessing famously (and problematically) proclaimed that action was the proper subject of literature he was also asserting that our experience of events can be ordered in organic form privileging some of these over others.[13] And this is to say that the world as we perceive it, ordered by time and events, is susceptible to narrative.[14]

The privileging of moments of psychological importance is fundamental to most of the shorter works of Pushkin: the moment when Evgenii confronts Peter's statue, when Silvio refuses his shot for the first time, when Hermann hears the story of the Countess's secret formula - these are indisputably salient moments in the temporal sense, but also in the psychological, for they are crucial to the psychological drama which unfolds in the relevant works. A deictic moment is not inherently a present moment, for theoretically any moment, whether (from the perceiver's point of view) past, present or future, can be privileged and invested with super-signification in relation to the rest of the undifferentiated temporal flow. Nevertheless any discrete event which we may care to select from the past was once itself a *now* and it is in the nowness rather than the pastness of such events that we seek their authenticity. For this reason, perhaps, events, as they are lectorially encountered in narrative, have the feel of present events. More than that, the lectorial experience presents us with a hierarchization of events, a prioritization whereby some are made to seem, if not more real, then more essential and fundamental than others. Herein lies the paradox of deictically privileged events in narrative: the reader is presented with a vicarious experience within his/her own receptional *now* which closely replicates his/her own hierarchical ordering of temporal experience. The fictional characters' *now* is marked by features which also define nowness for the reader.

The Russian word настоящий well sums up this equivalence: what is present is real; more pertinently, what is real is present. Reality, moreover, is the site where we experience past and present.[15] This synthesizing present, or in Dilthey's terms *nexus* (of past, present and future) is to be distinguished from the virtual present, the infinitesimal *point-instant*[16] in which we must logically acknowledge 'true' presentness to consist. The present is inevitably a precarious concept;[17] what we know it to be we cannot experience; what we experience seems constantly to resolve itself into either future or past. Ricoeur followed Augustine in calling the first of these apprehensions of time *intensio* and the second *distensio* and he defines our experience of presentness in terms of a constant oscillation between the two.[18] For Augustine, as for Schelling, the 'intensive' present constitutes true time, God's time, in Schelling's case precisely because it lacks distensio, which he regarded simply as a debased metaphorization of true time into the spatial categories of extension, length, distance etc.[19] Narrative, then, in aspiring to a mimesis of time, is confronted by a number of temporal features which can only be reproduced tropologically:[20] the mediation to the reader of another's presentness (when experience of time is essentially subjective);[21] reproduction of presentness in an essentially preterite medium; reproduction of an *ecstasy* which is constantly escaping definition and which is inherently unexperienceable.

Pushkin's narratives show a number of ways in which presentness may be mediated. Bethea argues convincingly that Pushkin brings the lyric principle into narrative (by which I take him to mean exactly the opposite principle to that associated with narrative) and that this manifests itself in a synoptic approach to the latter.[22] This effect is achieved, however, not so much at the price of temporality but rather by means of privileging certain moments in the structure so that these occlude the temporal process, attenuate its linearity and, in place of the onward rush associated with linear narrative, set up a reflexive system wherein, although the sequence of events proceeds, they are constantly referred back to a primal or evaluating moment for the protagonist, a kind of quasi-present. Such a moment is inevitably *epiphanic*.[23] It constitutes a *kairos*, a privileged or fateful time, which, exactly in the sense Dilthey intends, is of greater *value* than the rest of the temporal flow - *chronos* or, from another perspective, the before and after, past and future. It is this apparent power of the moment in its presentness to differentiate itself from the temporal flow and arbitrate both past and future which led Merleau-Ponty to privilege the present over the past and, unlike Heidegger, the future.[24] The epiphanic moment is the locus of maximal emotional intensity for the protagonist; often it seems to be the chief, sometimes the only significant moment in his life. When the latter is the case we have what has been termed *hypostasis*:[25] the emergence of the protagonist as a knowing subject.

Both Evgenii in *The Bronze Horseman* and Salieri in *Mozart and Salieri* experience such moments: Evgenii's confrontation with the horseman and Salieri's admission of his own envy are moments of tense and self-defining consciousness. The characters undergo a complex experience: on the one hand it is highly emotionally charged; on the other it is a moment of extreme intellectual clarity - the temporal flow either side of this moment is, as it were, sucked back into it, so that it becomes genuinely synchronic and synoptic. Evgenii's momentary insight spans not only his own past, present and future, but also that of St Petersburg and Russia itself; the whole of Salieri's past is unlocked by the single word 'завидую' ('I envy') and as an immediate consequence his future too is settled in advance. These synoptic moments, then, impart the impression of presentness by their compelling reality and their centrality in relation to the rest of the plot. In this way they compete with and foreshadow a more traditionally privileged moment of narrative closure - the conclusion, the infallible gateway to pastness.

However, there is a further important characteristic of these epiphanic moments in the case of Pushkin's narratives, one which acts perhaps as a counter-balance to the intensely solipsistic impression of time which the present model would otherwise convey. If the present moment is an eruption of *self-consciousness*, it is *ipso facto* synonymous with the emergent awareness of an *Other*. Given the stress in the romantic period on precisely this dialectic by Fichte, it is possible that the coincidence of an awakened self-consciousness in Pushkin's narratives with the emergence of an Other derives from a prevalent cultural or intellectual paradigm. One possible explanation of the generation of the Other as by-product of the epiphanic process is that suggested by Dilthey: the present is characterized by 'reflexive awareness' an instantaneous relating back of experience to ourselves.[26] It implies an almost instinctive awareness of what is ours and therefore presumably of any threat to this valuational *status quo*. The Other encroaches on the subject's *habitus* or possessive existence; the protagonist's social status, his dignity, his personal ambitions, in short not only what is his, but also what is due to him - all these are challenged or called into question. Out of the same (largely German) philosophical tradition comes the equation of self with will[27] which reinforces the sense of the self's assertive persistence through time; by corollary, however, the Other functions as another limiting will, with a competing chronology and teleology. In the works by Pushkin which we have already mentioned, and indeed in some others, the alteric component of the epiphany displays both of these salient features of the Other - value and will. Silvio's antagonist in the duel will not behave with the required decorum, and the former's sense of self-worth is threatened; Hermann obsessively covets the winning sequence at cards because his concept of himself is increasingly challenged by his non-possession of it; Evgenii's yearning for a future of domestic bliss is thwarted by the will of another - Peter. What is interesting in this case is that the clash of wills produces a reciprocal awakening into consciousness: it is not only Evgenii who becomes conscious in the moment of his challenging the statue; Peter awakens too. The will animates and the Other is animated by our will.

In structural terms the epiphanic moment is bounded on either side, before and after, by qualitatively less privileged events, though this positioning need not of course reflect the chronological order of these events. The Augustinian model is most appropriate here: the epiphany is the point of *intensio* - intensity in all senses of the word - while all other time extends indifferently either side of it. This model is superficially reminiscent of Freitag's pyramid,[28] but its dynamics are fundamentally different. Essential to narrative epiphany is that nothing after it is the same as before. It is a process of transformation, rather than simply a procession of events. For instance, the nature of the temporal process leading up to the epiphany has to be such as to adequately motivate its emergence. In effect this means one of two things: either the process, though psychological, is largely conditioned by external (exogenous) factors or it is endogenous: an internalized dialectic within the subject himself which culminates in epiphany.

Salieri, Hermann and Evgenii are all subject to pre-epiphanic processes, though they vary in the representational time afforded them in their respective texts. In the case of the first two, endogenous factors are clearly important. Thus Salieri's first monologue manages to encapsulate his whole biography up to the present moment of his awakening to the significance of Mozart. In Salieri's case, though, we can see that the seeds of his bitter harvest have not fallen upon unprepared ground: cumulative attitudes have made him ripe for just such a catastrophic awakening. The sparser characterization of Hermann's past, focusing on his parsimoniousness and fascination with card play, caution and passionate obsession, is suggestive of a dangerous inner conflict of opposites resolvable only by a powerful act of fulfilment or psychic integration, something close to enlightenment. Evgenii's moment of enlightenment, by contrast, is very much as the result of an impact from without: there is nothing in his earlier psychological profile, other than the most basic and everyday aspiration towards happiness, which prepares the ground for what happens to him.

What these three characters share in the long period of time which gestates their epiphany is a strong element of conformity. They emplot their lives, as Bethea puts it, following Lotman, 'consciously inserting' them 'into ancient plots' which require them to act in a certain way.[29] The degree of consciousness is admittedly variable: one can see it at its most striking in the voluntary privations which Salieri visited upon himself in his youth in the belief that they would transform him into a great composer. And indeed a stylistic symptom of these characters' conscious choice of such a role is the frequency of negative (or privative) generalizations in the characterization associated with such types: 'Evgenii did not fret / About his deceased kindred / Nor about the forgotten days of old'.[30] This lack of interest indicates a narrowing of perspective, an inscription into the workaday present: Hermann too 'did not touch even the interest on [his] capital and survived on his salary alone, denying himself the slightest extravagance'.[31] These characters display a well defined habitus; in Bourdieu's terms their subjective decision to pursue an end is determined by the objective criteria of its possibility.[32] In most cases the description of the habitus is ironic and the author imparts its vulnerability not by description alone, but by subtler formal and stylistic means: the epitome of Evgenii's life style is presented to us via a banal *skaz*, motivated by the hero's bout of insomnia. Salieri's is presented to us through a prism of bitterness since his biographical monologue is delivered in the aftermath of an epiphany of envy. The description of Hermann's habitus is withheld from us until after he has heard the story of the magic formula at cards. Thus it is that presentational criteria - siuzhetization - are used to undermine the status of the pre-epiphanic hero's hopes. Inscription into another's plot is essentially monologic[33] but the epiphanic moment which results in the hero's breaking out of that plot, or his being ejected, ushers in an ideological period in which the externalized hero juxtaposes himself with the previous plot, often painfully. Salieri sees God as the author of a plot which he now rejects as unjust, although, by corollary, as long as he believed himself have a meaningful part in it he voiced no complaint.

The Gypsies supplies an interesting variant on this pattern. The urban habitus of Aleko has to be inferred by the reader: it is largely omitted from the characterization system apart from some generalized reflections on civilization by the hero himself. The irony of the story is that the hero has undergone no real change of habitus, no epiphany, simply a change of location. It is left to the Old Man in the poem to suggest a plot, that of Ovid, which adequately analogizes Aleko's habitus and implicitly associates it with an imperial or metropolitan context.

There certainly are broad similarities between the sequence of events underlying the plot of Ovid's exile and that of Aleko. The former, like the latter, wins the trust of the indigenous people among whom he is exiled, but despite this cannot accustom himself to the 'wretched life' which is his lot.[34] Aleko, however, does not see the analogy. He interprets the tale of Ovid, as it has been told to him, as a lesson on temporal attrition, the laws of obsolescence, the sublime remoteness of antiquity and its consequent irrelevance to his own condition. The impression of remoteness is enhanced by the picturesquely eroded fragments of the Ovid story in the Old Man's *skaz*: it is a 'tradition among us', rather than a historical fact; the Old Man has forgotten 'the difficult name' of an individual who is central to European culture.[35] For the Old Man the mythologizing of Ovid's lot serves to detemporalize it or, at least, abolish the conventional signposts which would impart remoteness to it. Innocent of historical perspective he is able to see the exiled poet's fate as a still valid existential option, one corroborated by what he sees happening to Aleko. By contrast Aleko hears nothing but the inadequate retelling of what to him must be an already familiar plot. Ironically it is precisely the fragmentary nature of the plot as delivered by the Old Man, its legendary form, which confirms to Aleko its remoteness and closes off to him the personal analogy which is obvious to us and to the Old Man. He succumbs instead to an elegiac illusion. The fact that 'a rumbling from the grave, the voice of praise, / A sound passing swiftly from generation to generation' has become 'the tale of a wild gypsy / Beneath his smoky tent ...' increases for Aleko a sense of the enfeeblement of the past, its causal ineffectiveness, closing off from him the possibility of recognizing his own inscription in a cultural pattern, unlike, for instance, albeit belatedly, the humble Evgenii.[36]

The Bronze Horseman and *The Gypsies* have in common the presence of a metropolitan dimension, indeed, an imperial one, articulated through time. But there the analogy ends. In semiotic terms, that which reaches Aleko from the lips of the Old Man is the sign of an absent signifier. There is no causal relationship between the story of Ovid and that of Aleko and, as we have seen, Aleko's reaction to what is in effect a paraphrase of the 'official' story shows that Aleko does not identify with it. In the case of *The Bronze Horseman* however, the plot into which Evgenii is inscribed is both sign and cause.[37] The mythic foundation of Petropolis functions quite differently from the topologically and chronologically distant Augustan Rome momentarily evoked for Aleko out of a vanished past. The foundation of the city is also the cause of the city, the cause, too, of all who have lived in it, including Evgenii. In this way the city of St Petersburg itself is a story or plot, with its own author, Peter, who has supplied the setting and who has settled the fate of its inhabitants. The poetic voice of the poem too is in one sense inscribed into this plot. Part of the time, at least, this voice speaks as a civic poet, proud alike of the plot, the setting and the author, willingly embedding himself into it.[38] As Ricoeur has noted, we apprehend the past in two modes: *ne plus* and *encore*. While Aleko declares *ne plus* to his possible identification with Ovid, Evgenii is engulfed by the *encore* of St Petersburg's past - encore in its double meaning: *still*, that is, not receded into the past of non-being and *again* in the sense of repetition.[39] What is crucial is the persistence of the past in the present.

Thus far we have considered the psychological state of the hero in the extension before the epiphany and we have seen that motivational considerations make it receptive ground for the efflorescence of epiphany. The post-epiphanic extension fulfils quite a different role. In the first place it must valorize the preceding epiphany, otherwise it will deprive the latter of its status. Thus it exists to maintain the epiphany in its presentness, that is in its sustained reality, by affirming of it what, in Diltheyan terms, at least, is the most visible marker of the present: *value*. Epiphany is a moment of transformation, of psychic alteration: as such it must be retained in the memory; more than that - located centrally by the consciousness as a perpetual source of reference for the transformed self.[40] The epiphany, therefore, enforces a corroborative role on the temporal extension that follows it: epiphany can be defined as a past kept present by constant affirmation. We may say, indeed, that the epiphany is knowable by this latter affirmation and by the reiteration of such affirmation. Just as epiphany itself is by definition an inner event which may be marked externally[41] so its consequences are inward, but may also be marked externally. In the latter case the most obvious marker is a change of habitus, and habitus, indeed, overlaid by its own literal sense, since what will be marked is the repetition necessary to maintain the centrality of the epiphany.

In *The Blizzard* the remarkably chaste and reticent lifestyle of Maria is a source of local social interest: 'The neighbours, hearing about all of this were amazed at her constancy and awaited with interest the appearance of a hero destined to prevail over the poignant fidelity of this virginal Artemis'.[42] Constancy is in one sense admirable but here it is presented as resistance to the adaptability and adjustment characteristic of normal social existence. It thus has a specific social dimension but also a temporal one: the onlookers wonder at her behaviour and wait for it to end; it is a process of retainment and an outer manifestation of a hidden inner value rooted in the past. It might be added here that the irony of the story in this temporal context is that the epiphanic moment in *The Blizzard* is duplicated, shared equally between Burmin and Maria. Burmin therefore naturally displays the   retentive habitus and preterite orientation characteristic of the post-epiphanic being: '… but most of all … (over and above his tenderness and pleasant conversation, his interesting pallor and bandaged arm) most of all it was the silence of the young Hussar which fired her curiosity and imagination'.[43] She is comically blind to another in a situation identical with her own; indeed, Burmin is a central component of the primal situation which is responsible for her own similar behaviour.

There is, however, another reason, apart from the maintenance of its psychic centrality, why the epiphanic moment enforces subsequent tropes of endurance and repetition. As we have already noted, the epiphany entails *nowness*; it consists, indeed, of two elements, one temporal - the substantive - and an emotive, moral, intellectual, in short psychic element which is the qualifier: an *epiphanic moment*. But the moment itself defies definition: even if it is possible to deictically locate that moment in the narrative - 'he changed' - it is impossible verbally to invest this point-instant with a convincingly profound value: it is the opening of a second dimension of profundity as it were at right angles to the linearity of the narrative. For this reason, then, its import must be mediated tropologically. We can, for instance, locate the site of the inner wound dealt to Samson Vyrin. One feels that it must be at the moment of his 'surrender' or, as Pushkin puts it, *retreat*: 'The old man returned to his lodgings. His friend advised him to make an official complaint; but, having thought about it, the station-master shrugged his shoulders and decided to retreat'.[44] We know that this is a defining moment because in it the hero grasps the whole truth of his situation however unbearable it may be and in so doing resigns himself to accepting a radically modified personal and social situation. If we look back at the moments which precede it we will see that they are still replete with hope for the recovery of the old *status quo*. We may also mark here the word *retreat*, one particularly poignant for an old soldier. Yet the mere narration of this moment as narrative fact can show us nothing of its depth. For this we require a typological excursus out of the narrative and into the descriptive mode.

Description, if we are to follow the strict Lessingian view, is something annexed to narrative *ad lib.*, rather than an integral part of it,[45] and, indeed, a description of Samson Vyrin is supplied by the narrator precisely because of the rhetorical requirement to corroborate the depth of the experience which he has undergone. This is evident from a comparison of the perfunctory initial description of Vyrin ('a man about 50, cheerful and healthy-looking, in a long green coat with three beribboned medals on it') with the later one: 'It was indeed Samson Vyrin. But how old he had become! While he was copying out my travel documents, I looked at his grey hair, the deep wrinkles on the face long unused to the razor, at his bent back, and was amazed that three or four years could change a healthy fellow into a decrepid old man'.[46] This juxtaposition illustrates the degree to which the first description is expositional in nature, establishing a) the military origins of Vyrin and b) his good health. It is therefore subordinate in function to the second descriptive unit: a once proud old soldier has suffered an inner 'retreat' and is in decline. The second description, however, speaks not only of the invisible depth of an inner experience which we are not shown narratively, it also displays a semiotics of duration: facial stubble, wrinkles, a renunciation of enthusiasm for the present which speaks of a constant recurrence to the primary past event. The persistence of Hermann under Lizaveta Ivanovna's window is another outward manifestation of profound inner change, but in this story, with its Gothic-fantastic overtones, the achrony of dream and hallucination provide an added insight into the hero's psyche, and the depth of his emotional affectation, absent in the other narrative.

Suspense and resistance to closure are other devices whereby the hero's epiphanic experience and its sustained *nowness* may be tropologized. The polarization of critical views on this matter is worthy of note. For instance those who regard narrative as essentially teleological perceive it as moving inexorably towards a closure which is the key to all that has gone before.[47] On the other hand Hillis Miller asserts that 'A function of story telling is to keep the story telling going ... a function of all narrative is not to come to an end, but to keep the line, series or chain of repetition going. All story telling in continuing interminably wards off death'.[48] This is certainly the situation in *The Shot*, where the primal experience undergone by Silvio, the insult dealt to him by his opponent, leads to a sustained avoidance of pulling the trigger. When this act is finally accomplished the story ends.[49] However this is a feature of represented rather than representational time: duration is not invariably marked in the text by a monothematic prolongation of its verbal description. Indeed the converse is often the case: the terse revelation that the embittered Salieri has kept poison about him for seventeen years or that a hundred years have now elapsed since the event described in the introductory lines of *The Bronze Horseman* are highly effective evocations of time lapse in their respective contexts. And they owe their effectiveness to the oxymoronic hyper-contraction of what are otherwise sublime sweeps of fabular time. The omission itself accentuates the power of these gestative time-lapses. They are stripped down to their essentiality as sources of immense temporal significance.[50]

The Shot is worthy of closer scrutiny for its subtle manipulation of the the hero's habitus and the interesting play it makes with the lectorial expectations it arouses. The siuzhet enables Silvio's characterization to precede the revelation of his epiphanic moment (the duel) to narrator and reader, although the inferred fabula demands a reversal of this order. The personal isolation, monotony and flavour of self-enforced underfulfilment that are evoked by this characterization permit Silvio to be read initially as a pre-epiphanic character, destined to be torn out of his semi-detached existence by some profound inner event. It is only when Silvio offers the narrator a valedictory account of his duel that we appreciate that the habitus which confronts us here is in fact post-epiphanic, that, for instance, the honeycombed walls of Silvio's cottage are not an indication of pre-epiphanic boredom, but rather of post-epiphanic zeal and fanaticism. It may be arguable, then, that the presentation of pre- and post-epiphanic psychologies is largely a matter of montage or *Gestalt*, of their positioning, that is, in the expositional structure of the narrative. From a strictly receptional point of view this may be the case but, for this second post-epiphanic reading of Silvio's habitus effectively to supplant the first, there must be elements in the initial characterization which are rhetorically supportive of the revised reading, albeit subliminally. For instance at an early stage in *The Shot* the narrator declares that 'we imagined that an unfortunate victim of this terrifying skill lay on his [Silvio's] conscience'.[51] Tentative speculations have thus been made about a defining inner event in Silvio's past, but the youthful fantasizing which evokes them minimizes their impact on his characterization at this stage in the plot. The revelation of the duel shows them to have have been justified, but only imperfectly so: that which lies on Silvio's conscience is infinitely more complex than was first imagined, as indeed is his conscience itself.

Finally, before leaving this question of post- and pre-epiphanic characterization, we should note the situation in *The Queen of Spades* where the siuzhetization results in the immediate juxtaposition of both kinds of description:

1)   Hermann was the son of a naturalized German who had left him a little money. Firmly convinced that he must maintain his independence, Hermann did not even touch the interest on this capital, and survived on his salary alone, denying himself even the slightest extravagance. However, since he was both proud and reticent, his friends rarely had the opportunity of laughing at his excessive thriftiness. He was of a very passionate disposition and possessed a fiery imagination but a certain staidness saved him from the habitual follies of youth. So, for instance, although he was a born gambler, he never touched a card, on the grounds that his financial position, to use his own words, forbade him to *sacrifice the essential in the hope of acquiring the superfluous*. Even so he would spend whole nights at the card table, following the vicissitudes of the game with feverish animation ...

2)   The story of the three cards had strongly appealed to his imagination, and all night he could not get it out of his mind. 'What if,' he thought as he wended his way through St Petersburg the following evening, 'What if the old countess let me know her secret! ...'[52]

Passage 1 exhibits the characteristic foreshadowing of pre-epiphanic characterization: well-defined habitus centred on a frugality always vulnerable to the assaults of overpowering temptation and a precariously maintained armistice between contradictory psychic urges. Passage 2 by contrast argues the profundity of the inner change which has taken place in Hermann, by means of typically post-epiphanic evidence: the persistence of the epiphanic moment marks both its essential nowness and its transcendent value for the hero. The supersession of the second passage so closely upon the first narratively subordinates the former to the latter, obliterating his pre-epiphanic self more thoroughly than is the case with Evgenii in *The Bronze Horseman*; like Evgenii, however, this failure to nurture a personal past, makes him vulnerable to inscription into another's - the Countess'.

In conclusion, then, we can posit a narrative model in which the *intensio* of the epiphany, the privileged moment, the mimetic *now*, is mediated by two forms of extension which form the body of the narrative, the first conditioning the epiphany, the second corroborating its inherent value.

The second section of this chapter concentrates specifically on *The Bronze Horseman* as the most temporally self-conscious of Pushkin's narratives. We have discussed at some length the implications of Dilthey's notion that presentness is marked by value because it is the most challenging of his chrono-ethical equations. However, his equations of past with understanding and futurity with purpose provide their own complexities when applied to a text like *The Bronze Horseman*. The introduction to this poem would seem to provide an unalloyed example of Diltheyan purposiveness and futurity: Peter's thoughts are reproduced: 'From here we will threaten the Swede. / Here a city will be founded / To spite our haughty neighbour. / Here we are destined by nature / To cut a window through to Europe, / To stand steadfastly at the sea's edge'.[53] Here we have a true *distensio* in the 'distractive' sense (as Ricoeur interprets it) but such a distraction into the future paradoxically entails an intense deictic focus, a *here* from which to value it, and that *here* is both temporally and spatially located, is literally both here and now.[54] The purpose, furthermore, is one that befits the Diltheyan man of action: it is civically or socially oriented, and conforms to Aristotle's dictum from *The Politics*: 'Every community is established with a view to some good'.[55] There is thus a valuational element in such purposiveness, so that Peter's consciousness may be seen as a nexus of future aims born out of an evaluation of present potentials. *Pastness*, of course, is absent from this nexus; there is no allusion to Peter's past and the natural environment which encompasses the solitary Peter is an achronic Other which transcends the temporal ecstasies: a timeless wilderness. Peter, we must infer, has a valuational response to what is present to him, but, of course, a negative one: he wants to supplant it with futurity. Pushkin, by contrast, speaks from a temporal location which Dilthey considers to be appropriate to the poet who can contemplate life without being 'incited to action by what he perceives' because 'for the poetically inclined, value lies in every moment of life'.[56]

It is important to note that purposiveness in the present context is not an abstract; Dilthey defines purpose as an image or images connected with an attitude of expectation, and it is clear that rhetorically, at least, the purposive vein of Peter's musings is indeed enhanced by language which combines the eidetic with the anticipative: 'The flags of all nations will come here to us as our guests, / Across waves unknown to them till now, / And we will celebrate on the broad sea'.[57] Paradoxically, of course, because the poem's siuzhet is wrought out of a concrete historical fabula, this characterization of Peter is unavoidably analeptic: the molten moment of vision will inevitably be viewed through the hard lens of its realization in fact. As Bethea has pointed out, that which appears as 'случайность' (chance) in the instant of its occurrence may come to be viewed as 'провидение' (providence) in retrospect;[58] but such an imposition of closure occludes the erstwhile *nowness* of the past and the plurality of possible outcomes which precede concretization into historical fact. By analogy with the familiar temporal metaphor *foreshadowing* Morson sees these once potential and now discarded outcomes as 'sideshadowing' ultimate historical outcomes. A long and peaceful life with Parasha sideshadows Evgenii's brief and tragic history, while in the flood's re-assertion of its primæval power we have a sideshadowing which impinges unsettlingly on the history of a city.[59] St Petersburg is both place and narrative, topos and mythos, and, as narrative, it aspires, in Genette's terminology, to be *first* and to move towards a definitive closure of the process of foundation; but this the sideshadowed fluvial counter-plot will not permit it to achieve.[60]

We have already spoken of the deictic coincidence in the poem of time and space; since St Petersburg is both place and narrative there is a constant tropologization of one dimension by the other for elucidatory purposes. Peter's looking into the distance is a figurative representation of his future-oriented thoughts. The water which he surveys is, however, a paradoxical phenomenon: Heraclitus' famous observation that one does not step into the same river twice reflects the fact that a river is both *kinesis* and *topos*. And it is more generally true of water that we encounter it (or conceive it) either kinetically or topographically or in a processive combination of these modes. As Olga Sedakova puts it 'There is nothing humbler than water'[61] which is to say that, in its downward movement, it endlessly strives for stasis - *vis agendo consumitur* (force is consumed in action). This is a goal sublimely indifferent to human axiology: it is satisfied as much by an orderly system of canals as by the aftermath of inundation. It is water's inhuman teleology which makes it so powerfully symbolic in *The Bronze Horseman*. Moreover water in the poem is capable of representing time in both its quantitative and qualitative values: initially the flowing water emphasizes our perception of time as chronos - running swiftly past Peter while remaining the same - but at a later stage it becomes kairos: a raging flood, rising in spate to achieve its place in history as 'a terrible time'.

Over against the temporal is the spatial dimension of water: space without movement, a kind of temporal becalming. In this moment water erases all spatial signifiers: 'But he as though bewitched, / As though fastened to the marble, / Cannot get down! Around him / Water and nothing else! / While, back turned from him, / On its unshakable eminence / Sits the idol on his bronze horse, / Hand outstretched / Over the troubled Neva'.[62] This image is famous for the obvious parallelism between the two riders, but it is interesting too for the damming of time, in the evocation, perhaps, of a pure Schellingian moment. Space, which makes sense only in terms of the juxtaposition of objects within it, has been abolished and all that remains are two temporal signifiers - Peter and Evgenii - previously kept hidden from one another by the clutter of urban space, a clutter created by the historical process. Each is utterly bereft of any vestige of meaningful personal context: Peter because he is present only representationally - a signifier in the present of a non-existent past; Evgenii because the position he finds himself in is quite literally non-signifying - the 'leonine' monument of which he briefly comprises the human part is in no sense a commemoration of its accidental subject or his life.[63] This collocation of discrete but related moments in time is artificial and, ultimately, sterile: the two cannot communicate and Peter's back is turned towards Evgenii. This is not an evaluative *now* for Evgenii (that will come later) but it is for us; we are now afforded a synoptic vision of the elapsed hundred years. Time may be regarded as a sublime temporal flow or torrent, or we may view the present in juxtaposition with the past: then the two temporally remote moments are, as it were, *within sight* of one another and they seem neither alien (as the past is for Dilthey) nor, as it is for other thinkers, a locus of the familiar, the real and authentic,[64] but instead an ironic mixture of the two.

This, perhaps, is one typically Pushkinian perspective on the past, but there are others too. The different kinetic qualities of the river - its primæval unified 'неслася' (literally 'bore itself along') suggestive of autonomy, the 'державное течение' ('sovereign flow') of the civic *flumen* praised by Pushkin and the anthropomorphized depredations of the flood - can be seen as temporal metaphors for the three fundamental structural categories of the poem: nature, state and man.[65]

When the flood recedes (everywhere but in his fevered brain) Evgenii is able to draw physically near to the equestrian statue. 'Everything has returned to its former order'. The flood's recession is temporal as well as spatial and poets swiftly begin to consolidate its status as a historical event.[66] In what is, then, an entirely reinstated topography, the equestrian statue too becomes once more a remnant of the past. Evgenii's second encounter with Peter takes place in what Lovejoy terms *empirical time*: the time of the archæologist, the moment of inference from the relict signifier; but it is also an encounter *with* time, with the Diltheyan past, an alien other which can be approached only through understanding and insight.[67] In comparison the first encounter seems to exemplify Lovejoy's *abstract time*.[68] Evgenii has been transported back to the primal scene of the *urbs condita*; he is Remus at that moment to Peter's Romulus. But it is an abstract moment, a fictional *as if*. The poet himself asks 'Is he dreaming this?'[69] Time can be neither reversed nor revisited, but it can be reviewed and understood, constantly read backwards as the poem invites us to do.

Despite the temporal paradoxes introduced into the poem by Peter's persistence in monumental form, the plot of *The Bronze Horseman* is, in comparison with the other narratives which we have discussed, remarkably free from anachrony. The others, particularly *The Tales of Belkin* which lay the device bare, make particular play of subjective analepsis (a missing component from his past being supplied by the hero himself: Silvio's story of the duel, Samson Vyrin's tale of his lost daughter, Burmin's explanation to Maria or vice versa). In comparison with these *The Bronze Horseman* reads like a cosmogony. No subterfuges or blind alleys are encountered in our journeys to and from the past; no artificial suspense is created either. Thus far, in comparison at least, it reads much more like history. Yet the past still remains elusive and problematical; Peter's city is like Freud's psychic city[70] - a reef-like accretion of growths through time where nothing of the past is lost but maintains a sphinx-like semiotic presence which has to be interpreted painfully and at the risk of one's sanity. Mere linear narration is not sufficient to reproduce the passage of time; the past is in the present and must be read as much synchronically as diachronically.

NOTES

1. See my 'Lermontov's *The Demon*: Identity and Axiology' in *Russian Literature and Its Demons*, edited by Pamela Davidson, Berghahn Books, New York and Oxford, 2000, pp. 215-39.

2. Wilhelm Dilthey, *Selected Writings*, ed. and transl. H.P. Rickman, Cambridge University Press, Cambridge, 1976, p. 216.

3. Loc. cit.

4. Rudolf A. Makkreel, *Dilthey: Philosopher of the Human Sciences*, Princeton University Press, Princeton, 1975, p. 382.

5. M.Iu. Lermontov, *Sobranie sochinenii v chetyrekh tomakh*, ed. Ch. Zalilov et al., Izdatel'stvo khudozhestvennaia literatura, Moscow, 1964, II, p. 89 (my translation).

6. Meir Steinberg, *Expositional Modes and Temporal Ordering in Fiction*, The Johns Hopkins University Press, Baltimore and London, 1978, p. 14.

7. For this argument applied to the short story see Suzanne Hunter Brown, 'The Chronotope of the Short Story: Time, Character and Brevity' in Noel Harold Kaylor, ed., *Creative and Critical Approaches to the Short Story*, Edwin Mellon Press, Lewiston, 1997, pp. 182-213 (184).

8. Caryl Emerson, 'The Queen of Spades and the Open End', in David Bethea, ed., *Puškin Today*, Indiana University Press, Bloomington, Indianapolis, 1993, pp. 31-7 (37).

9. Savelij Senderovič, 'Pushkinskaia povestvovatel'nost' v svete ego elegii', *Russian Literature*, XXIV, 3, 1988, pp. 375-87 (384).

10. Lubomir Doležel, 'A Scheme of Narrative Time', in Ladislaw Matejka and Irwin Titunik, eds, *Semiotics of Art: Prague School Contributions*, MIT Press, London, 1976, pp. 209-17 (210).

11. Wilhelm Dilthey, *Hermeneutics and the Study of History*, ed. Rudolf A. Makkreel and Frithjof Rodi, Princeton University Press, Princeton, New Jersey, 1996, p. 230.

12. P.F. Strawson, *Individuals: An Essay in Descriptive Metaphysics*, University Paperbacks, Methuen, London, 1964 (first published 1959), pp. 118-19.

13. See Gotthold Ephraim Lessing, *Laokoon and How the Ancients Represented Death*, translated by E.C. Beasley and Helen Zimmern, G. Bell and Sons, London, 1914, pp. 91 ff.

14. J. Hillis Miller, *Reading Narrative*, University of Oklahoma Press, Norman, 1982, p. 227. See also Sebastian Gardner, 'Psychoanalysis and the Story of Time', in David Wood, ed., *Writing the Future*, Routledge, London and New York, 1990, pp. 81-97: 'The world in which narrative occurs is one that is, so to speak, predisposed to having stories told about it' (88).

15. Indeed 'memory ... and anticipation ... are only experienced as present events ...': E. Douka Kabitoglou, *Plato and the English Romantics*, Routledge, London and New York, 1990, p. 149.

16. A term originally used by Samuel Alexander (*Space, Time and Deity*, II, Macmillan, London, 1927 [for example, pp. 130-1]).

17. On this (particularly in the context of romantic æsthetics) see Niklas Luhmann, 'A Redescription of "Romantic art"', *MLN*, III, 3, 1996, pp. 506-22 (520).

18. Paul Ricoeur, 'The Human Experience of Time and Narrative' in Mario J. Valdes, ed., *A Ricoeur Reader: Reflection and Imagination*, Harvester/Wheatsheaf, Hemel Hempstead, 1991, pp. 99-116 (101).

19. For a concise summary of Schelling's concept of time see Arthur O. Lovejoy, *The Reason, the Understanding and Time*, Johns Hopkins, Baltimore, 1961, pp. 82 ff.

20. Originally Ricoeur's idea: see Paul Ricoeur, 'Narrated Time' in Valdes, op. cit., pp. 338-54 (348).

21. The view that time is a subjective (as opposed to objective) phenomenon is elaborated by Merleau-Ponty who contrasts it with space (the locus of objectivity). See Daniel Frank

Chamberlain, *Narrative Perspective in Fiction: A Phenomenological Mediation of Reader, Text and World*, University of Toronto Press, Toronto, Buffalo and London, 1990, p. 30.

22. '... his way of organizing the world, was not the notion of "plot" or tellable *mythos*', but rather 'poetic logosemantic *simultaneity* ...': David Bethea, 'Slavic Gift-Giving: The Poet in History and Pushkin's *The Captain's Daughter*' in Monika Greenleaf and Stephen Moeller-Sally, eds, *Russian Subjects: Empire, Nation and the Culture of the Golden Age*, Northwestern University Press, Evanston, 1998, pp. 259-73 (264). Hereafter 'Slavic Gift-Giving'.

23. On the nature and definition of epiphanic moments in narrative see David K. Danow, *Models of Narrative: Theory and Practice*, St Martin's Press, New York, 1997, pp. 21-2; 44-5.

24. According to Chamberlain, op. cit., p. 32, Merleau-Ponty privileges the present 'not only because it is when being and consciousness coincide, but also because it mediates past and future'. For Heidegger 'in a sense, the future comes before the present, for present action is a realization of future projects': Peter Marshall, *Nature's Web: Rethinking Our Place on Earth*, Cassell, London, 1992, p. 369.

25. By Emmanuel Levinas (in this context, at least): see Tina Chanter 'The Alterity and Immodesty of Time: Death as Future and Eros as Feminine in Levinas', in David Wood, ed., op. cit., pp. 137-54 (140).

26. Wilhelm Dilthey, *Introduction to the Human Sciences*, ed. Rudolf A. Makkreel and Frithjof Rodi, Princeton University Press, Princeton, N.J., 1989, p. 387 (hereafter *Introduction*).

27. Dilthey, *Introduction*, p. 356.

28. See Gustav Freitag, *Technique of the Drama*, translated by Elias J. Macewan, Chicago, 1908 (first published 1863), cited by Steinberg, op. cit., pp. 5 ff.

29. David H. Bethea, *Realizing Metaphors: Alexander Pushkin and the Life of the Poet*, University of Wisconsin Press, Madison, 1998, p. 128.

30. A.S. Pushkin, *Polnoe sobranie sochinenii v desiati tomakh*, second edition, ed. A.I. Korchagin, Izdatel'stvo Akademii nauk SSSR, 1957, IV, p. 384. Hereafter *Pss*. All subsequent references to Pushkin's works relate to this edition. Translations are my own.

31. *Pss*, VI, p. 331.

32. See Pierre Bourdieu and Jean-Claude Passeron, *Reproduction in Education, Society and Culture*, transl. Richard Nice, Sage Publications, London, 1997, pp. 156-8.

33. Bethea, *Realizing Metaphors*, loc. cit.

34. *Pss*, IV, p. 215.

35. *Pss*, IV, p. 214.

36. *Pss*, IV, p. 215.

37. A dual function which Ricoeur sees as characteristic of all traces of the past: See Ricoeur, 'Narrated Time' in Valdes, op. cit., p. 345.

38. On the civic voice see John Fennell, 'Pushkin' in John Fennell, ed., *Nineteenth-Century Russian Literature: Studies of Ten Writers*, Faber and Faber, London, 1973, pp. 16-38 (29).

39. Ricoeur, 'Narrated Time' in Valdes, op. cit., p. 347.

40. Danow, op. cit., p. 22.

41. Ibid., p. 44.

42. *Pss*, VI, p. 112.

43. *Pss*, VI, p. 114.

44. *Pss*, VI, p. 141.

45. F.K. Stanzel, *A Theory of Narrative*, translated by Charlotte Goedsche, Cambridge University Press, Cambridge, 1988 (first published 1984), p. 115.

46. *Pss*, VI, pp. 132; 134.

47. For example, Thomas M. Leitch, *What Stories Are: Narrative Theory and Interpretation*, Pennsylvania State University Press, University Park and London, pp. 42-62.

48. Hillis Miller, loc. cit.

49. In this context see Wolf Schmid's interesting discussion of the motivation of Silvio's hesitancy in his 'Three Diegetic Devices in Puškin's *Tales of Belkin*' in Benjamin Stolz et al., eds, *Language and Literature Theory: In Honor of Ladislaw Matejka*, Department of Slavic Languages and Literatures, Ann Arbor, Michigan, 1984, pp. 505-25.

50. As Chatman notes, contraction or summary of events or periods (rather than omission or full description) often foregrounds a 'problem of transition'. In the present case it takes the form of the paradox that, although a hundred years have passed, the past itself is very much present: Seymour Chatman, *Narrative Structure in Fiction and Film*, Cornell University Press, Ithaca and London, 1993 (first published 1973), p. 223.

51. *Pss*, VI, p. 86.

52. *Pss*, VI, pp. 330-1.

53. *Pss*, IV, p. 380.

54. 'The Human Experience of Time and Narrative' in Valdes, ed., op. cit., p. 101.

55. See Dilthey, *Introduction*, p. 120. One might also add here that Dilthey regarded legislation as one of the principal manifestations of the purposive principle, for to legislate is to control now in the interests of the future.

56. Wilhelm Dilthey, *Poetry and Experience*, ed. Rudolf A. Makkreel and Frithjof Rodi, Princeton University Press, Princeton, New Jersey, 1985, p. 230.

57. *Pss*, IV, p. 380.

58. Bethea, 'Slavic Gift-Giving', p. 269.

59. Gary Saul Morson, 'Time and the Intelligentsia: A Patchwork in Nine Parts with Loopholes' in Dwight Eddins, ed., *The Emperor Redressed: Critiquing Critical Theory*, University of Alabama Press, Tuscaloosa and London, 1995, pp. 81-100 (93). See also his 'Strange Synchronies and Surplus Possibilities: Bakhtin on Time', *The Slavic Review*, LII, 3, 1993, pp. 477-93.

60. Gerard Genette, *Narrative Discourse*, transl. Jane Lewis, Basil Blackwell, Oxford, 1980 (first published as *Discours du récit* in 1972), p. 48.

61. See *Autumn Waters Elegy*, translated by Robert Reid in Olga Sedakova, *The Silk of Time*, edited and introduced by Valentina Polukhina, Ryburn Publishing, Keele Universtiy Press, Keele, 1994, p. 63.

62. *Pss*, IV, p. 388.

63. Thus, while the Bronze Horseman itself is a fully ekphrastic presence in the poem, the parodic monument created by Evgenii is only partially so. For more on ekphrasis in this context, see chapter 6.

64. Danow, op. cit., p. 18.

65. These categories are from Miroslav Drozda, 'Povestvovatel'naia struktura "Mednogo vsadnika"', *Russian Literature*, XXIV, 3, 1988, pp. 349-61.

66. *Pss*, IV, p. 392.

67. Arthur O. Lovejoy, *The Revolt Against Dualism: An Inquiry Concerning the Existence of Ideas*, W.W. Norton and Co., New York, 1930, pp. 124-5.

68. Loc. cit.

69. *Pss*, IV, p. 388.

70. Sigmund Freud, *Civilization and Its Discontents*, translated by Joan Rivière, Hogarth Press, London, 1975, pp. 6-10.

Index

Akhmatova, A. 132, 156, 164
Alexander I 128, 131, 142, 150-152
Algarotti, F. 148-50, 152-3, 154, 156
Apuleius 16, 20
  The Golden Ass 16, 22-3, 32-3, 35 n. 31
Aristotle 200
  The Politics
Augustine 191-3

Bakhtin, M. 130-1, 182
Balzac, H. de 166
Batiushkov, K. 154, 172
  'Walk in the Academy of Arts' 154
Bayley, J. 86, n. 2, 117, 122, 135
Belyi, A. 139, 149
Bem, A. 3
Benkendorf, A. 151, 152
Berkhoffer, R. 179
Bergson, H. 117-18, 134
Berlin, I. 68, n. 27
Bethea, D. 2, 4, 6, 12 n. 2, 69 n. 45, 97, 102, n. 25, 192, 194, 201
Blake, W. 135
Blok, A. 117-18, 119, 125
Boileau, N. 104
Bourdieu, P. 194
  habitus 193-4, 196, 198-9
Briggs, A. 12, n. 1, 50, n. 19, 86, n. 2
Briusov, V. 24, 56-60
Bronevskii, B. 178-9, 181
Buber, M. 46
Bulgarin, F. 143, 178
Byron, Lord 30, 32, 54, 123, 179, 181

Callistratus 104, 108, 111-12

Catherine the Great 145-6, 148, 165, 182, 184
Chatman, S. 71, 206, n. 50
Chizhevskii, D. 41
Classicism 81, 148, 169
Cleopatra 7, 53-65
Coleridge, S. 50, n. 16, 113
Corneille, P. 54
Cornwell, N. 12, n. 11, 100, n. 10, 101, n. 17, n. 25

Dante 39-48
  Commedia 39, 42
  Inferno 39
  La Vita Nuova 40-1, 46
  Paradiso 45
  Purgatorio 42, 44
Davydov, S. 89, 101, n. 20, 102, n. 23
Debreczeny, P. 13 n. 21, 68 n. 16, 100, n. 11
Decembrists 44, 119, 122, 123, 126, 127, 142, 152, 163-5, 169-70, 171, 172
Derzhavin, G. 6, 107-8, 112, 113, 177
Dickens, C. 131
Diderot, D. 107, 109, 111, 112, 130
Dilthey, W. 10, 189-90, 191, 192, 193, 200-2
Dmitriev, I. 177, 184
Dolinin, A. 186, n. 5
Dostoevskii, F. 54, 56-61, 99, 130-1
  The Idiot 57
Driver, S. 14, 32
Du Bellay, J. 105
Dumas, A. 166

ekphrasis 103-113
Eliot, T.S. 58